李 萍 / 著

涉外
法律文书
写作

WRITING

WRITING LEGAL DOCUMENTS
CONCERNING FOREIGN AFFAIRS

中国法制出版社
CHINA LEGAL PUBLISHING HOUSE

序　言

随着世界经济全球化进程的不断加快，我国政府提出了“一带一路”和“粤港澳大湾区”发展战略。随着战略的实施，中国经济走出去越来越成为常态，中国与世界各国的合作与交流日益加强，各种涉外经济活动日益增多，对涉外律师的需求也日益增加。

党的十八届四中全会通过的《中共中央关于全面推进依法治国若干重大问题的决定》对发展涉外法律服务业作出了重要部署，提出建设通晓国际法律规则、善于处理涉外法律事务的涉外法治人才队伍。2017 年 5 月 27 日，司法部联合外交部、国家发改委、教育部、商务部、全国律协等 13 个部门召开了第一次发展涉外法律服务业联席会议，号召加快培养通晓国际规则、善于处理涉外法律事务的涉外法律人才。党中央和国家政策层面上的部署凸显了涉外法律工作的重要性，提出了培养涉外法律人才的紧迫性。

涉外法律人才需要具备两方面的能力：一方面，具有国际视野，能熟练运用外语，能在国际事务中发出自己的声音，并进行有效的交流与谈判，即精通外语（尤其是英语）；另一方面，通晓国际规则，精通国际谈判，能够参与国际法律事务，维护国家利益。简言之，涉外律师不但要求精通专业的国内国际法律，还要求具有优秀的外语水平。

而现实情况是，中国的高端外语人才寥寥无几。全国范围内，熟知国际法、国际贸易法和 WTO 规则的律师稀缺，这导致精通外语、能直接参与国际合作与国际竞争的国际人才极其匮乏。中国执业律师超 30 万，但涉外律师仅为1%。法律英语载体为英美法，也是一门专门用途英语（ESP），与普通英语又有显著区别。大多数的中国律师不具备英文基础，更不用提法律英语。

随着我国对外经济交往的加强和涉外法律体系的完善，对专业英文法律文书写作的需求越来越多也越来越高，同时对高层次、高质量懂法律专业英文的法律人才的需求亦更为迫切。但是，培养和培训各种层次懂法律专业英语的人才需要时间，在一段时间内恐怕难以适应我国“一带一路”经济发展战略的需求，所以，必须另行采取措施。

一个办法是通过出版有关涉外法律文书英文写作的指导性著作。目前，国内学者对于法律文书的写作研究，主要集中在法学院的教授或者老师，而且主要研究的是汉语法律文书，对于涉外法律文书研究较少，即使是少数的涉外法律文书研究，也主要集中于合同研究。不可否认，合同是涉外法律实务中应用较广的一种文书，但是，还有其他常见的非诉讼类涉外法律文书有待研究，如尽职调查报告、公司章程、出资协议书、保密协议、竞业限制协议、劳动合同书等。

在本书中，除了研究常见涉外法律文书英文写作之外，作者还从基础的法律英语特征层面展开深入研究，如研究法律英语的语言特征、句法特征、文体特征等，法律英语的特殊词汇现象，如专业词汇的使用、古英语和外来词的使用、词语并列现象等，同时还研究了法律英语的句法特征，如冗长句式、条件句的普遍存在、多用被动语态、名词的多重修饰等。此外，本书多处加注法律背景知识，旨在帮助读者更好地理解，并通过大量的实践工作案例，拓展涉外法律文书英文写作研究的广度和广度，为相关的法律英语学习者、研究者、应用者等提供指导作用。

除句法特征外，本书为涉外法律文书英文写作提供大量不同的写作方法和写作范例，并对有关专门的修辞用语甚至语法特点和写作习惯加以总结，借此可提炼有关涉外法律文书英文写作方面的规律，不但对助力涉外经济发展，助力“一带一路”和大湾区发展战略有重要意义，而且对提高国内涉外法律文书英文写作水平、提高涉外律师的办案能力，亦可起到良好的促进作用。

本书通俗易懂，具有很高的应用价值，可读性强，同时还具有专业性，适合作为法律英语学习者和研究者的参考书目，亦可作为希望提高法律英语水平的律师的重要参考书目。

本书的出版，得到了李萍主持的广东省教育厅青年创新人才类项目（人文社科）（项目名称：面向“一带一路”和大湾区发展战略的涉外法律文书英文写作在线咨询与编辑系统平台建构研究；项目编号：2018WQNCX252）以及李萍主持的北京理工大学珠海学院校级科研基金项目（项目名称：面向“一带一路”和大湾区战略的涉外法律文书写作研究；项目编号：XZ－2019－02）的资助。在本书付梓之际，笔者由衷地感谢北京理工大学珠海学院科研发展基金对于本书出版的支持！

2020 年春
于珠海

目　录

Contents

第一章　涉外法律文书概述

第二章　有形商品类涉外合同法律文书

第三章 服务类涉外合同法律文书

第四章 知识产权类涉外合同

第五章 用工类涉外合同法律文书

第六章 公司经营管理类常见涉外法律文书

第七章 接受客户委托类涉外法律文书

第八章 其他非诉讼类涉外法律文书

第九章 仲裁类涉外法律文书

第一章　涉外法律文书概述

第一节　法律英语的词汇特征

法律英语是一种专门用途英语（ESP），也是一种工具性语言（instrumental language）。美国法律语言研究权威梅林可夫（Mellinkoff）认为“法律英语”指 the English language of law，而加州大学的大卫（David）教授主张用 legal English 来表述“法律英语”。本书讨论的法律英语主要指以英语为母语的英美法（common law）国家的司法从业者，如律师、法学研究人员、法官、检察官等在以法律为职业和以法学研究为目的的过程中所使用的法律语言。有时候为了更易于理解法律英语的特点，会辅以我国法律条文作为例子从而更好地证明观点。

在对法律英语进行研究的过程中，Mellinkoff 针对法律英语的词语特点作了系统的分析，Crystal 和 Davy（1969）对法律文本的结构和组织进行了分析总结。他们认为：1. 法律语言是工具性语言；2. 法律文件具有不同于其他类文本的特征；3. 法律英语具有明确的特点；4. 法律语言使用了日常英语不采用的语义规则。为了更好地理解法律英语，本章节将从法律英语的词汇特征、句法特征、语法特征等方面展开详细分析。

词汇是构成法律英语的基本单元，因此法律英语的词汇研究是法律英语研究的关键。法律英语的词汇特征，主要体现在以下几个方面。

一、具有特殊法律涵义的普通词汇

法律语言中有很多词汇是由普通词汇转换而来，和法律专业术语不同的是，这类普通词汇在法律语境中却有着专业的涵义。准确地掌握这类专业词汇的涵义需要读者对所熟悉词语的法律含义有一定的积累，并且在一定的语境中进行逻辑分析，从而正确地理解。例如：

1. Damage

a. He maliciously damaged a car with a baseball bat.

b. The machines in the clothing factory were old and dangerous and one of the employees injured his hand. The employee sued the factory owners and got 5000 dollars in damages.

Damage 在普通语境中一般作及物动词，表示“损害、损毁、破坏”之意（a 句）。而在法律语境中，其经常见于侵权法中，一般指代“侵权人向被侵权人支付的损害赔偿金”，词性为名词，而且往往以复数形式出现。

2. Acceptance

a. The Party is being degraded by its acceptance of secret donations.

b. Acceptance cannot contain any suggested changes to the original offer. In addition, acceptance must be communicated and cannot be by silence.

c. Modification of acceptance of bill denotes acts on instruments that payers (acceptors) did - write and sign on the bills and eliminate his/her writings afterwards.

Acceptance 通常意指“接受”（a 句）。但是在合同法中，其意思为“承诺”，如 b 句所言，承诺不能够沉默作出，而必须通过某种方式让要约人知道，且承诺不能对要约作出任何改变，否则视为新的要约。而在 c 句中，acceptance 的意思为“承兑”，是票据法中的一种票据行为。c 句可翻译为汉语：承兑涂销是指付款人（承兑人）在已承兑的汇票上将其记载的承兑予以消除的票据行为。

由此可见，一个普通英语单词在法律文本中的意思与其通常涵义有很大的区别，而且，在不同的法律语境中，其涵义也有所差异（如句子 b 和 c）。要理解这几个句子，不仅要求读者具备英语语言基础，更要求具备一定的法律知识。

3. Consideration

a. This problem should be reserved for further consideration.

b. In consideration of all the Services provided by ALT Services Ltd., the Company shall pay the sum of 10,000 dollars subject to the provision of the Services and satisfactory completion of work.

Consideration 在普通语境中指“考虑”（a 句），而在合同法中，其涵义为

“对价”（b 句）。句子可翻译为：作为 ALT Services Ltd 所提供服务的对价，公司应依据所提供的服务和工作的圆满完成而支付 10,000 美元。

而这样的例子在法律英语中不胜枚举，对比如下：

例词	一般文本涵义	法律文体涵义
Counterpart	极相似的人或物、对手，对方	有同等效力的副本
Negligence	疏忽	过失
Assign	分配，指派	转让（合同）
Grace	优雅；善意；宽恕	还款或专利申请的“宽限期”
Royalties	皇室；王权	特许权使用费；版税
Award	奖励；授予	判决书
Action	行动	诉讼
Instrument	仪器	法律文件；票据
Party	政党	当事人
Service	服务	传票送达
Sentence	句子	法院判决
Brief	简要的	诉讼案件摘要
Motion	运动	议案
Summons	召集	传票
Balance	平衡	余额
Statement	陈述、声明	对账单
Provide	提供	规定
Policy	政策	保险单

二、外来词的使用

法律本属于上层建筑，而英美法从产生到形成时期英国的统治者均是讲法语的诺曼人，加之拉丁语的影响，因此法律英语中存在大量借用法语、古希腊语和古拉丁语中的专用词汇，包括成语和短语。法律英语中广泛使用拉丁词和拉丁词源的词语使语言严肃冰冷，而从法语借词则使法律语言显得高贵典雅。

另外，随着世界各国的交往日益频繁，国家间法律语言的互相借鉴和援引也随之增多，尤其是在国际交往中通用的法律用语。一些法律文献上常用的标准外来词已经在人们的日常生活中得到认可，其词源逐渐为人们淡忘。

常见的拉丁语外来词有：

ex post facto 追溯
versus 对抗
alibi 不在现场证据
ratio decidendi 判决理由
obiter dictum 判决附带意见
ad hoc 专门的
in rem 对物权
per se 本身
affidavit 誓章，证明
de facto 事实上
ex delicto 由于侵权；源自侵权
quorum 法定人数
alieni juris 他人权利
bona fide 真诚
habeas corpus 人身保护令
prima facie 表面的
sine die 无期限
ad hoc 特别地
ab initio 自始
ad idem 一致，相同
ex contractu 因合同，
et al …等人，以及其他人

常见的法语外来词有：

debt 债务
jury 陪审团
alien 转换
voir dire 照实陈述
proposal 建议
void 无效的
lien 留置权
quash 废除，撤销
estoppel 禁止反言

举例如下：

1. The decision of the judge in common law countries must form what is called the ratio decidendi of the case. This is the Latin for "the reasoning behind the decision". This is the part of the judge's words that provide the legal reasoning for his or her decision. Everything else the judge says is called obiter dictum. Obiter dictum is something that is not really necessary for the legal basis for the decision. Only the ratio decidendi is binding.

注：在英美法系国家，法官可以造法，即，法官的判决理由（ratio decidendi）可以成为法律，作为法官处理类似案件的依据，判决理由（ratio decidendi）具有强制约束力，而附带意见（obiter dictum）仅具有参考价值，不具

有强制约束力。ratio decidendi 和 obiter dictum 都是来自拉丁语的外来词，但是在法律英语中已经成为非常活跃的词汇并被广泛接受。

为了更好地理解 ratio decidendi，请看下面的例子：

2. An Actress was employed for a season, but was delayed by illness from taking up her role until a week after the opening night.（来自英国判例 Poussard v Spiers & Pond 1876）

Held: her employers were entitled to terminate the contract: her presence on the opening night was crucial to the contract.

该判例中，女演员因为生病导致不能依约出席开幕式，构成合同重大违约，守约方有权解除合同。其中 Held: her employers were entitled to terminate the contract: her presence on the opening night was crucial to the contract 就是我们所说的判决理由（ratio decidendi），该部分具有强制约束力。"Held"一词一般被翻译为："法院认为"。

为了更好地理解附带意见（obiter dictum），请看下面例子：

3. The defendants owned a block of flats on land leased to them by the claimants. By September 1939, many flats had become vacant due to outbreak of war. Consequently, the defendants were having difficulties paying their ground rent. The claimants agreed that they would accept reduced payments. The defendants continued to pay the reduced rent even when the flats refilled and the war was over.

The claimants brought a test case claiming arrears of rent for the last two quarters of 1945 (by which time the war had ended).（来自英国判例 Central London Property Trust v High Trees House 1947）

Held: the claimants were found to be entitled to the arrears they claimed, but it was also held (obiter dictum) that had they claimed for arrears prior to the end of the war this would have been refused. It would be unfair to allow them to go back on their promise on which the defendants had naturally relied. The claimants' gratuitous promise operated to suspend their rights to full payment while the extenuating circumstances in which the promise had been made continued to operate.

在上述法官观点中，obiter dictum 后面的内容，就是我们所说的法官的附带意见，该意见对于以后的案件具有指导性意义，但不具有强制性约束力。

另外，需要补充的是，上述判例确立了禁止反言原则（promissory estoppel），promissory estoppel 也被称为 High Trees doctrine（沿用判例名称：Central London Property Trust v High Trees House）。上述判例大概的意思是说：战争期间，房东同意给承租人降低房租，承租人信赖房东的诺言而同意继续租赁房子，但是战争结束后，房东不能食言向承租者追讨承租人在战争期间少交的房租，也即，禁止反言（promissory estoppel）。而战争结束后，由于租房市场的复苏，如果承租人继续按战争期间较低的租赁价格缴纳房租，则房东则有权主张正常价格的租金。

Promissory estoppel（禁止反言）来自拉丁语，该原则的大概意思是：under this principle, parties who gratuitously promise that they will not enforce existing contractual rights may lose their entitlement to do so if it would be unfair to allow them to go back on their promise; they are prevented (estopped) from breaking the promise.

另外，bona fide third party（善意第三人），null and void（无效）等外来词在法律英语中也很常见，针对其用法，此处不再赘述。

三、古英语的存在

古英语词汇在现代英语中已很少使用，但在各种类型的法律性文件中，依然随处可见。一些古旧词汇删除后，并不会对法律文件的解读有实质的影响，因此在英美国家要求法律语言“简明化”的呼声颇高，但一些律师和司法领域从业者认为，为了使法律文件中的语言简练、严谨，体现法律文句的权威性、严肃性和正规性，适当使用古旧词汇是必要的。因此，当我们在一些法律文件中看到这些词汇时，应该理解他们的含义。

其中常见的一种古旧词汇的形式是：副词 here/there + 介词。如“herein”“hereon”“thereby”“thereon”等。“here”通常的涵义为“在此文件中、在此合同中，或者在该条款中”，而“there”一般指上文提到的文件、合同、条款等。如：

The persons herein after named 指的就是“在本文件之后所提及的人”

The sum of money borrowed and the interest thereon shall be repaid in full on June 6. 此句中的“thereon”指该单词前面所述“sum of money borrowed”。

The titles to the articles are for convenience of reference only, not part of this contract and shall not in any way affect the interpretation thereof. （本协议）各条款之标题仅为查阅方便，非本协议之构成部分，也决不会影响合同的解释。其中“thereof”是指 of the said contract。

对于具备一定英语知识的人来说，用英文来解释常见的古旧词汇，会更有利于理解，如：

1. Hereby——by means of this document/with that words/with this action.

“I hereby accept your offer.”

兹接受你的要约。

“The undersigned hereby certify that the goods to be supplied are made in the USA.”

下列签署人兹证明所供应之货物在美国国内制造。

2. Herein——in this document.

“The price named herein is final and non-negotiable.”

合同中的价格是最终的、没有谈判余地的。

3. Hereto——to this contract.

“All disputes arising from the performance of this Contract shall, through amicable negotiations, be settled by the Parties hereto”.

对于因履行本合同所发生的一切争议，本合同双方应友好协商解决。

4. Hereinafter ——starting from this time/later in this document.

“ALT Electronics plc, hereinafter known as ‘the Company’.”

ALT Electronics plc 在此后被称为“该公司”。

5. Heretofore——earlier in this document/previously/before the time of writing.

“The property heretofore known as Downing House is renamed Appleby House.”

此前所提及的名为 Downing House 的物业被重新命名为 Appleby House。

6. Hereunder——in a later part of this document/under the terms of this agreement.

“The terms and conditions are listed hereunder.”

合同中所列条款。

7. Thereby——as a result of this or that action.

"Your client signed the contract and thereby entered into a binding agreement."

你的客户签署该合同并因此受合同约束。

8. Therein ——in or into a particular place or thing/in that/in there.

"The rented property and the furniture contained therein."

合同中所包含的租赁物业和家具。

9. Thereon ——on it/on there/on what I have just mentioned.

"The amount borrowed and the interest due thereon must be repaid by May 22, 2016."

所借本金和利息必须在2016年5月22日之前付清。

10. Thereinafter——later in that place or thing/later in what I have just mentioned.

"We were defined in that contract as the Company and we were known as the Company thereinafter."

在合同中，我们被定义为“该公司”，并在此后被称为“该公司”。

11. Thereto ——to it, to the thing that I have just mentioned.

"At the meeting we will discuss Mrs. Smith' will and all matters related thereto."

在会议上我们讨论了史密斯夫人的遗嘱及与遗嘱相关的所有问题。

另外，还有一些古旧词汇用来指代“本文件/合同/条款前面所提及的事物”，如 said, aforesaid, aforementioned, the same.

1. The contract between the claimant and the defendant was signed in August. Said contract was for the supply of goods.

该句中的“said contract”指代句子所述“The contract between the claimant and the defendant”.

2. The goods should be inspected by the Buyer upon delivery. All goods come with a delivery note. In the event that goods cannot be examined by the Buyer the aforementioned document shall be marked "not examined".

该句子中的 aforementioned document 指代句子中的 delivery note.

3. Any defective goods must be returned to the Supplier. Said goods must be correctly packaged.

该句中的"said goods"指代句子中的 defective goods。

4. Payment must be made upon delivery of the goods. The exception is where payment by invoice has been agreed. In the event of payment by invoice payment must be made within 30 days of receipt of the same.

该句中的" the same"指代句子中的 invoice。

四、词语并列现象

法律英语中经常出现一些近义词并列使用的现象，即，用两个或者三个意思相近或者相同的词构成一个短语以表达法律上本来只需要一个词就能表达的概念，这体现了法律语言的严肃性和法律文本的准确性和严密性，确保了整体含义的完整、准确。如：

1. The amendments to or alteration of this contract become effect only after they are signed by parties hereto and approved by the original approving authorities.

译文：该合同的任何修改只有在双方签署并由最初的审批机关批准后方生效。

2. If the contract shall duly perform and observe all terms, provisions, conditions and stipulations of the said Contract, this obligation shall be null and void but otherwise shall be and remain in full force and effect.

译文：如果承包人切实履行并遵守上述合同的所有条款、条件及规定，此义务即告终止，否则将保持完全有效。

除了上述两个句子中的 amendments to or alteration of, terms, provisions, conditions, and stipulations, null and void, in full force and effect 等词语并列现象外，其他常见的并列现象如下：

Any and all 全部

Any duties, obligations or liabilities 所有责任

Charges, fees, costs and expenses 各种费用

Covenants and agreements 合同、协议

Customs and usages 惯例

Free and clear of 无

Import duty and tax 进口税捐

Keep secrete and confidential 保密

Licenses and permits 许可

Packing and wrapping expenses 包装费

Rights and interests 权益

Settle claims and debts 清理债务

Ships and vessels 船只

Sign and issue 签发

Support and maintenance 维护

Use and wont 习惯、惯例

Null and void 无效

五、介词短语的使用

为了体现法律语言的严肃性，法律英语的措辞风格以严谨、庄重为主，多采用正式书面体。所谓法律文书中的正式词汇，不但指相对于口语用词而言的书面语用词，尤其指普通书面语体中不常用的正式程度较高的词汇或短语。如常见的书面体用语 according to，concerning/regarding/ with regard to，但是在法律英语中，一般采用正式程度更高的、表达相同概念的词汇如 in accordance with，pursuant to 及 in respect of。

1. The participants in the Joint Venture shall commence discussion with regard to the extension of the period of existence of the Venture and in the event of their agreeing upon such extension, they shall record such agreement in a written document signed by all of them not later than three years prior to the expiry of the current period.

译文：就本合资企业的存续时限的延期问题，各方应进行讨论；一旦各方就此达成一致，应形成书面协议，由各方在本合同期限到期之前的三年内签字生效。

本句中的三个介词短语 with regard to，in the event of，prior to 分别对应三

个介词 about，if，before。用介词短语代替，更好地体现了法律英语的正式性。

其他类似的用介词短语来代替介词的表达方式有：in the near future (soon)，until such times as (until)，on the part of (by)，at the present time (now)，during such time as (while)，due to the fact that (because)，notwithstanding (despite)，inclusive of (including)，referred to (named，called，mentioned) 等。

另外，法律英语中经常出现的两个正式介词或介词短语有：notwithstanding 和 inasmuch as。

Notwithstanding 的含义为：despite or in spite of something。如：:

2. The new law concerning the protection of the environment will come into force next year，notwithstanding a huge amount of opposition to it from industry.

译文：尽管有来自行业大量反对的声音，新的有关环境保护的法律将会在明年生效。

而 inasmuch as 的含义为：what you are saying in the rest of the sentence is true only in a limited way or to a certain extent。如：

3. The judge in the Court of Appeal held that the court of first instance made a mistake inasmuch as inadmissible evidence was taken into consideration.

译文：上诉法院的法官认为一审法院由于采信了不能采纳的证据导致作出了错误判决。

4. Caroline is a good lawyer inasmuch as she usually gets a good result in court. However，she is not very good at keeping up to date with important work.

译文：卡罗林总是能够取得好的诉讼效果，在这方面，她是个好律师。但是，她不太擅长跟进一些重要的工作。

六、专业词语的使用

法律英语的正式性还体现在一些专业词汇、甚至是生僻词汇的使用，以体现法律英语的严肃性和正式性。如：

1. The Licensee will notify the Licensor and shall assist the Licensor in taking such action as the Licensor deems appropriate.

句子中的 notify，assist，deem 相对于常用的 inform，help，think 要正式

很多。

2. The term "Effective date" means the date on which this Agreement is duly executed by the parties hereto.

该句中的 execute 相对 sign 要更加正式一些。

又比如用 premises 代替 place 来表示企业的经营场所，用 commence 代替 start，用 termination 或者 expiration 代替 end，用 comply with 代替 obey，用 subsequent to 代替 after，用 procurement 代替 purchase，用 term 代替 duration，用 aggregate 代替 total，用 undertake 代替 do 等。

七、情态动词的特殊法律内涵

在法律英语中，shall 和 may 是经常出现的两个情态动词，然而在法律英语中，这两个词的使用方法和普通英语有很大的区别。

（一）Shall 在法律英语语境中的使用

Shall 在普通英语中通常构成第一人称复数的将来时态。法律的主要功能有授权、使负担义务或禁止，shall 在法律英语中经常表示一种义务性约定，体现当事人必须承担的责任和义务，带有指令性和强制性，也同时体现法律文件的权威性和约束性。它通常被译为"应、应当"，如：

（1）The quality and prices of the commodities to be exchanged between the ex-importers in the two countries shall be acceptable to both sides.

译文：货物的质量和价格应当使进出口双方都能接受。

（2）The board meeting shall be convened and presided over by the Chairman. Should the chairman be absent, the vice-Chairman shall, in principle, convene and preside over the board meeting.

译文：董事会会议应由董事长召集、主持；若董事长缺席，原则上应由副董事长召集、主持。

（二）May 在法律英语语境中的使用

在普通英语中，may 一般在疑问句中用来提出请求，在陈述句中表示可能，或者表达祝福，但是在法律英语中，由于法律的强制性与指令性，may 的通常含义是"给予许可或给予某人做某事的授权"，是一种选择性约定，通常翻译为“可以”。如：

A civil juristic act may be in written, oral or other form. If the law stipulates that a particular form be adopted, such stipulation shall be observed.

译文：民事法律行为可以采取书面形式、口头形式或者其他形式。法律规定是特定形式的，应当依照法律规定。

从该句中，我们也可以更好地理解 shall 和 may 的区别。根据法理学相关知识，法律规则分为授权性规则和义务性规则，授权性规则是指规定人们有权做一定行为或者不做一定行为的规则，即规定人民的“可为模式”的规则，一般在这样的规则中会出现情态动词 may，表达一种选择性约定。而义务性规则是指在内容上规定人们的法律义务，即有关人们应该做出或者不做出某种行为的规则，一般在这样的规则中会出现情态动词 shall，表达一种义务性约定。上述法律条文的前半句是一种授权性规则，即，民事法律行为可以采取书面形式、口头形式或者其他形式，故用 may。而后半句是一种义务性规则，如果法律规定了特定形式，则应遵循特定形式，故用 shall。

八、法律英语的模糊性和精确性

根据 L. A. Zadeh 提出的模糊集合理论以及由此产生的模糊语言学，我们知道法律英语作为自然语言之一，必然具有模糊性，法律英语的模糊性不仅存在，而且具有自身的作用。社会生活的多样性和语言的限制性之间的矛盾造成法律英语必须具有概括性的特点，从而产生模糊。另外，由于法律具有滞后性，由于社会及经济的逐步发展，社会文化、人们的思想意识、法律标准也在发生深刻的变化，过去某些被律师及法律工作者认为是确定的法律名词现在又被提出质疑，从而产生了模糊性。如汉语法律文书中经常用到“情节严重”“数额巨大”“多次盗窃”“其他”“任何单位和个人”等词义模糊的词语，有很强的不确定性。英语法律语言也是如此，如 about, as soon as possible, necessary, average 等。

以《中华人民共和国刑法》为例。《中华人民共和国刑法》第 264 条规定：“盗窃公司财务，数额较大的，或者多次盗窃、入户盗窃、携带凶器盗窃、扒窃的，处三年以下有期徒刑、拘役或者管制，并处或者单处罚金；数额巨大或者有其他严重情节的，处三年以上十年以下有期徒刑，并处罚金；

数额特别巨大或者有其他特别严重情节的，处十年以上有期徒刑或者无期徒刑，并处罚金或者没收财产。”该法条中，存在三种法定刑，主要由盗窃的数额决定的，而“数额较大”“数额巨大”和“数额特别巨大”很显然是模糊的。《最高人民法院、最高人民检察院关于办理盗窃刑事案件适用法律若干问题的解释》第一条规定：“盗窃公私财物价值一千元至三千元以上、三万元至十万元以上、三十万元至五十万元以上的，应该分别认定为刑法第二百六十四条规定的‘数额较大’、‘数额巨大’、‘数额特别巨大’。各省、自治区、直辖市高级人民法院、人民检察院可以根据本地区经济发展状况，并考虑社会治安状况，在前款规定的数额幅度内，确定本地区执行的具体数额标准，报最高人民法院、最高人民检察院批准。”

比如在广东省，盗窃价值在 3000 元（二类地区 2000 元）以上为“数额较大”，而在贵州省，盗窃价值在 1000 元以上为“数额较大”。由此可见，即使司法解释规定了三种法定刑的入罪标准，但由于各省经济发展水平的差异，在数额认定标准上，也是有区别的。即使在一个省内，一类地区和二类地区的入刑标准也有所区别。但是，也正是由于法律语言的模糊性，在解释法律的时候，能够考虑各地实际情况，使得法律能够更好地得到适用。

同理，该法条中的“严重情节”“特别严重情节”也体现了法律语言的模糊性。由于模糊性具有包容原则，这使得法律能够得以更广泛的应用。

而有时候模糊性和精确性却是辩证统一的。如在传票“你已被本院传唤，请于接到本传票之日起 20 日内在本法院出庭”。翻译为英文：“You are summoned to appear and answer this action in the Court named above by filing an Answer along with the required answer fee within twenty (20) consecutive days from the service of this summons, not including the day of service. If the twentieth day is Saturday, Sunday or a legal holiday, then this time shall run until the end of the next day which is NOT a Saturday, Sunday or legal holiday.”

在英文翻译中，考虑到周末和法定节假日的影响，对于 20 日进行了详细解释，以更好地告知当事人诉讼法中关于送达期间的规定，体现了法律英语的精确性。

又如：Shipment: To be shipped on or before Feb. 28, 2014.

译文：2014 年 2 月 28 日前（含 28 日）装船。

on or before Feb. 28, 2014 增译为“2 月 28 日前（含 28 日）”，使得译文更加精确和严密，避免导致曲解。

针对法律英语的模糊现象，法律文本的中英文两种语言的转换中，除了使用上述的增译法之外，也可以采取省略法。如：

1. In all cases affecting ambassadors, other public ministers and consuls, and those in which a state shall be a party, the Supreme Court shall have original jurisdiction. In all the other cases before mentioned, the Supreme Court shall have appellate jurisdiction, both as to law and fact, with such exceptions, and under such regulations as the Congress shall make.

在英语中，such 是个模糊词汇，意思是“这样的”，但是在结构“with such exceptions, and under such regulations as the Congress shall make”，如果译为“国会有这样的例外和规定除外”，原文意思就没有得到恰当的表达。而如果省略翻译 such，翻译为“但国会规定为例外及另有处理条例者，不在此限”则显得简明清晰多了。因此，可以将上述句子翻译为：“在一切有关大使、公使、领事以及州为当事一方的案件中，最高法院有最初审理权。在上述所有其他案件中，最高法院有关于法律和事实的上诉受理权，但国会规定为例外及另有处理条例者，不在此限。”

英汉两种语言中均存在大量的模糊词语，但译者有时候可以直接采用直译的办法来处理这一现象，也可以很好地表达原文的信息。例如：

2. The applicant or the insured shall notify the Insurer in a timely manner of the occurrence of any insured event once it is known to them.

译文：一旦发生保险事故，投保人或被保险人应在知道后及时通知保险人。

3. Unless this account is paid within twenty days, we will take further measures.

译文：除非二十天内把款付清，否则我们将采取进一步的措施。

对于这句话中的“take further measures”，完全可以用“start legal proceedings”或“bring lawsuit”等来代替。但是用模糊词语“take further measures”使得表达更加含蓄、委婉，缓解了可能的诉讼给双方带来的紧张局面。

另外，通过意译法（free translation），根据原文的精神实质，使译文更忠实通顺地表达原文的思想内容而增加或减少适当的词语，而非机械地保持原文与译文在词量或字面含义上的对等，也有助于解决法律英语模糊性造成的在实务写作和翻译方面的困难，如：

4. The Insurer shall have the right to terminate the insurance contract, in the case that the applicant intentionally does not perform his/her obligation of making a full and accurate disclosure, or fails, due to gross negligence, to perform such obligation to the extent that it would materially affect the Insurer's decision whether or not to underwrite the insurance or whether or not to increase the premium rate.

译文：投保人故意或因重大过失未履行如实告知义务，足以影响保险人决定是否同意承保或者提高保险费率的，保险人有权解除保险合同。

Materially 本意是“本质上”，译文灵活处理，将其翻译为“足以”，显得更为简洁。

5. This Agreement may be immediately terminated by one of the Parties, without compensation from either side, in case of bankruptcy, winding up, or legal or factual, direct or indirect, taking over by a third party of the other party.

译文：如果一方破产、解散或在法律上或事实上直接或间接地被第三方所接管，另一方可立即终止本协议，任何一方无须就此做出赔偿。

原句中，one of the Parties 不能直译为“一方”，或者“任何一方”，而应根据语境灵活翻译为“另一方”。同理，the other party 应翻译为“一方”，表达协议终止的一种假设情形。

九、名词化结构的使用

“语法隐喻”这一概念是 Halliday 在《功能语法导论》（1985）中首先提出来的。根据系统功能语言学理论，语言是由音系层（phonology）、词汇语法层（lexico-grammar）和话语意义层（discourse semantics）构成的三层次符号系统，且三个层次之间是体现和被体现的关系，即，音系层体现了词汇语法层，而词汇语法层体现了话语意义层。体现方式大致有两种：（1）一致式（congruent form），即无标记形式；（2）非一致式（incongruentform），或隐喻式，即有标记形式。

所谓一致式，就是通过用名词体现事件过程的参与者，用动词体现过程本身，用形容词体现事物的特征，用副词或介词词组体现时间、地点、工具、方式等环境意义（circumstantial meaning），用连词体现逻辑意义，从而使词汇语法层所表达的表层意义和话语意义层所表达的深层意义彼此相同。但是，如果词汇语法层所表达的表层意义和话语意义层所表达的深层意义不一致，例如，用名词体现过程、用名词体现特征、用动词体现时间关系或因果关系等，使词汇语法层所表达的表层意义和话语意义层所表达的深层意义变得不一致，属于有标记形式，就是非一致式，这种现象也叫语法隐喻，其中名词化就是其中一种常见的形式。例如：

[a] The man drove the car too fast down the slope, so the brakes failed.

[b] The man's overrapid downslope driving of the car caused brake failure.

[a] 属于一致式，三个动作参与者分别用名词 the man，the car 和 the brake 表示，动词 drive 和 fail 分别表示两个过程，用副词词组 so fast 体现表示速度的环境意义，用介词词组 down the slope 体现表示方向的环境意义，由连词 so 体现表示因果关系的逻辑意义。而 [b] 则属于非一致式，三个动作参与者和环境意义都变成了名词词组中的修饰成分，逻辑意义变成了过程本身，而过程却通过名词化的使用变成了参与者。

作为语法隐喻的一种重要体现形式，名词化（normalization）就是"将过程和特性经过隐喻化，不再是小句中的过程或修饰语，而是以名词形式体现的参与者"（胡壮麟，1996），或者是"将小句通过变为名词或名词词组的方式，使表过程的动词或表性质的形容词具有名词特征，从而减少及物性小句，使自然语义句的信息密度增大"的一种表达形式（杨敏，2004）。

Quirk 等人（1985）从词性转换的角度对名词化作过界定，把它看作是"一个在形态上与小句谓语相对应的名词短语"。也有人将名词化视为动词或形容词用作名词这一语言现象。一般认为，名词化指的就是把某个过程或特征看作事物，并通过词性转换使得这种现象得以实现。

一般说来，语篇的技术性与名词化出现的频率是成正比的，即，语篇的技术性越高，名词化出现的频率越高。反之，名词化使用得越多，语篇的技术性越强（Halliday 1998b）。因此，科技、法律语篇作为技术性较高的语篇，名词化的语法隐喻出现的频率也较高。而小说、寓言等文学类语篇的技术性较低，名词化出现的频率较低。

学者王晋军从实证主义分析的角度对五种不同类型的语篇进行了分析统计，统计结果表明：名词化在法律语篇中的比例为 83.5%，科技语篇为 72.6%，新闻语篇为 40.3%，小说和寓言故事分别为 27.2% 和 0.7%。由此可见，法律语篇中充满大量的名词化结构，而且法律语篇的正式性、严谨性、准确性、庄重性等必然要求大量使用名词化结构。通过在法律语篇中使用语法隐喻，可以实现信息浓缩或虚化，从而泛化特定行为概念，虚化行为概念的主体和受体，增强法律的适用性。

以上分析表明，语法隐喻存在多种情形，名词化是最主要的情形，也是法律英语的典型特征。在运用法律英语的过程中，如何运用名词化结构，从而使法律英语文本简洁紧凑、信息密集、使法律英语文本符合规范的表达方式，可以从以下几个方面来运用名词化结构：

1. 将动宾结构转译成英文名词化结构

（1）公司股东依法享有资产收益、参与重大决策和选择管理者等权利。

Shareholders of a company shall be entitled to gains on assets, participation in major decision-making and selection of managers in accordance with the law.

（2）设立外资企业，必须有利于中国国民经济的发展，并且采用先进的技术和设备，或者产品全部出口或者大部分出口。

The establishment of foreign-invested enterprises shall be beneficial to the development of China's national economy; they shall use advanced technology and equipment or market all or most of their products outside China.

2. 将状语成分转译成英文名词化结构

无论本协议是否有相反规定，如任一方被法律诉讼或政府法规要求披露在此接收的保密信息时，该方应立即通知另一方上述要求，且应另一方的要求该方应配合另一方对此披露要求进行抗辩。除未能履行前款所述义务外，双方对于依司法程序或政府法规所做披露而造成的损失概不负责。

Notwithstanding any contrary provisions herein contained, should either party be faced with legal action or a requirement under governmental regulations to disclose Confidential Information received hereunder, such party shall promptly notify the furnishing party of such requirement, and upon the request of the furnishing party, shall cooperate with the furnishing party in contesting such disclosure. Except in connection with failure to discharge responsibilities set forth in the preceding sentence, neither party shall be liable in damages for any disclosure pursuant to judicial action or governmental regulations.

3. 将小分句转译为英文名词化结构

（1）限制民事行为能力人订立的合同，经法定代理人追认后，该合同有效，但纯获利益的合同或者与其年龄、智力、精神健康状况相适应而订立的合同，不必经法定代理人追认。

A contract concluded by a person with limited civil capacity for conduct becomes effective upon ratification by its legal agent (s), provided that a contract from which such person accrues benefits only or the conclusion of which is appropriate for his age, intelligence or mental health does not require ratification by his legal agent (s).

（2）只有在另一方事先书面同意、经董事会一致通过并经审批机关批准后，一方才可向第三方出售、转让或以其他方式处置（合称“转让”）其对合营公司注册资本享有的全部或部分权益。

A party may sell, transfer or otherwise dispose of (each a “transfer”) all or any part of its interest in the registered capital of the Company to any third party only with prior written consent of the other party, the approval of the Board and the approval of the Examination and Approval Authority.

（3）民事主体从事民事活动，应当有利于节约资源、保护生态环境。

Any civil activity conducted by civil subjects shall be conducive to saving resources and protecting the ecological environment.

4. 将“…的”结构转译为英文名词性结构

在法律文本中，会有大量的“…的”结构表述假设或者条件，对于此结构，也可以通过转过为名词性结构的方式进行处理。

（1）有限责任公司变更为股份有限公司的，或者股份有限公司变更为有限责任公司的，公司变更前的债权、债务由变更后的公司承继。

In the case of a conversion from a limited liability company into a company limited by shares or vice versa, the liability of the company before the conversion shall be assumed by the converted company.

（2）上市公司重大资产重组存在下列情形之一的，应当提交并购重组委审核。

Any of the following circumstances arising in a listed company's major assets restructuring shall be submitted to the Listed Company Merger and Reorganization Examination Committee for examination.

第二节 法律英语的句法特征

第一节主要研究了法律英语的词汇特征，本节将主要研究法律英语的句法特征。

法律英语的句法特征，主要表现在以下几个方面：（1）冗长句式；（2）条件句的普遍存在；（3）多用被动语态；（4）名词的多重修饰。

一、冗长句式

据专家统计，在法律文件中，句子的平均长度为 271 个单词。这造成了阅读英文法律文件的难度大大增加，这除了读者要求英文功底好之外，还需要具备相应的法律背景知识，才能够真正理解句子的含义。

但是，无论句子再长，也要遵循一定的语法规则，通过分析句子结构和句式特征，法律英语中的长难句也很容易被攻克。英语的五种基本句型为：

1. 主语 + 谓语（subject + verb）

It works.（药品/方法等）有效果。

2. 主语 + 谓语 + 宾语（subject + verb + object）

I like apples. 我喜欢苹果。

3. 主语 + 谓语 + 双宾语（间接宾语 + 直接宾语）（subject + verb + indirect object + direct object）

I will tell you the truth. 我会告诉你真相。

4. 主语 + 谓语 + 宾语 + 宾补（subject + verb + object + object complement）

You make me happy. 你使我快乐。

5. 主语 + 谓语（系动词） + 表语（subject + verb（link verb） + predicative）

You are beautiful. 你很漂亮。

以上五个句子代表的就是英语中最基本的五大句型，任何高难度的法律英语表达都是从这五大基本句型发展而来的。如下面的例子所示：

范例一：

The Buyer may, within 15 days upon arrival of the goods at the destination,
①　⑤

lodge a claim against the Seller for short-weight being supported by
②　③　④

Inspection Certificate issued by a reputable public surveyor.
⑥　⑦

分析方法：

针对以上句子，我们先找出句子主干：the buyer may lodge a claim against the Seller for short-weight，其中 the buyer 为主语，may lodge 为谓语，a claim 为宾语，against the Seller for short-weight 为宾语补足语，因此我们确认该句的基本句型为第四种句型（主语 + 谓语 + 宾语 + 宾补）。句子的主语和谓语被⑤（时间状语 within 15 days upon arrival of the goods at the destination）所隔离。结构⑥ being supported by Inspection certificate 是动名词结构，充当 short-weight 的后置定语，而结构⑦ issued by a reputable public surveyor 又为结构⑥中的 Inspection Certificate 的后置定语。

参考译文：

货物抵达目的港 15 天内，买方可以凭有信誉的公共检验员出示的检验证明向卖方提出短重索赔。

范例二：

"Confidential Information" shall mean and include any information and data
①　②　③

of a commercially sensitive nature that is not generally known to the public,
③　④

that is marked "confidential" or "proprietary", or identified as confidential at the time of disclosure,
⑤

or which by its nature or the circumstances surrounding its disclosure shall reasonably be regarded as confidential (regardless of whether such information is specifically designated as confidential and regardless of whether such information is in written, oral, electronic, or other form), ⑥

relating to the business, technology, research, manufacturing, marketing, products, samples, processes and/or customers or suppliers of a Party, ⑦

disclosed by the Disclosing Party to the Receiving Party under this Agreement. ⑧

分析方法：

本句子共包含 109 个单词，句子主干为 "Confidential information" shall mean and include any information and data of a commercially sensitive nature. 其中结构①为主语，结构②为谓语，结构③为宾语，可以确定本句的句型为第二种基本句型：主语 + 谓语 + 宾语。如果再细分，句子主干中的 of a commercially sensitive nature 应该为 information and data 的后置定语。两个 that 引导的从句，一个 which 引导的从句，均为非限制性定语从句，修饰 information and data。另外，relating to 引导一个现在分词非谓语结构，disclosed by 引导一个过去分词非谓语结构，也是做后置定语，修饰 information and data。Relating to 引导的 the business, technology, research, manufacturing, marketing, products, samples, processes and/or customers or suppliers 为名词并列，罗列保密信息所包含的范围。

因此，本句子虽然很长，但是里面大部分内容都是由起修饰作用为定语所组成：of a commercially sensitive nature，两个 that 从句，一个 which 从句，两个非谓语动词结构。

另外，对于三个非限制性定语从句而言，即，结构④⑤⑥，我们还可以进一步分析。结构④that is not generally known to the public，属于第五种句型：主语 + 谓语（系动词） + 表语；结构⑤that is marked "confidential" or "proprietary", or identified as confidential at the time of disclosure，也属于第五种句型：主语 + 谓语（系动词） + 表语；结构⑥which by its nature or the circumstances surrounding its disclosure shall reasonably be regarded as confidential (regardless of whether such information is specifically designated as confidential and regardless of whether such information is in written, oral, electronic, or other form) 比较复杂一

些。我们单独分析。

句子which by its nature or the circumstances surrounding its disclosure shall reasonably be regarded as confidential（regardless of whether such information is specifically designated as confidential and regardless of whether such information is in written, oral, electronic, or other form）中，which 为主语，shall reasonably be regarded as confidential 为谓语和表语，本句子主干也属于主语 + 谓语（系动词）+表语，只是主语 which 跟谓语表语部分被 by 引导的介词短语结构隔离开来，造成句子复杂。

综上，本句用了多个定语结构把保密的内容尽可能多的包含进去，体现了法律语言的精确性。

参考译文：

"保密信息"是指并包括任何不为公众所熟知的、具有商业敏感性的、已被标记为"机密"或"专有"，或在披露时被标识为机密的信息和数据，或其性质或围绕其披露的情况应合理地视为与业务、技术有关的机密信息（无论此类信息是否被专门指定为机密，并且无论该信息是书面、口头、电子还是其他形式），且该信息是披露方根据本协议向接受方披露的与商业、技术、研究、制造、营销、产品、样品、过程和/或一方的客户或供应商相关。

范例三：

The Franchisee, in further consideration of the grant of this license, agrees to pay
①　⑤　②
the Franchisor, without notice from Franchisor, on the tenth (10th) day after the
③　⑥　⑦
end of each Period, a non-refundable Advertising Fee (Brand Development Fee)
④
equal to two percent (2%) of the Franchisee's Gross Revenue.
⑧

分析方法：

本句子的主干为：The franchisee agrees to pay the Franchisor a non-refundable Advertising Fee，可以该句子确定属于第三种基本句型：主语 + 谓语 + 双

宾语。其中 the Franchisee 是主语，agrees to pay 是谓语，the Franchisor 是间接宾语，a non-refundable Advertising Fee 是直接宾语。

结构⑤中介词短语 in consideration of 引导方式状语，结构⑥为 without 引导方式状语，结构⑦为时间状语，结构⑧为 equal to 引导的后置定语，修饰 Advertising Fee。

参考译文：

作为授予本许可的进一步的对价，特许经营人同意无需特许人通知，在每个期间结束后的第十（10）日向特许人支付特许经营人总收入百分之二（2%）的广告费（品牌发展费），而且该费用是不可退还的。

范例四：

The Licensee shall keep secret towards third parties all the technical

① ② ⑤ ③

specifications for the products under license entrusted to him by the Licensor

③ ⑥

as well as all the other experience（know-how）transferred to the Licensee

④ ⑦

except as required by the purpose of this Agreement.

⑧

分析方法：

本句子的主干为：The Licensee shall keep all the technical specifications for the products under license as well as all the other experience（know-how）secret，其中 The License 是主语，shall keep 是谓语，结构③和④是两个并列宾语，结构⑤secret 是补语，可以确定该句子属于第四种基本句型（主语 + 谓语 + 宾语 + 宾补）。结构⑥是过去分词短语结构做后置定语，修饰结构③，结构⑦也是过去分词短语结构做后置定语，修饰结构④。结构⑧是一个让步状语结构。

这个句子与范例一均为主语 + 谓语 + 宾语 + 宾补，难点在于，本句中的宾补放到了宾语的前面，主要是因为两个并列宾语结构太长，为了保持句子的平衡，故作倒装处理。

参考译文：

对于许可方向其授予的许可项下产品的一切技术规范以及向被许可方转让的其他一切经验（专有技术），被许可均应予以保密，除非本协议另有要求。

总之，通过以上例子，我们可以看出，无论法律英语的句子多么复杂，都无外乎从五种基本句型发展到枝繁叶茂。由于存在定语、状语、补语等修饰结构，以及主语和谓语被隔离，倒装现象的存在等，使句子变得复杂。在分析复杂句子的时候，我们可以先找出句子主干，之后再剥离出定语、状语、补语等修饰结构，找出倒装、隔离结构，将句子结构层层剥离，就像剥洋葱一样，再复杂的句子也会迎刃而解。

二、条件句的大量存在

由于法律英语中经常表达的是假设情形 + 后果，因为存在大量的条件句，而条件句除了用 if 引导之外，为了突出法律英语的严肃性和准确性，经常用其他的结构代替 if。如：in the event of，in case（that），in case of，provided（that），should，where。下面分别举例子介绍：

范例一：

In the event of any loss caused by the delay in the delivery, the Representative can claim a compensation from the Manufacturer with a certificate and detailed list registered by the administration authorities of the Representative's site.

参考译文：

如果由于延误交货而造成任何损失，则授权代表可以向制造商主张赔偿，并提供授权代表所在地的管理机构提供的证书和详细清单。

范例二：

In case the Contract terminates prematurely, the Contract Appendices shall likewise terminate.

如果合同提前终止，则合同附录也应终止。

范例三：

Should all or part of the contract be unable to be fulfilled owing to the fault of one party, the breaching party shall bear the responsibilities caused therefrom. Should it be the fault of both parties, they shall bear their respective responsibilities according to actual situations.

参考译文：

如果由于一方过错而无法全部或部分履行合同，违约方应承担由此引起的责任。如果是双方的错，双方应根据实际情况承担各自的责任。

注：should 表达“条件”的时候，一般放在句首，表达一种虚拟语气，句子谓语用动词原形。

范例四：

Either Side can replace the representatives it has appointed provided that it submits a written notice to the other Side.

参考译文：

只要向另一方提交书面通知，任何一方都可以更换其任命的代表。

范例五：

Where a unit commits a crime, it shall be fined, and the persons who are directly in charge and the others who are directly responsible for the crime shall be imposed criminal punishment.

参考译文：

单位犯罪的，对单位判处罚金，并对其直接负责的主管人员和其他直接责任人员判处刑罚。

范例六：

Where a defendant is fined and the same is not forthwith paid, the officer may order the defendant to be searched.

参考译文：

凡被告人被判处罚款，但没有随即缴付罚款，长官可命令搜查被告人。

注：本句中的 the same 指的是前文的 fine（罚金），the same 的这种用法，我们在第一节法律英语的词汇特征已经介绍过，此处不再赘述。

三、多用被动结构

被动结构大量出现在法律英语中，其最大功能就是隐藏和弱化动作的行为者，在法律语境下就是隐藏和弱化法律主体，模糊对法律行为主体的认定，从而使法律语言显得更加客观公正。

范例一：

All construction projects shall be designed in compliance with the requirements for fortification against earthquakes and in conformity with the standard aseismatic design and shall be constructed in accordance with the design.

参考译文：

建设工程必须按照抗震设防要求和抗震设计规范进行抗震设计，并按照抗震设计进行施工。

范例二：

Any term or provision of this Agreement may be waived, or the time for its performance may be extended, by the party or parties entitled to the benefit thereof.

参考译文：

有权根据本协议规定获益的当事人可放弃本协议的任何条款或规定，或延迟本协议的履行时间。

范例三：

If any provision, or part of a provision of this Agreement is determined to be invalid, illegal or unenforceable by any rule or law, or public policy of any jurisdiction, all other provisions, or other parts of the provision of this Agreement shall nevertheless remain in full force and effect.

参考译文：

如本协议的任何条款或条款之一部分依照有关司法管辖区的法庭裁决、法律或公共政策而被确认无效、违法或不可执行，本协议的其余条款或条款之其余部分仍将完全有效。

范例四：

The formation of this Contract, its validity, interpretation, execution and settlement of disputes in connection herewith shall be governed by the laws of the People's Republic of China, but in the event that there is no published and publicly available law in the PRC governing a particular matter relating to this Contract, reference shall be made to general international commercial practice.

参考译文：

本合同的订立、效力、解释、执行及合同争议的解决，均受中华人民共和国法律管辖。中国颁布的法律对本合同相关的某一事项未作规定的，参照国际商业管理。

四、名词的多重修饰

在法律英语中，有时候为了使得语言更加精确，需要穷尽所有可能的情况，从而造成一个名词或者名词短语有多重修饰。

范例一：

The agent shall be responsible for damages and economic losses ① incurred by the Joint Venture Company ② solely due to the failure by the Agent to properly inform the Joint Venture Company of any amendments to the sales contract ③entered into by the Agent on behalf of the Joint Venture Company with a purchaser.

参考译文：

代理人应对仅因代理人未将其代理合营公司与买受人签订的*买卖合同的任何修改未能适当地通知合营公司*而使合营公司发生的损害和经济损失负责。

本句中，名词词组 damages and economic losses 后共有三个修饰结构：

① incurred by the Joint Venture Company

② solely due to the failure by the Agent to properly inform the Joint Venture Company of any amendments to the sales contract

③ entered into by the Agent on behalf of the Joint Venture Company with a purchaser

其中①是后置定语修饰 damages and economic losses，②是原因状语，对于

damages and economic losses 产生的原因进行说明，而③是②中 sales contract 的后置定语起修饰作用。因此，本句中存在两层修饰关系。

我们可以再回到在本节第一点冗长句式中的句子：

"Confidential Information" shall mean and include any information and data
①　②　③

of a commercially sensitive nature that is not generally known to the public,
③　④

that is marked "confidential" or "proprietary", or identified as confidential at the time of disclosure,　⑤

or which by its nature or the circumstances surrounding its disclosure should reasonably be regarded as confidential (regardless of whether such information is specifically designated as confidential and regardless of whether such information is in written, oral, electronic, or other form),　⑥

relating to the business, technology, research, manufacturing, marketing, products, samples, processes and/or customers or suppliers of a Party,　⑦

disclosed by the Disclosing Party to the Receiving Party under this Agreement.
⑧

该句子也是存在多重修饰。被修饰结构 any information and data 后共存在五个修饰结构：③④⑤⑥⑦⑧。

五、法律英语常用短语和词组

法律英语频繁出现一些短语和词组，其表达方式与中文表达不完全对应，造成理解困难。本节将主要介绍以下常见词组：otherwise, subject to, without prejudice to, for the purpose of, in respect of, save/except (for), notwithstanding。

（一）Otherwise

Otherwise 在普通英语中的含义有："不然，否则"；"在其他方面"；"别样，以另外方式"。在法律英语中，otherwise 一般指"除……以外"或"以其他方式"。应具体情况具体分析，一般要与上下文连贯。它常与前置的 unless, except 或 or，及后置的动词过去分词连用。

范例一:

A company secretary of a company may, unless it is otherwise provided in the Articles of Association of the company or by any agreement with the company, resign as company secretary at any time.

参考译文:

公司的公司秘书可随时辞去公司秘书职位，除非该公司的章程或与该公司订立的任何协议另有规定。

范例二:

Where a law or administrative regulation provides otherwise in respect of the method for calculation of damages and any limitation on damages, such provisions apply.

参考译文:

法律、行政法规对赔偿额的计算方法和赔偿额另有规定的，从其规定。

范例三:

The handling of administrative penalty cases by customs houses shall be governed by these Provisions, unless it is otherwise prescribed by any law or administrative regulations.

参考译文:

海关办理行政处罚案件适用本规定，法律、行政法规另有规定的除外。

范例四:

If an offeror expressly indicates, whether by stating a fixed time for acceptance or otherwise, that an offer shall not be revoked, then it is irrevocable.

参考译文:

如果要约人确定了承诺期限或者以其他形式明示要约不可撤销，则要约为不可撤销要约。

范例五:

In case one party delayed performance or otherwise breached the contract, thereby frustrating the purpose of the contract, the other party is entitled to rescind the contract.

参考译文：

当事人一方迟延履行债务或者有其他违约行为致使不能实现合同目的的，另一方有权解除合同。

范例六：

No person shall be held to answer for a capital, or otherwise infamous crime, unless on a presentment or indictment of a Grand Jury, except in cases arising in the land or naval forces, or in the militia, when in actual service in time of war of public danger.

参考译文：

无论何人，除非根据大陪审团的报告或起诉书，不得受判处死罪或其他不名誉罪行之审判，但发生在陆、海军中或发生在战时或出现公共危险时服现役的民兵中的案件，不在此限。

范例七：

A party who was unable to perform a contract due to force majeure is exempted from liability in part or in whole in light of the impact of the event of force majeure, except otherwise provided by law. Where an event of force majeure occurred after the party's delay in performance, it is not exempted from liability.

参考译文：

因不可抗力不能履行合同的，根据不可抗力的影响，部分或者全部免除责任，但法律另有规定的除外。当事人迟延履行后发生不可抗力的，不能免除责任。

有的时候，otherwise 更多的是起到舒缓语气到作用，并没有实质的意义，如下例：

范例八：

He shall have power, by and with the advice and consent of the Senate, to make treaties, provided two-thirds of the Senators present concur; and he shall nominate, and by and with the advice and consent of the Senate, shall appoint ambassadors, other public ministers and consuls, judges of the Supreme Court, and all other officers of the United States, whose appointments are not herein otherwise provided for, and which shall be established by law; but the Congress may by law vest the appointment of such inferior officers, as they think proper, in the President alone, in the courts of law, or in the heads of departments. (from Section 2-President to Commander-in-Chief Article, the Constitution)

参考译文:

总统有权缔订条约，但须争取参议院的意见和同意，并须出席的参议员中三分之二的人赞成；他有权提名，并于取得参议院的意见和同意后，任命大使、公使及领事、最高法院的法官，以及一切其他在本宪法中未经明定但以后将依法律的规定而设置之合众国官员；国会可以制定，酌情把这些较低级官员的任命权，授予总统本人，授予法院，或授予各行政部门的首长。

(二) Subject to

在法律英语中，subject to 一般指“遵从、遵守”；“根据”；“受制于”，如：

范例一：

This letter of Credit is subject to the Uniform Customs and Practices for Documentary Credits (1983 Revision), International Chamber of Commerce, Publication No. 500.

参考译文:

本信用证遵从国际商会第500号出版物，即《跟单信用证统一规则》。

范例二：

No state shall, without the consent of the Congress, lay any imposts or duties on imports or exports, except what may be absolutely necessary for executing its inspection laws; and the net produce of all duties and imposts, laid by any state on imports or exports, shall be for the use of the treasury of the United States; and all such laws shall be subject to the revision and control of the Congress.

参考译文:

未经国会同意，各州不得对进口货物或出口货物征收任何税款，但为了执行该州的检验法而有绝对的必要时，不在此限；任何州对于进出口货物所征的税，其净收益应归合众国国库使用；所有这一类法律，国会对之有修正和监督之权。

注：该句中，subject to 意思是指“受制于……”，参考译文作了意译处理。

再如：

Rates of Exchange is often subject to alterations.（汇率经常处于变动中）

范例三：

Subject to this clause, an appeal shall be brought in such matter and shall be subject to such conditions as are prescribed by rules made under Clause 4.

参考译文：

根据本条规定，这种情况下应提出上诉，并须受第 4 款订立的规则的限制。

注：本句中有两个 subject to 结构。其中第一个 subject to 的意思为“根据”，第二个 subject to 的意思为“受制于”。

范例四：

Subject to Clause 6, the Board shall have jurisdiction to inquire into, hear and determine the claims specified in the Schedule.

参考译文：

根据第 6 条的规定，仲裁处具备调查、审讯及裁决附表内指明的申索的司法管辖权。

（三）Without prejudice to

在法律英语中，without prejudice to 一般指“在不影响……的原则下”或者“不妨碍/损害……的情况下”。

范例一：

During the period of entrusted shareholding, Party A has the right to request Party B to transfer the shares held by it and the shareholders' rights involved to its own name or to any third party designated by it. For the formalities, relevant legal documents involved therein, without prejudice to Party B's substantive interests,

Party B must unconditionally agree and accept.

参考译文：

在委托持股期间，甲方有权随时要求乙方将其代持的股权及相关股东权益转移到自己或自己指定的任何第三人名下，乙方应无条件予以同意并及时予以配合协助和办理相关法律手续，届时涉及的相关法律文件，在不损害乙方实质利益的条件下，乙方须无条件同意并无条件承受。

范例二：

The employer may terminate this agreement without any period of notice or payment if the Employee at any time is guilty of serious misconduct or neglect or any other conduct in respect of the Employee's employment or personal life which may seriously adversely affect the interests of the Employer. Such termination shall be without prejudice to any other rights of the Employer against the Employee.

参考译文：

如果雇员的工作或个人生活中有严重不端、重大过失或任何其他行为，可能严重损害雇主的利益的，雇主可以终止本协议，且无需任何通知或支付经济补偿。该终止不应损害雇主对雇员的任何其他权利。

范例三：

Without prejudice to your power and discretions, we hereby authorize you or your agents to take any actions including but not limited to the following……

参考译文：

在不损害贵方权力和自由裁定权的前提下，本公司兹授权贵方或贵方代理人采取包括但不限于以下行为的权利……

（四）For the purpose of

For the purpose of 有两种含义：一是“就……而言”；二是“为了……（目的）”。

范例一：

For the purpose of any repossession pursuant to Clause 10 Party A or its agent shall be entitled to enter any relevant land or buildings with such transport as may be necessary.

参考译文：

就根据第 10 条进行的任何重新占有而言，甲方或其代理人有权凭借所需要交通工具进入相关土地或建筑物。

范例二：

For the purpose of this Agreement, "control" shall mean either the ownership of fifty-one percent or more of the ordinary share capital of the company carrying the right to vote at general meetings or the power to nominate a majority of the board of directors of the Company.

参考译文：

就本协议而言，"控制"系指拥有在股东大会上有投票权的百分之五十一或以上的公司普通股股本，或拥有任命公司董事会中多数董事的权利。

范例三：

A judge may, on the application ofan appellant who is in custody, order the appellant to be brought up to the court in custody for the purpose of attending his appeal or any application or any proceeding therein.

参考译文：

法官可应羁押中的上诉人的申请，为了使上诉人能出席其上诉或其中任何申请或法律程序而命令将他在羁押状态下带上法庭。

（五）In respect of

在普通英语中，in respect of 一般指"与…有关"，"就…方面"，其同义词组有：in connection with，in relation to，relating to，with reference to，of 等，但是在法律英语中，我们一般用正式程度较高的 in respect of 来表达此含义。

范例一：

The Licensee shall, at the request of the Licensor and at the Licensor's expense, give full cooperation to the Licensor in any action or claim brought or threatened to be brought in respect of the Licensed Trademarks, including joining at a party to any proceedings.

参考译文：

对于针对许可商标提起或威胁拟提起的诉讼或索赔，应许可方要求并由许可方支付费用，被许可方应给予许可方充分合作，包括作为当事人参与任何诉讼。

范例二：

The company shall pay taxes and enjoy preferential tax treatment in respect of its economic activities in accordance with the relevant laws and regulations of PRC and the relevant policies of the Industrial Park.

参考译文：

公司应根据中国的有关法律法规和工业园区的有关政策，就其经济活动缴纳税收并享受税收优惠待遇。

范例三：

Party A shall bear all the investment risks to the company to the limit of its capital contributions entrusted. Party B is not deemed to bear the obligation of maintaining and increasing the value of the capital entrusted by Party A. Therefore, Party A shall not claim compensation or indemnification from Party B in respect of the loss from the assets contributed.

参考译文：

甲方应以其委托出资的数额为限，承担对公司出资的一切投资风险，乙方不对甲方委托的出资承担保值增值义务，甲方不得就出资财产的盈亏要求乙方承担补偿或赔偿责任。

范例四：

You must pay to us or our nominee in pounds sterling or such other currency as we may require, the following sums without deduction or set-offs: our legal costs in respect of the signing of this agreement.

The Service Fee shall be due and payable whether or not you have received the service fee due to you in respect of any outlet under the relevant franchise agreement.

参考译文：

您必须以英镑或我们可能要求的其他货币向我们或我们的代名人支付以下款项，且不得扣除或抵销：与签订本协议相关的律师费。

无论您是否已收到根据相关特许经营协议就任何一家门店应付给您的服务费，服务费均应支付。

（六）Save/except（for）

Save 在普通英语中的含义是“拯救”，而在法律英语中则表示“除了…之外”。

范例一：

Save as is provided in this Clause, nothing in this Ordinance shall require the disclosure by a legal adviser of any privileged information, communication, book, document etc.

参考译文：

除本条另有规定外，本条例并不要求法律顾问披露任何特权信息、通讯信息、簿册、文件等。

范例二：

Save as provided in Clause 10, no payment of maternity leave pay or other sum may be made in lieu of the grant of maternity leave.

除第 10 条另有规定外，不得以支付产假薪酬或其他款项的方式代替给予产假。

范例三：

Save/Except as otherwise provided herein, all notices or demands sent by registered airmail shall be deemed received 8 days after they have been sent and notices or demands sent by telex shall be deemed received at the time of the dispatch thereof.

参考译文：

除本合同另有规定，所有通知和请求以航空挂号信寄出的，寄出后八日即视为送达，以电传方式发送的，则在发出时视为送达。

（七）Notwithstanding

Notwithstanding 在普通英语中很少见，但是法律英语中，其出现的频率还比较高。该词表达让步的语气，一般翻译为“即使”、“尽管”，作为连词使用，后面一般引导名词性短语或者让步状语从句，相当于 although/though/even if。

范例一：

This constitution, and the laws of the United States which shall be made in pursuance thereof, and all treaties made, or which shall be made, under the authority of the United States shall be the supreme law of the land; and the judges in every state shall be bound thereby, anything in the constitution or laws of any state to the contrary notwithstanding.

参考译文：

本宪法及依本宪法所制定之合众国法律，以及合众国已经缔结及将要缔结的一切条约，皆为全国之最高法律；每个州的法官都应受其约束，任何一州宪法或法律中的任何内容与之抵触时，均不得有违这一规定。

注：最后一句：and the judges in every state shall be bound thereby, anything in the constitution or laws of any state to the contrary notwithstanding，直译为：每个州的法官都应受其约束，即使该州的宪法或法律有相反规定。至于直译与意译的效果孰优孰劣，大家可以自己体会。

范例二：

If the party A places an order within the time designated in this offer, the price for the goods will remain firm notwithstanding any variation in the costs of producing the goods.

参考译文：

如果在要约指定的时间内，甲方下发了订单，则货物价格应保持不变，即使生产成本发生变化。

范例三：

Notwithstanding the foregoing, both parties agree that the foreign shareholder may sell or transfer all or part of its rights and interests owned by it in the registered capital of the Company to its affiliated party without restrictions of Article 5 and Article 6.

参考译文：

尽管有前述规定，双方同意，外方股东可将其在公司注册资本中拥有的全部或部分权益出售或转让给其关联方，而不受第 5 条和第 6 条的限制。

范例四：

Notwithstanding any other provisions to the contrary herein, insurance coverage and limits shall be subject to approval of all the parties.

参考译文：

即使本合同中有任何其他相反规定，保险范围和责任限制亦应当以各方同意为准。

（八） Any Person Who Does… Shall

大多数的法律条文表达的都是一种假设情形和行为后果，因此，“Any Person Who Does… Shall”句型出现的频率很高，也是一种非常简明、直接的表达方式。

范例一：

Any person who, without lawful authority or reasonable excuse, while having dealings of any kind with any other public body, offers any advantage to any public servant employed by that public body, shall be guilty of an offence.

参考译文：

任何人与其他公共机构进行任何事务往来时，无合法授权或合理辩解而向受雇于该公共机构的公职人员提供任何利益，即属犯罪。

范例二：

Any person convicted of an offence and sentenced to life imprisonment under the Criminal Law shall, by reason of such conviction, be disqualified to hold the post of director and office in a company for a period of 5 years after expiration of the sentence.

参考译文：

触犯《刑法》之罪名且被判处有期徒刑的，由于此判刑，自刑期届满之日起五年内不得担任公司的董事、高管。

范例三：

Any person who sets fire, breaches dikes, causes explosions, spreads poison, and employs other dangerous means that lead to serious injuries or death, or causes major losses to public or private property shall be sentenced to no less than 10 years of fixed-term imprisonment, life imprisonment, or death.

参考译文：

放火、决水、爆炸、投毒或者以其他危险方法致人重伤、死亡或者使公私财产遭受重大损失的，处十年以上有期徒刑、无期徒刑或者死刑。

第三节　常见合同通用条款

有关合同的定义，学者和立法者从不同的视角给出了不同的定义，其中最经典的为 Black's Law Dictionary 中的定义："an agreement between two or more parties creating obligations that are enforceable or otherwise recognizable at law"。

《中华人民共和国合同法》第二条规定："合同是指平等主体的自然人、法人、其他组织之间设立、变更、终止民事权利义务关系的协议。"中国法律框架下，一个有效合同的构成要素有：合同双方具有完全民事行为能力（legal capacity to contract）、成立合同的合意（agreement of mutual assent reached through offer and acceptance）、交易内容合法或者不违反公序良俗（not be illegal or contrary to public policy）。

英国法有关合同的定义为："a contract is a legally binding agreement concerning a bargain which is essentially commercial in its nature and involves the sale or hire of commodities such as goods, services or land"，根据英国法，一个合同必不可少的要素有：offer（要约），acceptance（承诺），consideration（对价），intention to create legal relations（建立法律关系的意图）。

美国法有关合同的定义为："a contract is a promise that one gives voluntarily and with the intent that the contract be enforceable at law”，根据美国法，一个合同必不可少的要素有：competent parties（适格当事人），legal subject matter（标的物合法），legal consideration（合法的对价），mutuality of agreement（合意），mutuality of obligation（双方互负义务）。

对比以上不同的定义可得出，合同的实质是合同当事人就合同标的进行的权利义务方面的约定，同时，合同应该是当事人的真实意思表示，且合同内容不得违法或者违反社会公序良俗。

同时，为了更好地理解 contract，还要区分以下几个概念：contract，agreement，covenant，indenture，deed，compact。

“Agreement”是指：although often used as synonym with“contract”，agreement is a broader term，e. g. an agreement might lack an essential element of a contract. 合同属于协议的一种，协议的范围比合同大，规定不如合同具体、规范。即：称作合同的，肯定也可称作协议；称作协议的，不见得符合合同的要求。

而 covenant，indenture，deed 主要针对不动产的转让，指经签字和转移的一方向另一方出让土地、租房或留遗产的书面协议，历史上的“房契”即 deed。Compact 指自然人、国家、州之间订立的协议、协定或合同，主要指国家间就共同关心的问题达成的协议，这意味着 compact 一词不大会出现在民事、商事合同中。在实务中，使用较多的是 contract 和 agreement。英文合同名称一般表达格式为：contract for XXX，XXX contract 或 XXX agreement，如：contracts for international sale of goods（国际货物销售合同），contracts for international technology transfer（国际技术转让合同），contracts for Sino-foreign joint ventures（中外合资经营合同），contracts for international engineering projects（国际工程承包合同），contracts for compensation trade（补偿贸易合同），contracts for Sino-foreign cooperation development of natural resources（中外合作开发自然资源合同），contracts for foreign labor services（涉外劳务合同），contracts for international leasing affairs（国际租赁合同），contract for sale of commodity houses（商品房买卖合同），property management contract（物业管理合同），tenancy agreement（租赁协议），outsourcing agreement（外包协议），technology transfer agreement（技术转让协议）。

本章将介绍十二个最常见的通用条款：合同序言条款、合同定义条款、语言与文本份数条款、合同生效条款、保证条款、不可抗力条款、知识产权条款、违约条款、合同解除与终止条款、通知和送达条款、争议解决条款、法律适用条款。接下来将就这十二个通用条款的写作展开分别论述。

一、合同序言条款（Preamble）

合同的序言（preamble）一般包括签署合同的日期和地点、当事人基本信息、当事人合法依据，以及订约缘由/鉴于条款（recitals or WHEREAS clause）。

当事人基本信息一般包含当事人名称、国籍、主要营业地或者住所地等信息，当事人合法依据（each party's authority）一般指当事人（一般指公司）合法存在所依据的法律，例如：a corporation duly organized and existing under the laws of…。订约缘由/鉴于条款则指签订合同的原因。

（一）合同序言范例

范例一：

This Contract is made this 20th date of June, 2019 in Zhuhai, China, by and between XXX (Full Name) Company under the Law of China, having its registered address in Zhuhai, its legal address being ________ (hereinafter referred to as the "Buyer") and ABC (Full Name) Company under the Law of ________, having its registered address in ________, its legal address being ________ (hereinafter referred to as the "Seller").

Whereas the Seller possesses know-how for the designing, manufacturing, and marketing of ________;

Whereas the Seller has the right and desires to transfer the above-signed know-how to the Buyer;

Whereas the Buyer desires to design, manufacture, sell and export by using the Licensor's know-how.

Therefore, in considering of the premises and the mutual conveniences, the Buyer agrees to buy, and the Seller agrees to sell the following goods on the terms and conditions as follows:

范例二：

Transferee (Party A):
Registered Address:
Legal representative:
Contact information:

Transferor (Party B):
Registered Address:
Legal representative:
Contact information:

In consideration of:

Party B is the legal owner of ________ formula (hereinafter referred to as "the Formula"),

Party B would like to transfer the above mentioned ________ formula to Party A for use, production, operation and sales,

Party A is willing to accept the "the formula" and agrees to pay Party B transfer fee,

After friendly negotiation between the two parties, the following agreement is hereby reached in accordance with the "Contract Law of the People's Republic of China".

附汉语版本如下：

受让方（甲方）：
住所地：
法定代表人：
联系方式：

转让方（乙方）：
住所地：
法定代表人：
联系方式：

鉴于：

乙方是________配方（以下简称"本配方"）的合法拥有者，

乙方向甲方转让上述________配方，供甲方使用、生产经营及销售，

甲方愿意受让"本配方"，并同意支付乙方转让费，

经双方友好协商，根据《中华人民共和国合同法》的规定，达成如下协议，并由双方共同恪守。

范例三：

XXX, a company incorporated under the laws of the Britain and having its registered seat at Gerengracht 649, 2045 CE London, the UK, and

YYY, a company incorporated under the laws of [____] and having its registered seat at [____] (the "Partner").

WHEREAS:

(i) XXX operates an online accommodation reservation system (the "System") through which participating Accommodations can make their rooms available for reservation, and through which visitors can make reservations at such Accommodations (the "Service");

(ii) XXX maintains and exploits its own websites, apps, platform, tools or other devices (collectively the " XXX Platform"), and also provides the Service and links to the Service on the websites, apps, platform, tools or other devices of third parties;

(iii) the Partner owns, controls, hosts and/or operates one or more websites, apps, platform, tools and/or other devices;

(iv) the Partner and XXX wish to make the Service available on the Partner Platform for the customers and visitors of the Partner Platform (s) and in such form and on such terms and conditions as set out in this Agreement.

HAVE AGREED AS FOLLOWS:

参考译文：

XXX，依英国法律成立的公司，注册地为英国伦敦 Gerengracht 649, 2045 CE，以及

YYY，依［____］法律成立的公司，注册地为［____］（下文简称“合作伙伴”）。

鉴于：

（i）XXX 运营在线酒店预订系统（下文简称“系统”），通过该系统，合作酒店可以提供房间供访问者预订，而访问者也可以预订此类酒店（下文简称“服务”）；

（ii）XXX 维护并开发自身的网站、应用程序、平台、工具或其他设备（下文统称“XXX 平台”），并提供服务及指向第三方网站、应用程序、平台、工具或其他设备上的服务的链接；

（iii）合作伙伴拥有、控制、托管和/或运营一个或多个网站、应用程序、平台、工具和/或其他设备；

（iv）合作伙伴和XXX希望借助合作平台向客户以及合作平台的访问者提供服务，服务形式及条款如本协议所述。

双方兹达成以下协议：

（二）当事人范例

有关当事人（parties）的写作，有不同的格式，仅列举以下几种供参考：

范例一： This contract/agreement is made and entered into by and between ________ (hereinafter referred to as "Party A") and ________ (hereinafter referred to as "Party B");

范例二： THIS AGREEMENT is made the ____ th day of (month), ________ (year) by and between ________, a company incorporated in ________ (country) and having its registered office/principal place of business/head office at ________ (address) (hereinafter called "the Company") of the one part and ____ (ID No: ____) of (domicile) (hereinafter called "the Manager") of the other part;

范例三： Effective as of ________ (date) this Agreement is made and entered into between ________ (hereinafter referred to as "Party A") and ________ (hereinafter referred to as "Party B").

范例四： Party A: ________________ Ltd. ("licensor")

Party B: ________________ Co., Ltd. ("licensee")

This agreement is made and entered into the 20th day of December 2018 by and between Party A and Party B.

◆ 知识点梳理

1. the contract is made and entered into by and between…：“…与…订立合同”，此结构中的made and entered into，by and between均属法律英语的词汇并列现象。

2. terms and conditions，“条款”，词语并列现象。

3. hereinafter referred to as，“以下简称”，古英语（hereinafter）的使用。

4. licensor，licensee，“许可人，被许可人”。

二、合同定义条款（Definitions）

范例一：

In these Articles, words and expressions defined in the Companies Law shall have the same meaning and, unless otherwise required by the context, (a) the singular shall include the plural and vice versa; (b) the masculine shall include the feminine and the neuter and references to persons shall include companies and all legal entities capable of having a legal existence; (c) "may" shall be construed as permissive and "shall" shall be construed as imperative; (d) a reference to a dollar or dollars (or $) is a reference to dollars of the United States of America; and (e) references to a statutory enactment shall include reference to any amendment or re-enactment thereof for the time being in force.

在这些条款中，《公司法》中定义的词语和表达方式应具有相同的含义，除非上下文另有规定：（a）单数应包括复数，反之亦然；（b）男性应包括女性和中性，对人的提述应包括公司和所有合法存在的法人实体；（c）"may"应解释为"允许的"，"shall"应解释为"必须的"；（d）提及美元或 $ 是指美利坚合众国的美元；及（e）对法规的提述须包括该法规当时有效的任何修订或重新制定。

范例二：

Unless the context otherwise requires in this agreement, word denoting the singular includes the plural and vice versa, and word denoting any one gender includes all genders, and word denoting person includes a natural person, body corporate, unincorporated association and partnership.

除本协议另有所指，表示单数的词包括复数，反之亦然；表示一个性别的词包括所有性别；表示人的词包括自然人、法人团体、非法人团体以及合伙组织。

范例三：

For the purpose of this Agreement, "Affiliate" of any party to this Agreement means any corporation which, directly or indirectly, controls such party or is controlled by such party or is under common control with such party, where "Control" means power or ability to direct the management and policies of the controlled corporation through ownership of or control of more than fifty-one percent of the voting shares of the controlled corporation by contract or otherwise.

就本协议而言，本合同中所提到之任何一方当事人之“关联企业”，系指直接或间接控制该当事人，或受该当事人控制，或与该当事人受控于同一企业。前述“控制”指通过合同或其他方式，掌握受控企业百分之五十一以上之股东投票权，从而拥有主导该企业之经营与政策的能力与权力。

范例四：

In this Agreement, save where the context otherwise requires or the Agreement otherwise provides, capitalised words and expressions shall have the meanings given to them in Appendix 1.

在本协议中，除非上下文中另有要求或协议另有规定，大写词语和表述的含义如附录 1 规定。

三、语言与文本份数条款（Language and Copies）

语言与文本份数条款一般出现在合同尾部，表明合同共签署几份、合同以何种语言签订，以及每种语言的效力等。

范例一：

This contract is made out in two originals, each copy written in Chinese and English languages, both texts being equally valid. In case of any divergence of interpretation, the Chinese text shall prevail.

范例二：

This contract is in both Chinese and English. In case of discrepancy between the interpretations of the two versions, the Chinese version shall prevail.

The contract is in duplicate, and each party holds a counterpart of it. The two counterparts have equal legal effect.

本合同中英文两种版本。两种版本的解释发生不一致时，以中文版本为准。

本合同一式两份，甲乙双方各执一份，具有同等法律效力。

范例三：

This agreement may be executed in any number of counterparts and they shall have the same effect as if the signatures on the counterparts were on a single copy of the agreement.

◆ 知识点拓展

In duplicate　一式两份

In triplicate　一式三份

In quadruplicate　一式四份

In quintuplicate　一式五份

In sextuplicate　一式六份

In septuplicate　一式七份

In octuplicate　一式八份

In nonuplicate　一式九份

In decuplicate　一式十份

四、合同生效条款（Validity）

范例一：

This contract shall take effect upon signature of both parties or their legal representative or duly authorized representative, affixed with corporate official seal. The contract is valid for ________ years, from month ________ date ________ year ________ to ________ month ________ date ________ year ________.

本合同自双方或双方法定代表人或其授权代表人签字并加盖单位公章之日起生效。有效期为____年，自____年____月____日至____年____月____日。

范例二：

This Agreement shall become effective upon signature of the representatives of both parties hereto, affixed with corporate seal.

This agreement is valid from the date of signature to two years after the date of acceptance. Upon expiration of the agreement, this agreement may be renewed through mutual agreement. If the parties do not raise an objection within 10 working days after the expiration of the agreement, the service terms of this agreement will automatically renew for one year.

本协议自双方代表签字、盖章之日起生效。

本协议有效期为自签订之日起到通过验收后两年。协议到期后，经双方协商可续签本协议。如双方在协议到期后 10 个工作日内未提出异议，则本协议服务条款自动延续一年。

范例三：

The terms of this contract are the full and complete agreement between the parties on the brokerage matters. The amendment to this contract shall be valid only after the written consent of both parties and signed and sealed by both parties. Matters not covered in this contract shall be settled separately by the parties.

本合同条款为双方就居间事项达成的完整协议。本合同的修改需经双方书面同意，并经双方签字盖章后方才有效。本合同未尽事宜，由双方另行协商解决。

五、保证条款（Representations and Warranties）

Representations（陈述）与 Warranties（保证）本来是两个概念。按照权威的 Black's Law Dictionary 的解释，"representations（陈述）"的含义是"a representation of fact—either by words or by conducts, made to induce someone to act, esp., to enter into a contract（通过言辞或行为呈现某种事实，以促使相对方做出相应行为，比如订立合同）"。合同保证条款中的"representations（陈述）"大多用来说明当事人的主体资格或权利能力、行为能力等问题。而"warranties（保证）"则指"an express or implied promise that something in furtherance of the contract is guaranteed by one of the contracting parties; esp., the seller's promise that the thing being sold is represented or promised（合同一方提供的明示或默示的保证条款，尤其是在买卖合同中卖方向买方做出的质量保证）"。但是，基于两者都是当事人针对过去曾经发生或现在存在，并可能影响合同效力的事实，所以现在的英文合同经常将两者连用，构成一组并列词组"represent and warrant"或"representations and warranties（陈述与保证）"。

保证条款又分为“明示保证（express warranties）”和“默示保证（implied warranties）”。明示保证在合同中明确约定，如有关起重机的跨度、提升高度、提升速度、运行电压等的保证，属于明示保证，而默示保证则是对所售商品或服务所有权或法律上的保证（statutory warranties），如顾客买部手机，手机能够正常通话是默示保证，电暖风能够致暖也是默示保证，无需卖方就此做出书面或者其他形式的明示保证或者承诺。

范例一：

Party A represents and warrants that there are no conditions at, on, under, or related to, the real property constituting all or any portion of the Land which presently or potentially pose a hazard to human health or the environment, whether or not in compliance with law, and there has been no manufacture, use, treatment, storage, transportation, or disposal of any hazardous or toxic substance, pollutant, or contaminant on the Land nor any release of any hazardous or toxic substance, pollutant, or contaminant into or upon or over the land.

Party A further represents and warrants that the Land is free and clear of any and all claims, charges, easement, encumbrances, lease, covenants, security interest, liens, option, pledge, rights of others, or restrictions, whether imposed by agreement, understanding, law, equity or otherwise.

甲方陈述和保证，构成土地全部或任何部分的房地产，其内部、上面、下面或其相关的部位现在不存在、也不可能存在危害人身健康或环境的情况（无论是否符合法律规定），且土地上从未生产、使用、处理、储存、运输或处置过任何危险的或有毒的物质、污染物或致污物，土地内部、上面或上空亦未曾释放过任何危险的或有毒的物质、污染物或致污物。

甲方进一步陈述和保证，土地不存在任何权利主张、抵押、地役权、障碍、租约、契约、担保权益、留置权、期权、质押、他人权利或限制，无论是以协议、谅解备忘录、法律、衡平法还是其他方法设定的。

范例二：

Party B guarantees the technicality, practicality and reliability of “the Formula” and warrants that the technical secret does not infringe on the legal rights of any third party. Should a third party accuse Party A of technical secret infringement, Party B shall take relevant actions to eliminate the allegation and compensate Party A for the economic losses suffered therefrom.

参考译文：

乙方保证“本配方”的技术性、实用性、可靠性，并保证本项技术秘密不侵犯任何第三人的合法权利。如发生第三人指控甲方实施技术秘密侵权的，乙方应该采取相关行动消除该指控，并赔偿甲方因该指控所遭受的经济损失。

范例三：

Party B warrants that Party B has all the intellectual property rights of the software under the contract. In case of any intellectual property disputes with the software sold by Party B to Party A, Party A shall not bear any joint and several liability. Party B warrants that the software under this contract or any right granted to Party A will not infringe on any third party's intellectual property rights such as copyright, patent, trademark etc. , nor violate the exclusive right of information of any third party, nor exist any pending litigation against the software of Party B.

乙方承诺乙方拥有合同标的软件的全部知识产权，若乙方向甲方出售的软件存在知识产权纠纷，甲方不承担任何连带责任。乙方保证本合同项下软件或其授予甲方的权利不会侵犯任何第三方的著作权、专利权或商标权等知识产权或其他权利，不违反任何第三方的信息专有权，也没有其他针对乙方拥有本软件权利的未决诉讼。

范例四：

If any of the above representations and warranties of a Party are not accurate in all material respects on the date hereof, then such Party shall be deemed to be in material breach of this Contract.

如果在本合同签订日，一方上述陈述与担保的任何一项与实际情况有实质性不符，则该方构成重大违约。

范例五：

Seller warrants that all products sold hereunder shall be free from defects in materials and workmanship for a period of six (6) months from the date of Buyer's receipt (warranty). In the event of a breach of this warranty, Seller shall, at Seller's option, either (i) repair the applicable product at the original FOB point of delivery, (ii) refund an equitable portion of the contract price, or (iii) furnish replacement equipment or parts, as necessary to the original FOB point of delivery. Except as specifically set forth in the preceding sentences, Seller makes no warranties either express or implied with respect to the products sold hereunder.

卖方保证根据本合同所售的所有产品的用料和工艺自买方收货之日起六（6）个月内均无瑕疵（“保证期”）。一旦违反本保证，卖方可自行选择：（i）在原先 FOB 交货地点修复瑕疵产品；（ii）返还合同价的对等金额；或（iii）在原先 FOB 交货地点提供替换产品或部件。除上句具体规定外，卖方对根据本合同售出的产品不做任何其他明示或默示保证。

范例六：

The Partner warrants that it will diligently maintain the content of the Partner Platforms and keep the Partner Platform (s) up-to-date and accurate. The Partner shall promptly correct any errors or omissions on the Partner Platform (s) after becoming aware of such errors or being notified by XXX.

合作伙伴保证积极维护合作平台的内容，并保持合作平台上内容的时效性和准确性。发现合作平台上有错误或接到 XXX 的错误通知后，合作伙伴应立即更正此类错误或遗漏。

范例七：

Parties warrant that in the event of an infringement or breach by the one Party of its obligations under this Clause 6, the burden of proof is carried by the Party in breach.

双方保证，如果一方违反了第 6 条规定的义务，由违约方负举证责任。

◆ 知识点拓展

1. infringement or breach of obligations，“违反义务”；infringement or breach of obligations 属于法律英语的并列现象。

2. burden of proof，“举证责任”。

在民事诉讼法中，一般采取“谁主张，谁举证”的证明标准，当一方不能完成举证责任的时候，则面临不利的法律后果。

3. 常见保证条款的常见句式归纳如下：

Party A warrants that…

Party A guarantees…

Party A represents and warrants that…

Party A and Party B hereby undertake that…

Party A makes no warranties…

六、不可抗力条款（Force Majeure）

不可抗力条款是指双方订立合同时不能合理预见、不能克服的障碍，当发生不可抗力的情形时，违约方不承担违约责任，但是要及时通知对方不可抗力的存在以及对履行合同的影响。

大多数合同中都会有不可抗力条款，不可抗力条款是一个可以使违约方免责的条款，所涵盖的情形由双方协商确定，但大多数包括两种情形：第一，超出合同双方或其中一方合理控制范围的类似事件，如罢工（strike）、暴动（insurrection）、战争（war）、恐怖主义事件（terrorism）、革命（revolution）、内战（civil war）、爆炸（explosion）、禁运（embargoes）、政府行为（acts of government）、检疫限制（quarantine restrictions）；第二，自然灾害，如火灾（fire）、旱灾（drought）、洪灾（flood）、地震（earthquake）、海啸（tsunami）、台风（typhoons）、飓风（hurricane）、火山（volcano）、山体滑坡（landslide）、雪崩（avalanche）。

另外，针对不同类型的合同，不可抗力条款中所列举的不可抗力事件应有所不同，如影响电子行业的不可抗力事件和影响房地产行业的不可抗力事件应是不一样的。

（一）不可抗力的定义

范例一：

"Force Majeure" means an event that cannot be reasonably controlled, unforeseeable or even foreseen by the parties to the contract, which obstructs, affects or delays the performance of any or all of its obligations under this contract. The event includes, but is not limited to, acts of government, natural disasters, war, network congestion or disruption, hacking attacks, or any other similar event.

The party suffering from the force majeure event may temporarily suspend the performance of the obligations under this contract until the impact of the force majeure event is eliminated, and neither party shall be liable to the other for breach of contract; however, the best efforts should be made to overcome the incident and mitigate its negative impact.

参考译文:

“不可抗力”是指本合同双方不能合理控制、不可预见或即使预见亦无法避免的事件，该事件妨碍、影响或延误任何一方根据本合同履行其全部或部分义务。该事件包括但不限于政府行为、自然灾害、战争、网络堵塞或中断、黑客袭击或任何其他类似事件。

遭受不可抗力事件的一方可暂行中止履行本合同项下的义务直至不可抗力事件的影响消除为止，并且无需为此而承担违约责任；但应尽最大努力克服该事件，减轻其负面影响。

范例二:

“Force Majeure” shall mean all events which are beyond the control of the Parties to this Contract, and which are unforeseen, unavoidable or insurmountable, and which prevent total or partial performance by either of the Parties. Such events shall include, but not limited to, earthquakes, typhoons, flood, fire, war, strikes, riots, acts of government, changes in law or the application thereof or any other instances which cannot be foreseen, prevented or controlled, including instances which are accepted as Force Majeure in general international commercial practice.

参考译文:

不可抗力指超出本合同双方控制范围、无法预见、无法避免或无法克服，使得本合同一方部分或完全不能履行本合同的事件。这类事件包括但不限于地震、台风、洪水、火灾、战争、罢工、暴动、政府行为、法律规定或其适用的变化，或者其他任何无法预见，无法避免或者无法控制的客观情况，包括在国际商务实践中通常被认定为不可抗力的事件。

（二）不可抗力的后果

范例一：

Party A agrees that Party B shall not be liable for: any losses; damage, including consequential damages; detention; delay or failure to perform in whole or part resulting from causes beyond the control of Party B, including but not limited to: acts of God, fires, strikes, insurrections, riots, embargoes, delays in transportation, inability to obtain supplies, or requirements or regulations of the government or any other civil or military authority. Delays or non-performance excused by this provision shall not excuse payment of any amount due hereunder owed at the time of the occurrence.

参考译文：

甲方同意乙方不必非为乙方所能控制的因素而引起的损失、包括间接损害在内的损害、扣留、全部或部分的履行迟延或履行不能而负责。此等因素包括但不限于：天灾、火灾、罢工、叛乱、暴动、禁运、运输迟延、无法取得原料、政府或其他军事或一般机关之法令规定或要求。依本条款免除履行迟延或履行不能之责任的当事人并不因此而免除支付到期买卖价款之义务。

范例二：

In the event of a force majeure event which results in one party's failure to perform the contract, the party abovementioned shall notify the other party of the accident as soon as possible, and negotiate with the other party to extend the time limit for performance of the contract. The damage incurred by the other party shall not be claimed. Every effort shall be made to ensure that the impact of force majeure event is minimized and that normal trade is fully restored in accordance with the contract.

（三）不可抗力发生后的通知义务

范例一：

If the shipment of the contracted goods is prevented or delayed in whole or in part by reason of war, earthquake, flood, fire, storm, heavy snow or other causes of force majeure, the seller shall not be liable for non-shipment or late shipment of the goods of this contract. However, the seller shall notify the buyer by phone/fax/email and furnish the latter within 5 days by registered airmail with a certificate issued by the China Council for the Promotion of International Trade (China Chamber of International Commerce) attesting such event or events.

参考译文:

如果由于战争、地震、洪水、火灾、风暴、大雪或其他不可抗力原因而导致合同货物的全部或部分装运被阻止或延迟，则卖方对未装运或迟交装运不承担责任。但是，卖方应通过电话/传真/电子邮件通知买方，并在5天内通过航空挂号信的方式提供中国国际贸易促进委员会（中国国际商会）颁发的此类事件的证明。

范例二:

Should a Party be directly prevented from performing this Contract or be delayed in performing this Contract by an event of Force Majeure, such as earthquake, typhoon, fire, flood, war and other unforeseen events, the occurrence and consequences of which are unpreventable and unavoidable, the affected Party shall notify the other Party by telephone without delay and, within fourteen (14) days thereafter, provide information regarding the event of force majeure and valid certificate thereof, explaining the reason for its inability to perform all or part of this Contract or the delay in performance hereof. Such certificate as proof of the existence of force majeure shall be issued by the notary public office at the locality where the event of force majeure occurred. The parties shall, through consultation, decide whether to terminate this Contract, or release part of the affected Party's responsibilities to perform this Contract, or delay the performance hereof.

参考译文:

如合同一方由于不可抗力事件（如地震、台风、火灾、洪灾、战争以及其他不可预见的事件，该事件的发生和后果无法阻止、无法避免）的发生而无法履行本合同或迟延履行本合同，则受影响的一方应立即以电话通知另一方，并在事发后的十四（14）日内提供不可抗力事件的信息和有效证明，解释其无法履行全部或部分合同或迟延履行本合同的原因。不可抗力事件发生的证明应由该事件发生地公证处出具。合同方应通过磋商决定是否终止合同，或减轻受影响一方履行本合同的责任，或迟延履行本合同。

七、知识产权条款（Intellectual Property）

知识产权是一种智力成果，指“权利人对其智力劳动所创作的成果和经营活动中的标记、信誉所依法享有的专有权利”，主要包括著作权（copyright）、专利权（patent）、商标权（trademark）和商业秘密（trade secret）四种。知识产权能够为权利人带来经济价值，充分体现了“知识就是财富”这一真理。

《与贸易相关的知识产权协议》（TRIPS Agreement，Agreement on Trade-Related Aspects of Intellectual Property Rights）是世贸组织最重要的文件之一，是有关国际知识产权保护中最具影响力和效力的国际公约，其规定了著作权的最低保护期为50年，发明专利的最低保护期为20年，并要求世贸组织成员国商标权的保护期为7年。在保护期内，知识产权直接受法律保护。

知识产权条款主要出现在技术开发合同、技术秘密转让合同、知识产权许可协议等。在该类合同中，相应方对会自己所开发、转让的知识产权进行权利正当性声明或者不侵权声明或者保证，因此知识产权条款实质上是保证条款的延续。具体例子如下：

范例一：

Party A owns or possesses the Intellectual Property which consists of its trademarks, trade names, service names, service marks, service mark registrations, patents, patent rights, copyrights, inventions, licenses, approvals, government authorizations, trade secrets and rights necessary to conduct its business as now conducted. To the knowledge of Party A, there is no claim, action or proceeding being made or brought against Party A regarding any of the foregoing Intellectual Property items.

参考译文：

甲方拥有或享有以满足经营目前业务所需而使用的知识产权，包括其商标、商号、服务名称、服务标记、服务标记注册专利、专利、专利权、版权、发明、许可证、核准书、政府授权书、商业秘密和商业权利。据甲方所知，没有任何一方就上述知识产权项目对甲方提出权利主张或提起诉讼。

知识点补充：

action or proceeding“诉讼”，“action”与“proceeding”均有“诉讼”的意思，在上述例子中并列出现，属于法律英语的并列现象。具体使用方法如下例句：

He is considering taking legal action against the hospital.

他正考虑起诉这家医院。

to bring legal proceedings against sb. 向某人提起法律诉讼

有关“提起诉讼”的表达方式归纳如下：

File/issue a claim

Start proceedings（律师经常使用的非正式表达方法）

Take legal action against sb.

Bring legal proceedings against sb.

另外，民事诉讼中的双方当事人分别为原告（plaintiff，claimant）和被告（defendant），“plaintiff”是在美国的用法，在英国原告一般用“claimant”。一个完整的民事诉讼程序，简而言之可归纳为：原告提起诉讼（issue a claim）、法院送达起诉状（serve a claim）给被告、被告答辩（respond to a claim）、开庭审理（hear a case）、法院作出判决（make a judgment）。

范例二：

The R&D personnel shall warrant that the R&D achievements delivered to the principal do not infringe on the legal rights of any third party. In case a third party accuses the principal of technical infringement, the R&D personnel shall bear the consequential legal liability arising from the violation of rights of the third party.

参考译文：

研究开发人应当保证其交付给委托人的研发成果不侵犯任何第三人的合法权益。如发生第三人指控委托人实施的技术侵权的，研发人应承担由侵犯第三者权益而引起的相应法律责任。

范例三：

Party B guarantees the technicality, practicality and reliability of “the Formula” and warrants that the technical secret does not infringe on the legal rights of any third party. Should a third party accuse Party A of technical secret infringement, Party B shall take relevant actions to eliminate the allegation and compensate Party A for the economic losses suffered therefrom.

Party B shall warrant that it is the legal owner of this formula, and that "the Formula" is not patented by others when the contract is signed.

In the course of the performance of this contract, Party A has the right to terminate the contract and require Party B to bear the corresponding liabilities if a third party applies for a patent or obtains a patent with the same technology or formula.

参考译文：

乙方保证"本配方"的技术性、实用性、可靠性，并保证本项技术秘密不侵犯任何第三人的合法权利。如发生第三人指控甲方实施技术秘密侵权的，乙方应该采取相关行动消除该指控，并赔偿甲方因该指控所遭受的经济损失。

乙方应当保证自己是本配方的合法所有者，而且"本配方"在合同订立时尚未被他人申请专利。

在本合同履行过程中，如出现第三方就同一技术或配方申请专利或获得专利权的情况，甲方有权解除合同，并要求乙方承担相应责任。

范例四：

Party B warrants that it enjoys legal and valid ownership of the transferred technology, and there is no infringement of any third-party rights. Should any third party claim any tort liability to Party A on the transferred technology, or should Party A incur any damages due to the use of the transferred technology, Party B shall be responsible for handling the matter and undertake all losses caused to Party A.

参考译文：

乙方保证对转让技术享有合法有效的所有权，不存在侵犯任何第三方权益的情形，如有任何第三方就转让技术向甲方主张任何侵权之债，或者由于甲方使用转让技术造成损害的情形，乙方应当负责处理并承担由此给甲方造成的一切损失。

八、违约条款（Breach Clause）

根据英国的合同法，合同条款根据重要性可分为条件条款（condition）和保证条款（warranty）。重要的条款为条件条款（condition），次要条款为保证条款（warranty）。违反条件条款（condition）和保证条款（warranty）的法律后果是不同的。一般而言，如果合同一方违反了条件条款，则守约方可以解除合同，同时要求违约方支付损害赔偿金。而如果一方违反了保证条款，守约方是无权要求解除合同的，仅有权主张损害赔偿金。在中国的合同法中，合同条款没有此方面的划分。

范例一：

Default in payment: In case the principal fails to pay the corresponding sum to the R&D personnel within the time limit stipulated in this contract and the attachment hereof for no reason, daily liquidated damages of 0.05% of the overdue payment shall be paid to the R&D personnel.

Default in delivery: In case the R&D personnel fails to complete the R&D work and pass acceptance within the time limit stipulated in this contract and the attachment hereof for their own reason, daily liquidated damages of 0.05% of the total contract value shall be paid to the principal.

Default in other clauses: In case any party to this contract violates the obligations stipulated in the contract, except as otherwise provided in this contract, the party in breach shall pay liquidated damages to the non-breach party according to 1% of the total contract value. The party in breach shall be liable for the loss, if there is, incurred by the non-breach party.

Maximum amount: The cumulative aggregate of all liquidated damages and compensation paid by the party in breach under this contract shall not exceed 100% of the total contract value.

参考译文：

付款违约：如果委托人无故未在本合同及附件规定的期限内向研究开发人支付相应的价款，每延迟一日，应向研究开发人支付应付而未付金额的万分之五的违约金。

交付违约：若研究开发人因研究开发人自身原因未在本合同及附件规定的期限内完成开发工作并通过验收，每延迟一日，应向委托人支付相当于合同总金额万分之五的违约金。

其他条款违约：本合同任何一方违反合同所规定的义务，除本合同另有规定外，违约方应按合同总金额1%的金额向对方支付违约金。若给对方造成损失的，违约方还应赔偿。

最高额度：本合同项下违约方支付的所有违约金及赔偿金的累积总额不超过本合同总金额的100%。

范例二：

In case Party B violates the provisions of Article 3 and 6 in this contract, Party B shall pay Party A liquidated damages of 20% of the amount payable in this contract and compensate Party A for all losses incurred.

In case Party A fails to pay the transfer fee to Party B on time, Party A shall pay Party B daily overdue arears of 0.01% of the amount payable.

In case either party breaches the contract, it shall bear the corresponding liability for damages and compensate the non-breach party for any reasonable expense (including but not limited to investigation fees, attorney fees, travel expenses, court costs, etc.) in the course of protecting its lawful rights and interests.

参考译文：

如果乙方违反本协议第三条、第六条的规定的，乙方应当向甲方支付本合同约定应付款总额20%的违约金，并赔偿由此给甲方带来的所有损失。

如果甲方不按时向乙方支付转让费的，甲方应按照每延迟一日，向乙方支付万分之一/日的滞纳金。

如果任何一方违约，应承担相应的赔偿责任及支付守约方为保护其合法权益而支付的合理费用（包括但不限于调查费、律师费、差旅费、诉讼费等合理费用）。

范例三：

After the entry into force of this Agreement, the parties shall perform their obligations and agreements in a comprehensive, appropriate and timely manner in accordance with this Agreement and all the annexes and schedules. In the event that any party to this Agreement violates the provisions in this Agreement, including all the annexes and schedules hereof, it shall constitute a breach of contract.

The parties agree that, except as otherwise provided in this Agreement, the liquidated damages for this Agreement are 10% of the total investment of the Investor.

In the event of a breach of contract, the defaulting party shall pay the non-breaching party liquidated damages and compensate the non-breaching party for any losses incurred.

The payment of liquidated damages does not affect the right of the non-breaching party to require the defaulting party to compensate for the loss, continue to perform the agreement or cancel the agreement.

参考译文：

1. 本协议生效后，各方应按照本协议及全部附件、附表的规定全面、适当、及时地履行其义务及约定，若本协议的任何一方违反本协议包括全部附件、附表约定的条款，均构成违约。

2. 各方同意，除本协议另有约定之外，本协议的违约金为投资方投资总额的 10% 。

3. 一旦发生违约行为，违约方应当向守约方支付违约金，并赔偿因其违约而给守约方造成的损失。

4. 支付违约金不影响守约方要求违约方赔偿损失、继续履行协议或解除协议的权利。

◆ 知识点拓展

遵守合同：honor the contract, abide by the contract

违反合同约定：violate/breach terms or condition of the contract

违约方：party in breach, breaching party, breach party

守约方：non-breach party, non-breaching party, non-defaulting party

违约金：liquidated damages

赔偿金：compensation, damages

构成违约：constitute a default or breach of contract

未完全履行或错误履行合同义务：any incomplete or mistaken performance of any obligations provided hereunder

未能履行合同规定的主要义务：fail to perform its material obligations in

the contract

重大违约、实质违约：material breach of contract

根本违约：fundamental breach of contract

违约方需负责守约方所有的债务、损失、损害，包括合理的律师费和诉讼费在内的各种开支：the party in breach shall be liable to the non-breach party for all liabilities, losses, damages, costs and expenses (including reasonable attorney fees and court costs); the breaching party shall hold the non-breaching party harmless and against any and all liabilities, losses, damages, costs and expenses (including reasonable attorney fees and court costs)

对守约方应负责任：be liable to the non-breach party for …

补偿守约方…损失：to indemnify or reimburse the non-breaching party for…

九、合同解除（Rescission/Dissolution of a Contract）与终止条款（Termination of a Contract）

合同解除（rescission/dissolution of a contract），是指合同当事人一方或者双方依照法律规定或者当事人的约定，依法解除合同效力的行为。只要法定或者约定的合同解除事由出现，当事人一方有权通知另一方解除合同。

所谓合同终止（termination of a contract），指合同当事人双方在合同关系建立以后，因一定的法律事实的出现，使合同确立的权利义务关系消灭。很多人往往会把合同终止和合同解除混为一谈，而事实上两者并不是一回事。

合同终止仅使合同关系发生将来消灭的效力，不具有溯及既往的效力，因此不能产生恢复原状的法律后果；而合同解除使合同关系发生既往消灭的效力，具有溯及既往的效力，因而对已履行的合同将产生恢复原状的后果。

（一）合同解除条款（rescission/dissolution of a contract）

作为合同体系的一项法律制度，合同解除具有以下法律性质：

第一，合同解除适用于有效成立的合同。合同只有在有效成立后、履行完毕前才发生合同解除的效力。可撤销合同及无效合同因属于效力瑕疵或欠缺合同要素的合同，不受合同解除制度调整。

第二，合同解除必须具备一定条件。为避免当事人滥用合同解除制度，从而维护合同的严肃性和社会经济生活的稳定性，法律规定合同解除必须具备法定条件或约定条件，禁止当事人任意解除合同。所谓法定解除，是指由法律规定在一定条件下解除合同的行为。例如，《合同法》第 94 条规定了五种情形：（1）因不可抗力致使不能实现合同目的（If the purpose of a contract cannot be reached due to force majeure）；（2）在履行期限届满之前，当事人一方明确表示或者以自己的行为表明不履行主要债务（If a party, prior to the expiration of the performance term, expresses explicitly or expresses by its action that it shall not perform its main debt obligations）；（3）当事人一方迟延履行主要债务，经催告后在合理期限内仍未履行（If one of the parties delays the performance of a major obligation, and fails to do so within a reasonable time limit after being urged to do so）；（4）当事人一方迟延履行债务或者有其他违约行为致使不能实现合同目的（If the purpose of a contract cannot be realized because a party delays performing its debts or commits other actions in breach of the contract）；（5）法律规定的其他情形（If other circumstances specified by the law occur）。

所谓约定解除，是指当事人在合同中约定解除合同的条件，当出现解除合同的条件时，合同解除。当然，当事人不必在订立合同时就约定解除合同，也可以事后经协商一致解除合同。

第三，合同解除必须有解除行为。我国法律没有采纳当然解除主义，即具备合同解除条件，就可以解除合同。因此，当事人要解除合同，必须有解除行为。合同解除分为两种：第一种是双方协商一致解除合同；第二种是享有法定或约定解除权的一方作出解除合同的意思表示。合同解除方必须具有法定或约定解除权，没有解除权的解除行为不发生法律效力。

第四，合同解除的效力是使基于合同而发生的债权债务关系（合同关系）消灭。理论上存在两种观点，第一种观点认为合同解除权的效力是合同关系自始消灭。所谓合同关系自始消灭，是指当事人负有恢复原状的义务，亦即合同解除的效力溯及既往。第二种观点认为合同解除权的效力是合同关系向将来消灭。所谓合同关系向将来消灭，是指合同关系自解除时消灭，合同解除前的关系仍然存在，亦即合同解除不溯及既往。我国《合同法》第 97 条规定：合同解除后，尚未履行的，终止履行；已经履行的，根据履行情况和合同性质，当事人可以要求恢复原状、采取其他补救措施，并有权要求赔偿损失（After the rescission of a contract, the performance of any obligations which have not been performed shall be terminated; where obligations have already been performed, based on the nature of the performance that has been provided and the nature of the contract, a party may demand the other party to restore it to the original state or adopt other remedial measures, and shall have the right to demand compensation）。由此可见，我国合同法采纳的是第一种观点，即合同解除的效力溯及既往。

范例一：

In case the following circumstances have made the performance of this contract unnecessary or impossible, the contract may be dissolved:

a. Force majeure;

b. Written agreement by both parties;

c. Others.

参考译文：

出现下列情形，致使本合同的履行成为不必要或不可能的，可以解除本合同：

a. 发生不可抗力；

b. 双方书面协议终止；

c. 其他。

范例二：

In case the other party fails to perform its obligation in the contract within the time limit agreed upon in this Contract, and fails to eliminate such breach or take remedial measures within 30 days following the receipt of the notice thereof from the non-breaching party, and still again fails to perform the Contract within the time limit allowed for delayed performance, the non-breaching party shall be entitled to rescind the contract by a written notice to the defaulting party and still have the right to claim damages from the defaulting party.

参考译文：

如果合同一方未能在合同规定的时限内履行合同义务，并在收到守约方的通知后 30 天内未能消除违约行为或采取补救措施，而且在被允许推迟履行的期限内仍未履行合同，在此情况下，守约方应书面通知违约方解除合同，同时有权要求违约方赔偿损失。

（二）合同终止条款（termination of a contract）

合同终止条款（termination of a contract）是基于合同履行完毕、仲裁裁决或法院判决或合同双方当事人合意等法律事实，导致合同法律关系归于消灭。同时，需要注意合同终止（termination of a contract）与合同中止（suspension of a contract）是不一样的。合同终止是指完全结束双方当事人的合同法律关系；合同中止是指合同在履行期间因故暂时停止履行，待造成中止的原因消除后，合同继续履行。

中国的《合同法》第 91 条规定了七种合同终止的情形：（1）债务已经按照约定履行（all obligations have already been performed as agreed）；（2）合同解除（the contract has been dissolved）；（3）债务相互抵销（obligations have been offset against one another）；（4）债务人依法将标的物提存（the obligor has lodged the subject matter of the contract in accordance with the law）；（5）债权人免除债务（the obligee has released the obligor from its obligations）；（6）债权债务同归于一人（all obligations and all obligatory rights under the contract are owed and enjoyed by the same person）；（7）法律规定或者当事人约定终止的其他情形（any other situation in which the law requires termination or the parties agree on termination）。由此可见，合同解除只是合同终止的一种情形。

范例一：

In the following circumstances, the contract will be terminated immediately after either party to this contract requests to terminate this contract by giving written notice to the other party:

(1) The other party has a fraudulent act;

(2) the other party is bankrupt or has been declared bankrupt, or the other party has been liquidated or has been dissolved; or

(3) The other party has been unable to carry out its normal business activities.

参考译文：

在以下情形下，本合同的任何一方均有权向另一方发出书面通知要求终止本合同，合同将立即终止：

（1）另一方存在欺诈性的行为；

（2）另一方破产或被宣告破产，或另一方已被清算或已经解散；或者

（3）另一方当事人已无法进行其正常的业务活动。

范例二：

This agreement is valid for three years and is automatically terminated after the investor holds the equity or the target company completes the share repurchase. Since the expiration of the term of this agreement, the new investment project of the target company has nothing to do with the investor, and the investor no longer holds any interest in the investment project of the target company.

参考译文：

本协议有效期三年，以投资方持有股权或目标公司完成股权回购后自动终止。本协议期限届满之日起，目标公司新的投资项目与投资方无关，投资方不再对目标公司的投资项目享有任何权益。

十、通知和送达条款（Notice and service）

通知条款源于英美法系中关于合同成立理论中的投邮主义（post rule）。根据英美法，成立合同需具备四个要素：要约（offer），承诺（acceptance），对价（consideration），建立法律关系的意图（intention to establish legal relations）。要约人（offeror）向受要约人（offeree）发出要约后，受要约人如有兴趣，即向要约人发出承诺，而承诺一经投邮，即视为已经送达。按照此原则，受要约人只要将做出承诺的书信投入邮箱或电报交邮局发出，承诺即生效，合同就成立。即使邮局疏忽，使承诺在传递中遗失，也不妨碍承诺的效力。从这个角度讲，接收方须承担风险。可以说，投邮主义是一种风险分配机制（risk allocation mechanism）。

将投邮主义应用到现代的通知条款中举例如下：某人用其持有的某个公司的股权做质押向银行借款，借款合同中约定，在逾期还款时，银行通知他

立刻还款，否则在邮寄出催款通知的五天后仍未能还款的话，借款人即构成违约，银行会取消他赎回质押物的权利。于是，银行以邮寄的方式将通知发送给了借款人。不幸的是，这封信偏偏在递送过程中弄丢了，最终借款人的股权被银行没收。可以说，借款人无计可施，因为在他签订借款合同时，即同意了合同中基于“投邮主义”的通知条款。

与投邮主义相对立的是到达主义（receipt rule），该原则主张受要约人的承诺要到达要约人时才生效。如果把到达主义的概念运用到上述例子中，借款人可以在和银行签订合同时指出：通知必须要在送达接收方时方才生效。这样借款人就将风险转移给银行，如果银行没有将通知成功送达给他，就无权没收他的股权。

实务中，起草合同时，双方通常会因权利、义务以及违约责任条款直接关系到合同各方的权益而花费较多篇幅设定，却忽视了看上去不那么重要的通知条款，从上述例子可以看出，通知条款与合同各方的权益是紧密联系的。通知是否已经送达给对方，有时候是区分合同各方权利和义务的关键所在。比如，一方是否适当地行使了优先权，是否适当地宣告了对方违约，或者是否适当地提出了赔偿请求，可能取决于通知的形式、内容、时间、交付方式及通知的有效送达。

因此，对于守约方而言，通知条款的作用是防止对方不接收相关书面文件，在发生纠纷时无法取得相关证据。例如，合同中通常会设定单方变更或者解除合同权，一旦满足条件，守约方将要向违约方发送通知行使单方变更或解除权。但是，我国对于通知往往采用“到达主义”（receipt rule），即，只有在发送方发送了通知且接收方接收到通知时通知才视为送达。发送方除了证明自己完成了送达义务还需要证明对方已经收到通知。只要对方不配合，送达就很难完成。实务中，接收方故意躲藏不接收或者拒收通知情形比较普遍。因此，在起草通知条款时，应注意以下方面：

第一，明确的联系方式。联系方式通常包括联系人、传真、电子邮件、住所等。首先，合同中应当有明确的联系方式，如果缺失，即使合同约定了单方变更或解除权，也因没有约定联系方式而无法行使；其次，联系方式应当准确无误，否则，相对方会以联系方式错误而没有收到作为理由抗辩；最后，联系方式应当是合同相对人本人或其授权指定联系人，否则，相对方会以联系方式的所有人非其合法授权人、无权处理合同相关事务而进行抗辩。

第二，明确的送达标准。我国《民事诉讼法》只规定人民法院送达法律文书的形式和认定标准，诉讼方式人不配合送达时，法院可以采取留置送达、公告送达等特殊方式送达。对于民商事主体而言，法无禁止即自由，民商事主体可以在合同中明确约定送达的标准，比如，通过电子邮件送达的，可以约定通知的信息发送至合同中对方指定的电子邮箱内即视为送达，即使对方没有打开电子邮件，也可视为对方已经收到通知。

第三，如通讯地址、联系方式发生变化，应及时通知对方。当通讯地址、联系方式发生变化的时候，应立即书面告知对方，否则对方有可能将重要通知文件发往旧的地址而导致无法正常接收文件，最终导致无法估量的损失。实务中，经常有当事人因地址变更未通知对方，导致没有收到法院的传票、起诉状等文件，未能参加庭审提出抗辩，最终导致法院缺席判决，损失巨大。

"到达主义"的通知条款如下例：

A notice is deemed to have been received as follows:

a. If a Notice is delivered in person, or sent by Registered or Certified Mail, or nationally/internationally recognized overnight courier, upon receipt as indicated by the date on the signed receipt.

b. If a Notice is sent by facsimile, upon receipt by the party giving or making the Notice of an acknowledgement or transmission report generated by the machine from which the facsimile was sent indicating that the facsimile was sent in its entirety to the Addressee's facsimile number.

c. If a Notice is sent by e-mail, upon acknowledgement of receipt of contents of email.

有的通知会给接收方带来不利的后果，接收方会故意逃避或拒绝签收。"投邮主义"避免了这种风险，银行给客户发送的一般通知往往采用"投邮生效"，如下例：

Any notice:

Sent by repaid registered post will be deemed to have been received on the 5th (fifth) business day after posting.

Sent by ordinary mail will be deemed to have been received on the 7th (seventh) business day after posting.

Delivered by hand will be deemed to have been received on the day of delivery.

Sent by telefax or email will be deemed to have been received on the 1st (first) business day after the date is was sent.

更多通知条款的例子如下：

范例一：

All the notices (including any invoice or report) authorized or required by and between Seller and Buyer at set out in any of the articles herein shall be made in writing in Chinese and English, and delivered by hand, courier, or registered mail to the following address or other address informed by both Parties in writing.

Party A:

Address for Notice:

Attention:

Telephone:

Facsimile:

Party B:

Address for Notice:

Attention:

Telephone:

Facsimile:

Notices are effective when received by the recipient during the recipient's regular business hours. Notices shall be deemed to have been received: (1) upon confirmed receipt of delivery if delivered by hand; (2) upon confirmed transmission if sent by fax: (3) upon acknowledgement of receipt if sent by registered mail or courier; (4) upon acknowledgement of receipt of contents of email (other than auto-reply) if sent by email.

If the time of such deemed receipt is not during customary hours of business, notice shall be deemed to have been received at 8: 00 a. m. on the first day of business thereafter.

参考译文：

本合同所有条款规定的买卖双方授权或要求的所有通知（包括发票和报告）均须采取中英文书面形式，并且采用专人递送、快递或挂号信送至下方地址或双方书面通知的其他地址。

甲方：

地址：

接收人：

电话：

传真：

乙方：

地址：

接收人：

电话：

传真：

通知只有在接收方于其正常工作时段内收到方才有效。通知在以下情形视作收悉：（1）如果由专人递送，于确认收到之时；（2）如果经传真发出，于确认传送成功之时；（3）如果以挂号信或快递方式发出，于确认收到之时；（4）如果经电子邮件发出，于电子邮件内容确认收到之时（但不包括自动回复）。

范例二：

Written notice may be sent by facsimile to the numbers listed above, but such notice shall not be effective unless the sender receives a return facsimile acknowledging receipt of the notice. Notice shall be deemed received when actually delivered to the recipient as demonstrated by courier records. E-mail notice shall be deemed received when actually delivered to the recipient as demonstrated by "sent records". Facsimile notice shall be deemed received upon receipt by the sender of an acknowledgment as described. The addresses and transmittal numbers set forth above can be changed only by written notice that complies with the requirements of this Article and the notice shall be issued in [3] days after the addresses and transmittal numbers changes, otherwise the previous information is still effective.

书面通知可通过上述传真号发送，但发件人收到收件人传真回执表明收到通知后，该通知方能生效。如果快递记录显示已交付收件人，该通知应视为收到。如果电子邮箱记录显示已发送，该通知应视为收到。传真通知在发件人收到上述确认后应视为收到。以上所述任何信息若有变更，须根据本条规定在变更后［3］日内发出书面通知，否则视为原信息仍为有效。

范例三：

All notifications, files, and data mutually issued by both parties arising from the performance of this Agreement should be served according to the address, fax or e-mail specified in this Agreement; any party shall notify the other party in writing in the occasion of relocation or changing the phone, fax or e-mail.

If sent by fax, the fax is deemed served upon the issue; if by mail, the mail is deemed served on the date of posing or registering; if by e-mail, the message is deemed served when sent successfully.

参考译文：

甲乙双方因履行本协议而相互发出或者提供的所有通知、文件、资料，均以本协议所列明的地址、传真或电子邮件送达，如果一方迁址或者变更电话、传真、电子邮件的，应当以书面形式通知对方。

使用传真方式的，在发出传真时视为送达；以邮寄方式的，挂号信寄出或投邮日视为送达；使用电子邮件方式的，邮件发送成功视为送达。

◆ 总结：

1. 通知发送方式的句型如下：

—— [Notice] shall be delivered/sent/given/addressed by [manner] to [addressee & address].

—— [Addresser] shall notify/deliver/send [addressee] [notice] by [manners] to [addressee & address].

2. 通知生效时间的句型如下：

到达生效：

upon confirmed/acknowledged delivery/transmission…

upon receipt as confirmed/indicated by…

投邮生效：

upon the delivery at/to…

at the time of sending or the next business day

upon/on the [number] business day after…

after [number] (business) days

另外，delivered 可用来表述“发送方式”，如 shall be delivered by courier，也会被用在“生效时间”的表述中，如 shall be deemed delivered，在这两种表达中，delivered 分别被译为“寄送”和“送达”。

Served 一般用来表达“送达”，如 If a notice is sent by fax, the fax is deemed served upon the issue.

十一、争议解决条款（Dispute Resolution Clause）

合同双方发生争议后，一般有以下几种解决方法：协商（negotiation）、调解（mediation）、仲裁（arbitration）、诉讼（litigation）。合同中，双方当事人一般会约定在发生争议的时候协商解决，协商不成的时候再选择通过诉讼或者仲裁的方式解决。有些当事人约定发生争议后即可以通过诉讼又可以通过仲裁的方式解决争议，这种既约定仲裁又约定诉讼的争议条款一般认定无效，一旦发生纠纷，通常情况下是由有管辖权的人民法院解决。

在国际商事领域，仲裁由于具有一裁终局性（finality）、中立性（neutrality）、灵活性（flexibility）、保密性（confidentiality）等优势，其使用的频率要远远大于诉讼。而且根据《纽约公约》（承认和执行外国仲裁裁决的公约，Convention on the Recognition and Enforcement of Foreign Arbitral Awards），仲裁的效力是受各国司法强制力保障实施的，这就避免了协商、调解、诉讼结果难以得到他国承认和执行的问题。因此，仲裁协议是我们研究的重点。

范例一：

The two parties agree by consensus that any disputes arising in this contract and its performance will be settled through negotiation. If the negotiation fails, the competent people's court at Party A's place will have jurisdiction over the case.

The conclusion, performance, interpretation and settlement of disputes of this contract shall be governed by the laws of the People's Republic of China, excluding the application of all other conflict laws.

参考译文：

双方协商一致同意，因本协议及其履行过程中发生的任何争议都协商解决，协商不成的，由甲方所在地有管辖权的人民法院管辖。

本协议的订立、履行、解释及争议的解决均适用中华人民共和国法律，并排除其他一切冲突法的适用。

范例二：

Any dispute arising out of or in connection with this contract, including any issues regarding its existence, validity or termination, shall be referred to and finally resolved by arbitration in Singapore in accordance with the Arbitration Rules of the Singapore International Arbitration Centre ("SIAC Rules") for the time being in force, which rules are deemed to be incorporated by reference in this provision. The Tribunal shall consist of ________ arbitrator (s) to be appointed by the Chairman of the SIAC. The language of the arbitration shall be ________.

This Agreement shall be construed in accordance with and governed by the law of ________ (name of the country or state).

参考译文：

任何由本合同引起或与本合同相关的争议，包括其是否存在、有效、终止等问题均应提交新加坡，根据新加坡国际仲裁中心当时有效的仲裁规则（SIAC 规则）进行最终解决，该规则应被视为已经合并到本条款中。仲裁庭应由该中心主席指定的________仲裁员组成。仲裁语言应当为________。

本合同应该根据________（国际或州的名称）法律进行解释并受该等法律管辖。

范例三：

The parties acknowledge that they intend to establish a mutually beneficial relationship and that, to this end, they will strive to resolve any disagreements between them through amicable negotiations. Nevertheless, if a dispute does arise that they are unable to resolve otherwise, the parties will submit it to binding arbitration before the [name of arbitration commission] . The arbitration will be conducted in [place], unless the parties have agreed otherwise. Any arbitration award or decision shall be final, non-appealable, and binding, and it may be submitted to a court with jurisdiction for enforcement.

参考译文：

双方同意他们将建立互惠关系，并尽力通过友好协商解决彼此争议。但是，如果使用这种方法不能解决问题，双方应将争议提交给（名称）仲裁机构。该仲裁机构应在（地点）进行仲裁，除非双方另有约定。仲裁裁决应当是终局性的、不得上诉的、并有约束力的，并且可以提交给同一司法区域内的法院申请执行。

范例四：

Any dispute arising from or in connection with this contract shall be settled through friendly negotiation between the two parties. Should the negotiation fail, either party may file a lawsuit in the court with jurisdiction over the matter in the lessor's domicile.

The costs incurred in litigation (including but not limited to case acceptance fees, travel expenses, reasonable attorney fees, etc.) are borne by the losing party.

In the case of partial disputes in the contract, during the settlement of the dispute, the parties shall continue to execute the contract terms unrelated to the dispute.

参考译文：

凡因本合同引起的或与本合同有关的任何争议，由双方通过友好协商解决。协商不成，任何一方可以向出租人住所地有管辖权的人民法院提起诉讼。

因诉讼发生的相关费用（包括但不限于案件受理费、差旅费、合理的律师费等）均由败诉方承担。

在合同存在部分争议的情况下，解决争议期间，双方仍应继续执行与争议无关的合同条款。

范例五：

Any disputes, controversies, differences or claims (collectively referred to as disputes) arising out of the conclusion, entry into force, interpretation or performance of this Agreement shall be settled through friendly negotiation.

If the dispute cannot be settled within ________ days after one party has notified the other party in writing of the dispute, either party may submit the dispute to the ________ Arbitration Commission, with the arbitral tribunal consisting of three arbitrators. The arbitration shall be conducted in accordance with the arbitration rules in force at the date of signing this Agreement.

The arbitral award shall be final and binding upon all parties.

Unless otherwise determined by the arbitral tribunal, the arbitration fee, attorney's fees and other professional advisor fees shall be borne by the losing party.

参考译文：

各方之间就本协议的订立、生效、解释或履行产生或引起的任何争议、纠纷、分歧或权利主张（统称：争议）均应通过友好协商解决。

如果争议不能在一方书面通知另一方存在争议后的____日内解决，任何一方均可将争议事项提交________仲裁委员会，由 3 名仲裁员组成仲裁庭，按照在本协议签订之日有效的仲裁规则进行仲裁。

仲裁裁决均为终局裁决，对各方均具有约束力。

除非仲裁庭另有裁定，仲裁费用、律师费用和其他专业顾问费用应由败诉方承担。

十二、法律适用条款（Choice of Law Clause）

法律适用条款是指在国际商务活动中，营业地分处不同国家的当事人之间订立的法律选择条款。由于各国政治、经济、法律制度不同，在发生争议的时候，涉及选择哪个国家法律解决争议的问题，因此也就产生了法律冲突和法律适用问题。当事人在合同中明确宣布合同适用何国法律的条款被称作法律适用条款或法律选择条款。

因为当事人（及其律师）对本国法律更为熟悉，他们通常希望本国法律成为适用协议项下所有争议的准据法。

范例一：

This agreement shall be interpreted and construed according to, and governed by, the laws of China, excluding any such laws that might direct the application of the laws of another jurisdiction. The courts located in [Jurisdiction Convenient to All Parties] shall have jurisdiction to hear any dispute under this Agreement.

参考译文：

本协议受中国之法律管辖，并依其进行解释，但可能导致适用另一司法管辖区法律的法律除外。位于［对各方均方便的司法辖区］的法院对本协议项下的任何争议均有管辖权。

范例二：

This contract shall be governed by and construed in accordance with the laws of the State of [franchisor's state], except for matters arising from or concerning Section ____ which shall be governed by and construed in accordance with the laws of the State of [franchisee's state].

参考译文：

本协议除因第____条而起或与之有关的事项应当由［特许经营者所在州］之法律管辖并依其进行解释外，受［授予特许经营权者所在州］之法律管辖，并依其进行解释。

范例三：

The construction, validity and performance of this Agreement shall be governed by and construed in accordance with the applicable laws of Singapore without regard to its conflict of law rules.

本协议的解释、效力、履行受新加坡法律的约束，并依其解释，排除冲突法规则的适用。

总结：法律适用条款的基本句式结构通常为：The formation, validity, interpretation, performance and settlement of disputes of this agreement/contract shall be governed by and construed in accordance with the law of ____.

或者：The laws of [country name] (without giving effect to its conflicts of law principles) govern all matters arising out of or relating to this Agreement, including, without limitation, its validity, interpretation, construction, performance, and enforcement.

第二章 有形商品类涉外合同法律文书

在前一章中，本书已经对法律英语的词汇及句法特征、常见合同通用条款进行了详细的分析，在此基础上，后续章节将根据各类合同或其他法律文书的内容特征分析其特殊条款英文撰写的技巧。

在涉外经济活动中，买卖标的物千差万别、包罗万象，可以是有形商品如飞机汽车轮船，可以是无形商品如法律咨询服务、金融服务等，也可以是知识产权如商标权、专利权等。由于买卖标的物种类繁多，合同条款的撰写也十分多变。本章节将主要对有形商品买卖行为中涉及的常见法律文书的撰写进行分析和研究。本章节将涵盖以下常见类型的合同：一、国际货物销售合同，二、OEM 合作协议，三、涉外建设工程合同。

第一节 国际货物销售合同

国际货物买卖是传统和古老的国际贸易方式，其中“货物”一般指有形的和可以移动的物，其范围非常广泛，只要相关国内法不禁止即可以作为买卖标的。“国际性”可以有很多标志，如以当事人营业地为标准、以行为发生地为标准、以货物跨越国境为标准或以当事人国际为标准等。当前国际货物销售领域一个重要的公约是 1980 年由联合国国际贸易法委员会（UNCITRAL）制定的《联合国国际货物销售合同公约》（United Nations Convention on Contracts of International Sales of Goods; CISG），该公约以当事人的营业地为标准，规定国际货物买卖合同是指营业地分处于不同国家的当事人之间订立的合同（Contract of International Sale of Goods means “contracts of sale of goods between parties whose places of business are in different States”）。

适用该《公约》需满足以下三个条件：1. 销售货物是为了商业的目的；2. 合同当事人的营业地位于不同的国家；3. 合同当事人营业地所在国家是公

约的缔约国。然而，即使满足了以上三个条件，合同当事人也可能在合同中通过法律选择条款（choice of law clause）排除（exclude/opt out）公约的适用，如："this contract shall be governed by the laws of China applicable to domestic contracts of sale, and shall not be governed by the United Nations Convention on Contracts for the International Sale of Goods, 1980"，即，"本合同适用于中国国内买卖合同方面的法律，而不受联合国国际货物销售合同公约（1980）的约束"。

本节将主要研究国际货物销售合同中的特殊条款，如商品描述条款、价格条款、装运条款、单证条款、支付条款、保险条款、包装条款、检验和索赔条款等。

一、货物描述条款（Description of Goods）

货物描述内容一般包括货名、品质、数量、单价、价格术语，有时还包括合同号码、货物包装要求等。价格术语常用的有 CIF、CFR、FOB、FCA、CIP、CPT 等，其中装运港交货的三个价格术语 CIF、CFR、FOB 最常用，例如：

范例一：

Description of Goods: 4500 PCS of Stainless Steel Spade Head S821/29099, USD 12.3 per pc, according to Sales Contract No. B67DE23600 dd. November 12, 2019 Rotterdam (Intercoms 2010)。

参考译文：

货物描述：4500 件不锈钢铲头，货号为 S821/29099，根据 2019 年 11 月 12 日签订 B67DE23600 号合同，每件 12.3 美元，CIF 鹿特丹（2010 通则）。

现在大多时候为了简明的需要，买卖双方直接用表格或者列表的方式描述商品，如：

范例二：

This contract is made by and between the Buyer and Seller, whereby the buyer agree to buy and the Seller agree to sell the undermentioned commodity according to the terms and conditions stipulated below:

Commodity and specifications	Quantity（数量）	Unit price（单价）	Total value（总价）

范例三：

This sales contract is made by and between the Seller and the Buyer, whereby the buyer agree to buy the undermentioned goods according to the terms and conditions stipulated below：/ 此销售合同由卖方与买方订立，买方同意根据以下条款购买以下商品：

<table>
<tr><th>Description of goods</th><th>Quantity（数量）</th><th>Unit price（单价）</th><th>Amount（总价）</th></tr>
<tr><td rowspan="2">100% CNT T-shirts No. 123
Women's trousers style 456
Five PCT more or less in quantity and amount are acceptable/ 100% 纯棉 T 恤，货号 123，女士裤子，款号 456。允许数量和总价 5% 上下的浮动</td><td>5 ,000 PCS
5, 000 PCS</td><td rowspan="2">CIF OSLO （Incoterms 2010）
USD 14. 00
USD 16. 00</td><td>USD 70, 000
USD 80, 000</td></tr>
<tr><td>10, 000 PCS</td><td>USD 150, 000</td></tr>
</table>

二、价格条款（Clauses of Price）

除了上文介绍的《联合国国际货物销售合同公约（CISG）》是国际商法的重要渊源之外，国际贸易惯例也是国际商法的重要渊源。国际贸易惯例是在长期的国际贸易实践中形成的习惯做法，不具有普遍的法律约束力，通常由当事人在实践中选择适用，而且，一经选择，即对当事人具有约束力。其主要作用是：一方面，可以补充现有法律规定的不足，明确合同条款具有的含义，更好地确定当事人的意图和权利义务关系；另一方面，国际贸易惯例促进了国际贸易规则的统一，减少了当事人的分歧和争议。

《国际贸易术语解释通则》（International Rules for the Interpretation of Trade Terms, INCOTERMS）是由国际商会（ICC）在 1936 年制定的，后于 1953 年、1967 年、1976 年、1980 年、1990 年、2000 年、2010 年作了七次修订。该通则对工厂交货（EXW）、离岸价（FOB）以及到岸价（CIF）等 13 种贸易术语作了详细的解释，具体地规定了买卖双方在交货方面的权利与义务。该通则在国际上已经得到广泛的承认与采用，是国际货物买卖的最重要的贸易惯例。

国际贸易术语属于国际贸易惯例，表现为一组字母和简短概念的组合，表达商品的价格，因此贸易术语又被称为“价格术语”或“交货条件”。国际贸易术语的主要功能在于划分买卖合同双方当事人之间的责任、风险、费用，并反映价格构成、交货条件。在国际货物买卖合同中，国际贸易术语构成了合同条款的重要组成部分。

国际贸易术语的分类有很多方法，INCOTERMS 2000 按卖方承担义务由小到大，用英文字母 E、F、C、D 排列，将贸易术语分成四组：

1. E 组。该组只有一个贸易术语 EXW，全称为 EX Works（named place），意思是工厂交货（指定地点）。

2. F 组。包括三个贸易术语：FAS，全称 Free Along-side Ship（named port of shipment），意思是船边交货（指定装运港）；FOB，全称为 Free on Board（named port of shipment），意思是船上交货（指定装运港）；FCA，全称为 Free Carrier（named place），意思是货交承运人（指定地点）。

3. C 组。包括四个贸易术语：CFR，全称为 Cost and Freight（named port of distination），意思是成本加运费（指定目的港）；CIF，全称为 Cost，Insurance and Freight（named port of destination），意思是成本、保险费加运费（指定目的港）；CPT，全称为 Carriage Paid to（named place of destination），意思是运费付至（指定目的地）；CIP，全称为 Carriage Insurance Paid to（named place of destination），意思是运费、保险费付至（指定目的地）。

4. D 组。包括五个贸易术语：DAF，全称为 Delivered at Frontier（named place），意思是边境交货（指定地点）；DES，全称为 Delivered Ex Ship（named port of destination），意思是目的港船上交货（指定目的港）；DEQ，全称为 Delivered Ex Quay（Duty Paid）（named port of destination），意思是目的港码头交货（关税已付）（指定目的港）；DDU，全称为 Delivered Duty Unpaid（named place of destination），意思是未完税交货（指定目的地）；DDP，全称为 Delivered Duty Paid（named place of destination），意思是完税后交货（指定目的地）。

INCOTERMS 2010 在 2000 年版本上进行了修订，按照适用的运输方法不同，可分为以下两组：

1. 适用于任何运输模式的贸易术语（Incoterms that apply to any mode of transport）：

EXW：Ex Works 工厂交货

FCA：Free Carrier 货交承运人

CPT：Carriage Paid To 运费付至

CIP：Carriage and Insurance Paid To 运费、保险费付至

DAT：Delivered at Terminal 运输终端交货

DAP：Delivered at Place 目的地交货

DDP：Delivered Duty Paid 完税后交货

2. 仅适用于海运和水路运输的贸易术语（Incoterms that apply to sea and inland waterway transport only）：

FAS：Free Along-side Ship 船边交货

FOB：Free on Board 船上交货

CFR：Cost and Freight 成本加运费

CIF：Cost，Insurance and Freight 成本、保险费加运费

贸易术语的使用，大大简化了当事人的贸易谈判、合同订立的过程，同时明确了买卖双方相关的权利义务。应该注意的是，国际贸易术语属于国际贸易惯例，具有选择性、非强制约束的特点，如当事人可以在合同中约定适用《国际贸易术语解释通则》2000 年版，或者约定《国际贸易术语解释通则》2010 年版，也可以约定合同不适用《国际贸易术语解释通则》，这都不影响合同的生效与履行。

与普通法系国家进行国际贸易时，尤其需要注意的是，在普通法国家，如英国，在国际贸易术语方面存在其自己的判例法，在国际贸易合同当事人没有明确适用哪一规则时，法院往往适用其判例法，从而可能与当事人的真实意图相违背。例如，如不特别注明，香港法院即适用香港有关贸易术语的判例法。

最新的贸易术语的具体解释和举例如下：

1. EXW（“Ex Works”）EXM（工厂交货）

The seller makes the goods available to be collected at their premises and the buyer is responsible for all other risks，transportation costs，taxes and duties from that point onwards.

卖家在其所在地把货物交付给买家，买家承担从收到货物之后的所有的风险，交通费以及税费。

Example:

Goods are being picked up by the buyer from the seller's premises in Birmingham. The term used in the contract is "EXW Birmingham".

例：

货物需要买家在卖家所在地伯明翰提货。这个术语在合同中是"伯明翰工厂交货"。

如下图所示：

2. FCA ("Free Carrier") FCA（货交承运人）

The seller gives the goods, cleared for export, to the buyer's carrier at a specified place. The buyer is then responsible for getting transported to the specified place of final delivery. This term is commonly used for containers travelling by more than one mode of transport.

卖方办理了清关手续后把货物在一个特定的地点交给买方。然后买方负责把货物运送到最终的目的地。这个术语在需要多种交通方式的集装箱货运中经常用到。

如下图所示：

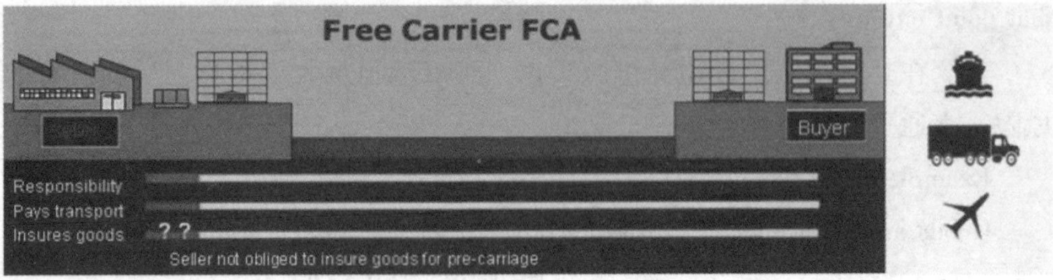

3. CPT（“Carriage Paid To”）CPT（运费付至）

The seller pays to transport the goods to the specified destination. Responsibility for the goods transfers to the buyer when the seller passes them to the first carrier.

卖家负责把货物运至指定地点。责任在货物经过第一承运人之后转移到买家手中。

如下图所示：

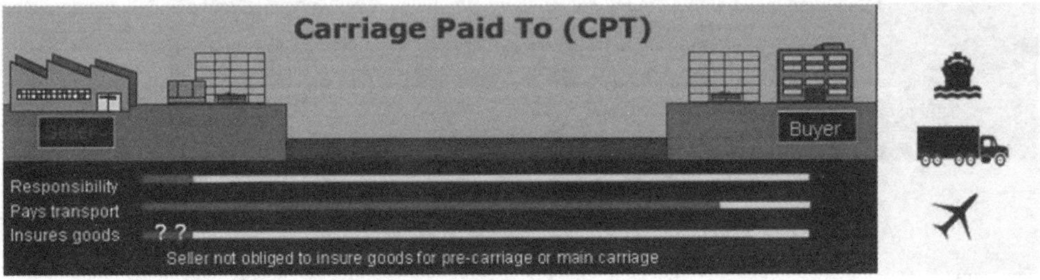

4. CIP（“Carriage and Insurance Paid”）（运费、保险费付至）

The seller pays for insurance as well as transport to the specified destination. Responsibility for the goods transfers to the buyer when the seller passes them to the first carrier.

CIP（“Carriage and Insurance Paid”）is commonly used for goods being transported by container by more than one mode of transport. If transported only by sea, CIF is often used.

卖方支付货物保险和交通费用到指定地点。对货物的责任在卖家把货物转给第一个承运人之后转移到买家手中。

运费保险费付至一般用在被多种交通方式承运的集装箱运输中。如果仅有海运，一般使用到岸价。

如下图所示：

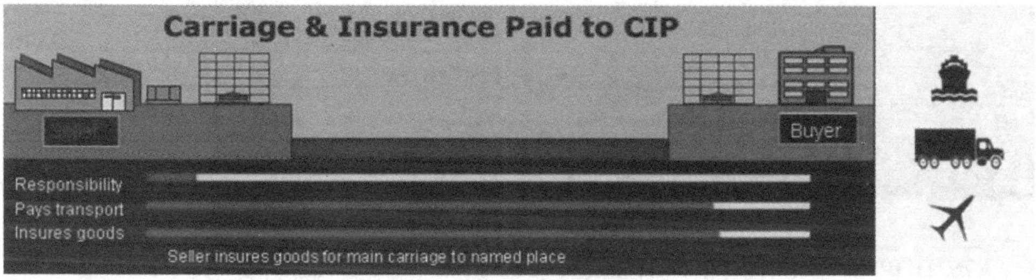

5. DAT（"Delivered at Terminal"）（目的地港交货）

The seller pays for transport to a specified terminal at the agreed destination. The buyer is responsible for the cost of importing the goods. The buyer takes responsibility once the goods are unloaded at the terminal.

卖家支付费用把货物运送到指定地点的特定港口。买家负责支付进口货物的费用。卖家从货物在港口卸货之后承担责任。

如下图所示：

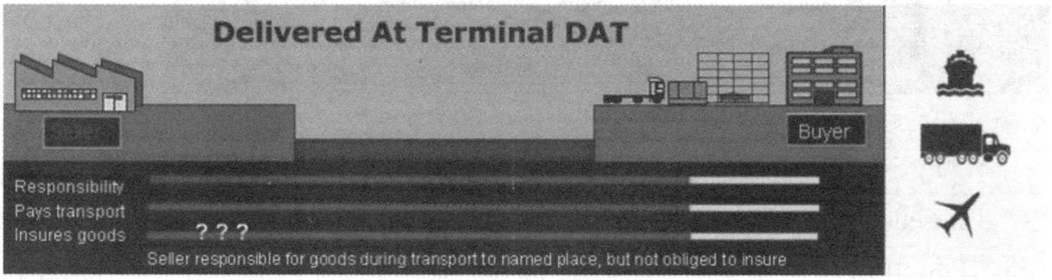

6. DAP（"Delivered at Place"）（目的地交货）

The seller pays for transport to the specified destination, but the buyer pays the cost of importing the goods. The seller takes responsibility for the goods until they're ready to be unloaded by the buyer.

卖家支付运费把货物运输到指定地点，但是买家需要支付进口费用。卖家对货物负责一直到货物被买家卸货完毕。

如下图所示：

7. DDP (“Delivered Duty Paid”)(完税后交货、税后交货)

The seller is responsible for delivering the goods to the named destination in the buyer’s country, including all costs involved.

卖家负责把货物运送到买家所在国的指定地点，并且支付所有相关费用。

如下图所示：

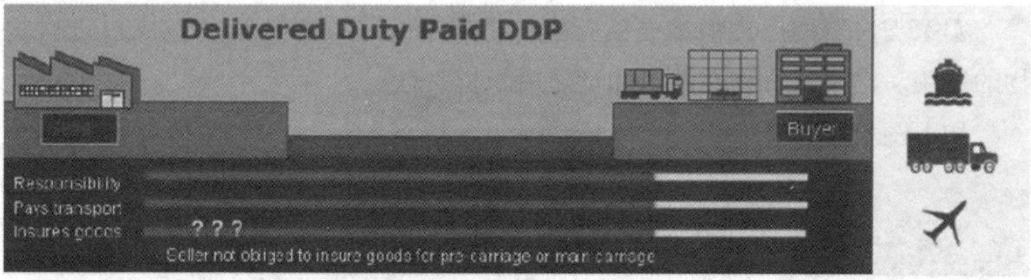

8. FAS (“Free Alongside Ship”)(船边交货)

The seller puts the goods alongside the ship at the specified port they’re going to be shipped from. The seller must get the goods ready for export, but the buyer is responsible for the cost and risk involved in loading them.

This term is commonly used for heavy-lift or bulk cargo (e. g. generators, boats), but not for goods transported in containers by more than one mode of transport (FCA is usually used for this).

卖家把货物运送到指定的发货港口的船边。卖家必须确保货物可以发货，但装货的风险和费用由买家承担。

这个术语在重物或者大件货物（比如发动机，船只）的运输中比较常用，但是不适用于多种交通方式运送的集装箱运输（货交承运人适用于这种情况）。

如下图所示：

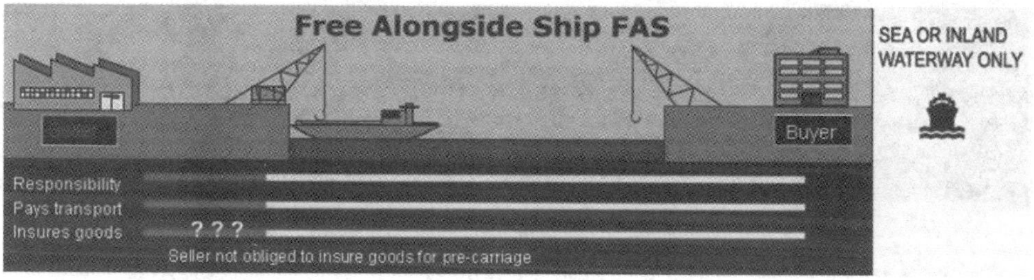

9. FOB（“Free on Board”）（船上交货价）

The seller must get the goods ready for export and load them onto the specified ship. The buyer and seller share the costs and risks when the goods are on board. This term is not used for goods transported in containers by more than one mode of transport（FCA is usually used for this）.

卖家必须确保货物可以出口并且将货物装载到指定的货船上。买家和卖家分担货物在货船上的相关成本和费用。这个术语不适用于多种交通方式的集装箱运输（货交承运人适用于这种情况）。

如下图所示：

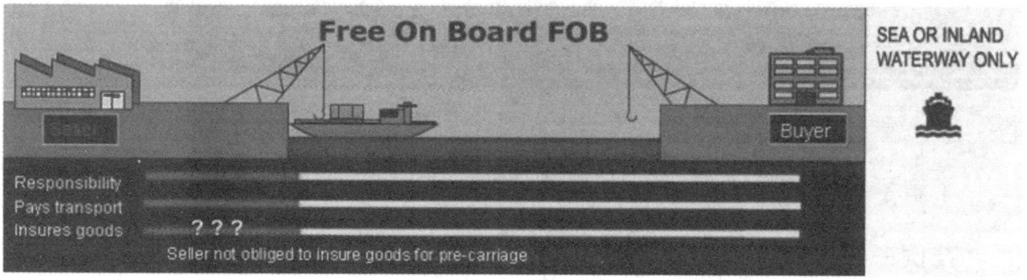

10. CFR（“Cost and Freight”）（成本加运费）

The seller must pay the costs of bringing the goods to the specified port. The buyer is responsible for risks when the goods are loaded onto the ship.

卖家负责把货物运送至指定港口的费用。买家从货物装载到货船上开始承担风险。

如下图所示：

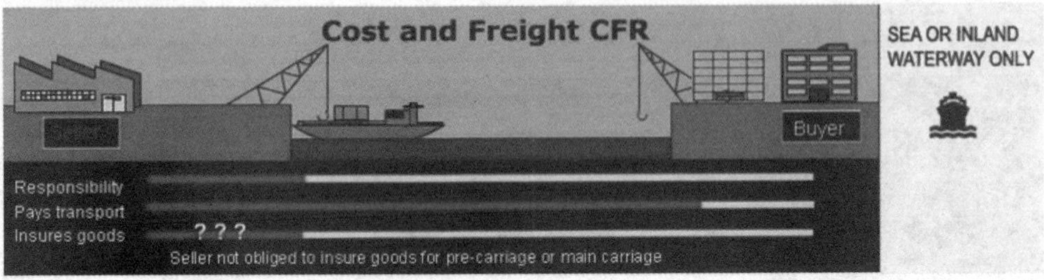

11. CIF（“Cost, Insurance and Freight”）（成本、保险费加运费）

The seller must pay the costs of bringing the goods to the specified port. They also pay for insurance. The buyer is responsible for risks when the goods are loaded onto the ship.

卖家负责把货物运送至指定港口的费用。卖家也要支付相关的保险费用。买家从货物装载到货船上开始承担风险。

如下图所示：

（注：以上解释和图示来自 alpha 法律检索系统）

了解了以上贸易术语，就很容易理解国际贸易中的价格条款，如：

范例一：

All prices stated are Ex-Works（Incoterms 2010）the Company's offices in Zhuhai China.

参考译文：

所有的价格均为中国珠海公司办公地工厂价（Incoterms 2010）。

范例二：The terms FOB, CFR, or CIF shall be subject to the International Rules for the Interpretation of Trade Terms（Incoterms 2010）provided by International Chamber of Commerce（ICC）unless otherwise stipulated herein.

参考译文：

除非另有规定，FOB、CFR、CIF 均应按照国际商会制定的《2010 年国际贸易术语解释通则》解释。

范例三：

The unit price sated in the contract is CIF New York.

参考译文：

合同中的单价为纽约到岸价。

三、装运条款（Clauses on Shipment）

装运条款通常包括装运期、是否允许分批和转运以及起讫地点的规定，以及装运中涉及的单证问题。

常见的装运期条款如下：

范例一：

Shipment must be effected not later than March, 12, 2020.

参考译文：

货物不得迟于 2020 年 3 月 12 日装运。

范例二：

From China Port to Singapore not later than May 10, 2019.

参考译文：

自中国口岸装运货物驶往新加坡不得迟于 2019 年 5 月 10 日。

范例三：

Latest date of shipment：March 23, 2020.

参考译文：

最迟装运日期：2020 年 3 月 23 日。

分批装运、转运的常见条款如下：

范例四：

With/without partial shipment/transshipment.

参考译文：

允许（不允许）分运/转运。

范例五：

Transhipment is allowed provided "through" Bills of Lading are presented.

参考译文：

如提交联运提单允许转运。

范例六：

Transhipment Prohibited (not allowed/per permitted)

参考译文：

不允许分运/转船

范例七：

Transshipment is authorized in Macao.

参考译文：

允许在澳门转运。

范例八：

Partial shipments allowed, but partial shipments of each item not allowed

参考译文：

允许分运，单个品种的货物不得分运

范例九：

Shipment from China to New York by steamer in transit Singapore not later than 15th August, 2018 of the goods specified below.

参考译文：

承载以下货物的轮船不得迟于2018年8月15日从中国中转新加坡转运到纽约。

范例十：

The Goods shall be shipped within ________ days after receipt of L/C allowing transshipment and partial shipment.

参考译文：

收到可转船及分批装运之信用证后________天内装运。

范例十一：

The Sellers shall ship the goods within the time as stipulated in Clause (9) of this Contract by a direct vessel sailing from the port of loading to China Port. Transhipment enroute is not allowed without the Buyers' consent. The goods shall not be carried by vessels flying of the countries not acceptable to the Buyers. (For CRF terms)

参考译文：

卖方应在本合同第（9）条规定之时间内，将货物由装船口岸直接船运到中国口岸，在未经征得买方同意前，中途不得转船。货物不得用悬挂买方不能接受国家的旗帜的船只装运。

范例十二：

The shipping space for the contracted goods shall be booked by the Buyers or the Buyers'shipping agent, China National Chartering Corporation. The Sellers shall undertake to load the contracted goods on board the vessel nominated by the Buyers on any date notified by the Buyers, within the time of shipment stipulated in the Clause (9) of this Contract.

参考译文：

装运本合同货物的船只，由买方或买方运输代理人在中国租船公司租定舱位。卖方应负责将所订货物在本合同第（9）条规定的装船期限内按买方所通知的任何日期装上买方指定的船只。

范例十三：

Ten to fifteen days prior to the date of shipment, the Buyers shall inform the Sellers by cable of the contract number, name of vessel, ETA of vessel, quantity to be loaded and the name of shipping agent, so as to enable the latter to contact the shipping agent directly and arrange the shipment of the goods. The Sellers shall cable in time the Buyers of the result thereof. Should, for certain reasons, it become necessary for the Buyers to replace the named vessel with another one, or should the named vessel arrive at the port of shipment earlier or later than the date of arrival as previously notified to the Sellers, the Buyers or their shipping agent shall advise the Sellers to this effect in due time. The Sellers shall also keep close contact with the agent of XXX.

参考译文：

货物装运前10—15日，买方应电告卖方合同号、船只名称、船只预计到港日期（(Estimated Time of Arrival)、装运数量及船运代理人的名称，以便卖方可与该船运代理人联系及安排货物的装运。卖方应将联系结果及时报告买方，如买方因故需要变更船只或有关船只提前或推迟到达情况发生，买方或船运代理人应及时通知卖方。卖方亦应与XXX代理保持密切联系。

◆ 知识点梳理

与运输有关的表达方式有：

海洋运输	Maritime transport
铁路运输	Railway transport
公路运输	Road transport
航空运输	Air transport
邮政运输	Post transport
集装箱运输	Container transport
管道运输	Pipeline transport
多式联运	Multimodal transport
转船	Transhipment
分批装运	Partial shipment
中转新加坡	In transit Singapore
船只预计到港日期	ETA（Estimated Time of Arrival）

四、单证条款（Clauses on Documents）

国际贸易单证（Documents）是合同履行的必要手段，是对外贸易经营管理的重要工具，并为保障买卖双方的权益提供重要支撑。

信用证项下要求提交的单据通常有商业发票（Commercial Invoice）、提单

(Bill of Lading)、保险单或保险凭证（Insurance Policy/Certificate)、汇票(Draft 或 Bill of Exchange)、原产地证（Certificate of Origin)、检验证书（Inspection Certificate)、受益人证明书（Beneficiary's Certificate)、装箱单（Packing List）等。

常见条款如下：

范例一：

Documents required

参考译文：

需要下列单据

范例二：

Documents marked XX below

参考译文：

（需提交）下列标注 XX 的单据

范例三：

Drafts must be accompanied by the following documents marked XX

参考译文：

汇票需随附下列注有 XX 标志的单据

范例四：

参考译文：

… available against surrender of the following documents bearing out credit number and the full name and address of the opener

参考译文：

（议付时）以提交下列注明本信用证编号及开证人详细姓名、地址的各项单据为有效

注：此句中，surrender 的意思是指“提交”。

范例五：

Accompanied by the following documents marked XX in duplicate

参考译文：

须随附下列注有 XX 标志的单据，一式两份

注：信用证一般都具体说明提供单据的份数，常见的词组有：

In（duplicate，triplicate，quadruplicate，quintuplicate，sextuplicate，septuplicate，octuplicate，nonuplicate，decuplicate）

一式两份（三、四、五、六、七、八、九、十份）

范例六：

Shipping Documents：

The Sellers shall present the following documents to the paying bank for negotiation of payment：

（a）Full set of clean on board，"freight prepaid" for CFR Terms or "freight to collect" for FOB Terms，ocean Bills of Lading，made out to order and blank endorsed，notifying the Branch of China National Foreign Trade Transportation Corporation at the port of destination；

（b）Five copies of signed invoice，indicating contract number and shipping marks；

（c）Two copies of packing list and/or weightlist with indication of measurement；

（d）One copy each of the certificates of quality and quantity or weight，as stipulated in the Clause 5 of the Terms of Delivery；

（e）One duplicate copy of the cable advice of shipment，as stipulated in the Chause 2 of the Terms of Delivery.

参考译文：

装船单据：

卖方凭下列单据向付款银行议付货款：

（a）填写通知目的口岸中国对外贸易运输公司分公司的空白抬头、空白背书的全套已装船清洁海运提单（如系成本加运费（CFR）条款则注明"运费已付"，如系离岸价（FOB）条款则注明"运费到付"；

（b）已签署的发票 5 份，注明合同号及装船唛头；

（c）注明尺码的装箱单/或重量单 2 份；

（d）本交货条款第 5 条规定的品质检验证明书及数量或重量证明书各 1 份；

（e）本交货条款第 2 条规定的装船港通知电报副本 1 份。

范例七：

The Sellers shall despatch one copy each of the duplicates of Bill of Lading, Invoice and Packing List to the Buyers' receiving agent, the Branch of China National Foreign Trade Transportation Corporation at the port of destination.

参考译文：

卖方需将提单、发票及装箱单副本各 1 份随船带交目的口岸买方收货代理人中国对外贸易运输公司分公司。

范例八：

Immediately after the departure of the carrying vessel, the Sellers shall airmail one set of the duplicate documents to the Buyers and two sets to the Branch of China National Foreign Trade Transportation Corporation at the port of destination.

参考译文：

船启航后，卖方立即将 1 份全套单据副本航空邮寄买方，另 2 份航空邮寄目的口岸的中国对外贸易运输公司分公司。

范例九：

The Sellers shall present the following documents to the paying bank for negotiation/collection, or to the Buyers in case of payment by M/T.

1. Full set of Negotiable Clean on Board Ocean Bills of Lading marked "FREIGHT TO COLLECT" and made out to order, blank endorsed, and notifying the China National Foreign Trade Transportation Corporation and the port of destination;

2. Parcel post receipt, indicating postage/Air Way Bill;

3. Insurance Policy or Certificate, covering War risk and all risks including TPND, Breakage and Leakage irrespective of percentage and indicating "In the event of loss or damage request for survey upon arrival of the cargo at the port of destination

to be made to the China Commodity Inspection Bureau of that port";

4. Invoice in quintuplicate, indicating contract number and shipping mark;

5. Packing List in duplicate with indication of both gross and net weights, measurements and quantity of each item packed;

6. Certificate of Quality and Quantity/Weight and Testing Report, each in duplicate issued by the manufacturers;

7. A true copy of cable to advise the Buyers of shipment immediately the goods are loaded on ship.

参考译文:

卖方应将下列单据提交付款银行议付货款/托收付款，如为信汇付款，下列单据应径寄买方:

1. 全套可议付的清洁已装运海运提单，空白抬头，空白背书，注明“运费到付”，并通知到货口岸中国对外贸易运输公司;

2. 邮包收据注明邮费/空运提单;

3. 保险单或保险证明书注明投保战争险和一切险，包括提货不着险、破碎险、渗漏险，无免赔额，并注明“货物到达后如发现残损情况，须向到货口岸之中国商品检验局申请检验”;

4. 发票五份，注明合同号、唛头;

5. 装箱单两份，注明毛、净重和所装货物的品名重量;

6. 由制造厂签发的质量和重量证明书及检验报告各两份;

7. 货物装船后发给买方的装船通知复印件。

◆ 知识点梳理

单证条款中经常涉及的术语:

Freight prepaid	运费已付、运费预付
Freight to collect	运费到付
Made out to order	空白抬头
Blank endorsed	空白背书
Clean on board ocean Bills of Lading	已装船清洁海运提单
negotiation	议付

国际货物买卖合同中常见的单证有：

Import license	进口许可证
Export license	出口许可证
Commercial invoice	商业发票
Bill of lading	海运提单
Airway bill (AWB)	航空运单
Packing list	装箱单
Weight list	重量单
Measurement list	尺码单
Certificate of origin	原产地证书
Certificate of inspection	检验证书
Inspection certificate of quality	品质检验证书
Inspection certificate of quantity	数量检验证书
Inspection certificate of sanitary or certificate of health	卫生（健康）检验证书
Veterinary certificate	兽医检验证书
Inspection certificate of hold	验舱证书
Conformity certificate	合格证
Letter of credit, L/C	信用证
Draft, bill of exchange	汇票
Insurance certificate	保险凭证
Policy	保险单

五、支付条款（Clauses of Payment）

国际货物买卖中常见的支付方法有：汇付（Remittance）、银行托收（Collection）、信用证（letter of credit, L/C）。

（一）汇付（Remittance）

汇付又称买方直接付款（Direct payment by Buyer），指由买方主动地把货款付给卖方的一种付款方式。汇付主要有以下三种：

1. 信汇（mail transfer，M/T）：指汇出行应汇款人的要求，将支付授权书通过邮寄方式寄给汇入行，由汇入行指定收款人解付一定金额的汇付方式。

2. 电汇（telegraphic transfer，T/T）：由汇款人委托汇出行用电报、电传等电讯手段发出汇款委托通知书给收款人所在地的汇入行，委托他将款项解付给指定的收款人。

3. 票汇（remittance by banker's demand draft，D/D）：是指应汇款人要求，汇出行开立以其国外代理行或联行为付款人的即期汇票，由汇款人将汇票寄交收款人，收款人凭此汇票向付款人（汇入行）收款。

（二）托收（Collection）

托收是卖方向买方开立汇票（此处的汇票为指己汇票），委托银行向买方收取货款的一种结算方式。卖方为出票人及受款人，买方为受票人。

托收的程序如下：

1. 委托人出具汇票，向托收行提出托收申请，填具托收指示书，附具或不附具装运单据。

2. 托收行接受申请后，委托债务人所在地的代理人传达托收指示，并寄交有关单据。

3. 代收行按托收指示，向债务人提示有关单据，在付款人付款后通知托收行，托收行即向委托人付款。

如图所示：

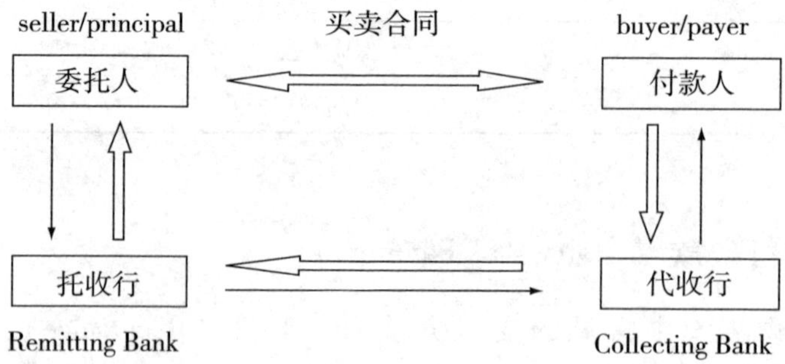

托收又分为光票托收与跟单托收。

1. 光票托收（Clean Collection）：指卖方仅开具汇票委托银行向买方收取款项，而不附任何装运单据，通常只用于收取货款尾数、佣金、样品机等项费用（Clean collection means collection of financial document not accompanied by commercial documents）。

2. 跟单托收（Documentary Collection）：指卖方在开具汇票时，还要将有关装运单据交给委托银行，委托银行向买方收取货款（Documentary Collection means collection of financial document accompanied by commercial documents）。

跟单托收又进一步可分为付款交单与承兑交单。

（1）付款交单（Document against Payment，D/P），指代收行在受票人支付了全部货款以后才将有关装运单据交付给受票人的一种托收方式（The documents shall be delivered to the buyer on actual payment of the bill）.

由此可见，付款交单对于卖方而言是非常安全的交易方式。

（2）承兑交单（ Document against Acceptance，D/A），指代收行在受票人承兑了有关汇票以后就将有关单据交付给受票人的一种托收方式（The documents shall be delivered to the buyer on acceptance of the bill），即，交单在先，付款在后。而这里的汇票肯定是远期汇票，如以 6 个月为期。待汇票到期，代收行向进口商提示付款。

注：D/P 与 D/A 相比，D/P 风险小，因为 D/A 虽表示承兑，但却存在不付款的风险。D/A 也可以理解为卖方给予买方的资金融通。

（三）信用证（letter of credit，L/C）

信用证是银行根据进口商（买方）的请求，开给出口方（卖方）的一种保证承担支付货款责任的书面凭证（ "Credit means any arrangement，however named or described，that is irrevocable and thereby constitutes a definite undertaking of the issuing bank to honour（香港表示付款，大陆表示兑付）a complying presentation."（UCP600 第二条），即："信用证是指一项不可撤销的安排，无论其名称或描述如何，该项安排构成开证行对相符交单予以承付的确定承诺"（定义来源：跟单信用证统一惯例 Uniform Customs and Practice for Documentary Credits 第二条）。

注：国际商会于 1930 年制定了《商业跟单信用证统一惯例》，供各银行和银行公会自由采用。1993 年修改的第 500 号出版。2007 年 7 月 1 日，第 600 号出版，即 UCP600。

作为国际商法的重要渊源之一，国际商会所制定的 UCP 适用于几乎所有的国际信用证交易（International Chamber of Commerce's Uniform Customs and Practices for Documentary Credits（UCP）governs virtually all international letters of credit transaction)。

信用证交易的当事人有：

1. 开证申请人（Applicant/Account party）：the buyer

2. 受益人（Beneficiary）：the seller

3. 开证行（Issuing Bank）：the buyer's bank

4. 通知行（Advising Bank）：受开证行委托，将信用证通知受益人的银行(bank in the beneficiary's country delivers the credit to the beneficiary)

5. 议付行（Negotiating Bank）：means the purchase by the nominated bank of drafts（drawn on a bank other than the nominated bank）and for documents under a complying presentation, by advancing or agreeing to advance funds to the beneficiary on or before the banking day on which reimbursement is due to (to be paid the nominated bank)。

此处需要注意的是，议付强调的是对汇票和单据的买入行为。

信用证下所需单据（Documents commonly requires by a letter of credit）如下：

Certificate of origin 原产地证书

Export license 出口许可证

Health inspection certificate 安全检验证明

Commercial Invoice 商业发票

6. 付款行（Paying Bank）：是开证行指定担任信用证项下付款或充当汇票付款人的银行。

7. 保兑行（Confirming Bank）：Bank that independently promises to pay, accept, or negotiate a credit, as appropriate, when the documents specified in the credit are presented to it.

信用证交易流程如下图所示：

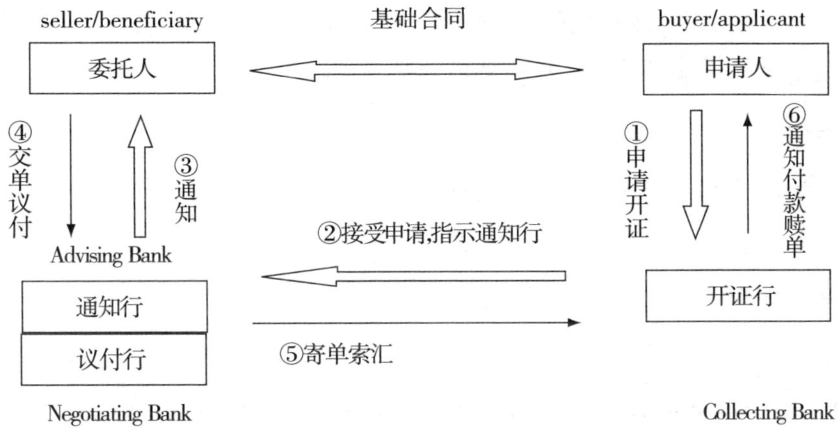

信用证的种类有：

◇可撤销信用证（Revocable L/C）VS. 不可撤销信用证（Irrevocable L/C）

不可撤销信用证：指一经开出，在有效期内，未经受益人及有关当事人的同意，开证行不得片面撤销或修改的信用证。

Irrevocable：can not be altered without the beneficiary's express consent.

可撤销信用证：是指开证行可以不经过受益人同意，也不必事先通知受益人，在议付行议付货款之前，有权随时修改信用证的内容或撤销信用证。

◇保兑信用证（Confirmed L/C）VS. 不保兑信用证（Unconfirmed L/C）

保兑的信用证是指开证行开出的信用证又经另一家银行保证兑付的信用证。

Confirmed：A second bank adds its endorsement to the credit.

不保兑信用证：未经保兑的信用证。

◇可转让信用证（Transferable L/C）VS. 不可转让信用证（Untransferable L/C）

可转让信用证（Transferable L/C）：是指受益人（第一受益人）可以要求通知行或付款行将信用证全部或部分转让给另一个或数个受益人（第二受益人）使用的信用证（It permits a beneficiary to transfer the credit to a second beneficiary；Transferable credit means a credit that specifically states it is "transferable"）。

了解了以上有关国际货物买卖的几种付款方式后，我们再学习以下常见的有关汇票和付款条款的写作范例就容易多了：

范例一：

Drawn under contract No. VK-4653-68。

参考译文：

第 VK-4653-68 号合同项下开立。

范例二：

Being amount of 1, 000 cartons Apple under Contract No. 667NM65。

参考译文：

系第 No. 667NM65 号合同项下 1000 箱苹果之金额。

范例三：

Covering 600 cartons of garments shipped from Zhuhai to Hong Kong under Contract No. 90GD003。

参考译文：

清偿第 No. 90GD003 合同项下自珠海至香港的服装 600 箱。

范例四：

We hereby issue our irrevocable documentary letter of credit No. XXX available, at 60 days after B/L date by draft。

参考译文：

兹开立不可撤销跟单信用证（号码：XXX），提单签发后 60 天汇票支付。

范例五：

Draft at 90 days sight. We are authorized to pay interest at the rate of 9% p. a. for full invoice value at maturity. Invoice and draft must show the amount of interest.

参考译文：

该条款是 90 天远期汇票，见票后起算。开证行被授权按年息 9 厘计息到付款。发票与汇票上必须显示利息金额。此条款表明货款金额连同利息都可在见票 90 天后在信用证项下支付。

范例六：

Drafts at 180 days sight drawn on Saitama Bank Ltd. , Tokyo Office. Usance drafts drawn under this L/C are to be negotiated at sight basis. Discount charges and acceptance commission are for account of accountee。

参考译文：

该条款由日本银行开来，汇票开立远期见票 180 天付款，但可即期议付，其贴现费和承兑费均由开证人负担。对受益人来说是即期信用证，通常称为假远期信用证。

范例七：

Invoice and drafts to be drawn on full CIF value but the beneficiary is to be paid 5% less as commission payable to openers and this should be incorporated on bank schedule.

参考译文：

该条款发票和汇票都开列货款全额，但议付行付给出口人货款时，必须扣除 5% 佣金；同时，他向开证行索汇，也只收取 95% 货款，5% 佣金在议付行寄送单据给开证行的表格上批明即可。

范例八：

Payment is to be made by irrevocable letter of credit payable against sight draft accompanied by a full set of shipping documents.

参考译文：

付款方式是以不可撤销的信用证下的即期汇票支付，随附全套装船单据。

范例九：

Date on which the documentary credit must be notified to seller: ________ days before date of delivery。

参考译文：

必须向卖方通知跟单信用证的日期：交货日前________天。

范例十：

Terms of payment

1. Payment by L/C：One month before shipment，the Buyers shall establish with Bank of China，Guangzhou an Irrevocable L/C in favor of the Sellers，to be available against presentation in Guangzhou of the shipment documents stipulated in Clause 12 hereof.

2. Payment by Collection：After delivery is made，the Sellers shall send through the Sellers，bank draft drawn on the Buyers together with the shipment documents specified in Clause 12 hereof，to the Buyers through the Buyers bank，the Bank of China，Guangzhou，for collection.

3. Payment by M/T：Payments to be effected by the Buyers not later than ________ days after receipt of the shipment documents specified in Clause 12 hereof.

参考译文：

付款条件：

1. 信用证付款：货物装运前一个月，乙方应由广州中国银行开立以卖方为受益人的不可撤销的信用证，凭本合同第 12 条规定的装运单据交到广州（银行）后付款。

2. 托收付款：货物装运后，卖方应将以买方为付款人的汇票连同本合同第 12 条所列各种装运单据，通过卖方银行寄交买方银行即广州中国银行转交买方，并托收货款。

3. 信汇付款：买方收到本合同第 12 条所列装运单据后，应于________天内信汇寄款。

◆ 知识点梳理

与付款有关的术语如下：

Remittance	付汇
Mail transfer，M/T	信汇
Telegraphic transfer，T/T	电汇
Remittance by banker's demand draft，D/D	票汇
Collection	托收
Clean Collection	光票托收

续表

Documentary Collection	跟单托收
Document against Payment, D/P	付款交单
Document against Acceptance, D/A	承兑交单
Letter of credit, L/C	信用证
Revocable L/C VS. Irrevocable L/C	可撤销信用证 VS. 不可撤销信用
Confirmed L/C) VS. Unconfirmed L/C	保兑信用证 VS. 不保兑信用证
Transferable L/C VS. Untransferable L/C	可转让信用证 VS. 不可转让信用证
Draft at sight , sight draft, demand draft	即期汇票
Time draft, usance draft	远期汇票

六、保险条款（Clauses of Insurance）

一般来说，保险条款所涉及的内容有保险金额（insured amount）、投保险别（coverage/types）、保险费（premium）、保险凭证（insurance certificate）等。因为保险条款与价格条款有着必然的联系，所以采用不同的价格条款，投保人不同，保险条款的订立方法亦不相同。

1. 在以 EXW、FAS、FOB、FCA、CFR、CPT 贸易术语签订合同时，保险条款可作如下规定："保险由买方办理。"（insurance is to be covered by the buyer.）

2. 在以 DEQ、DES、DDU、DDP 贸易术语签订合同时，保险条款可作如下规定："保险由卖方办理。"（insurance is to be covered by the seller.）

3. 在以 CIF 或 CIP 贸易术语签订合同时，保险条款须明确规定投保人、投保险别以及确定保险金额的方法和保险适用条款，并注明该条款的生效时间。

保险金额（amount insured）是指保险公司可能赔偿的最高金额，习惯上按发票金额加 10% 预期利润和业务费用。也可根据国外客户要求提高加成数。

保险金额的加成、保险险别的选择和适用的保险条款，都需在合同中作相应规定。在 CIF、CIP 合同中，保险条款可作如下规定："由卖方按发票金额的 110% 投保一切险和战争险，按 1981 年 1 月 1 日中国人民保险公司海洋运输货物保险条款投保"（Insurance is to be covered by the Sellers for 110% of the invoice value against All Risks and War Risks as per Ocean Marine Cargo Insurance Clauses of the People's Insurance Company of China dated Jan. 1，1981）。

在国际货物买卖中，按照承保范围的从低到高，三个主险分别是：平安险（free from particular average，F. P. A.）、水渍险（with particular average，W. P. A.）、一切险（All Risks，A. R.）。要区分三个险种，我们需要先了解avarage的含义。

在海上运输保险的语境中，avarage的含义是海损，其又分为单独海损（Particular average）和共同海损（General average），分别是指：

◇Particular average（单独海损）：a loss that is borne solely by the owner of the lost property（ship or cargo）（指货物非人为的意外而发生的损失，并且只涉及船舶或货物的一方利益，与他方利益无关）；For example：partial damage of cargo by sea water is a particular average（因海水导致的货物部分受损为单独海损）；

◇General average（共同海损）：a sacrifice made for the common safety of both the cargo and the ship（指在同一海上航程中，船舶、货物和其他财产遭遇共同危险，为了共同安全，有意地、合理地采取措施所直接造成的特殊牺牲、支付的特殊费用，共同海损的理念是：为大家牺牲的财产，应由大家来补偿）。

平安险的英文是free from particular average，字面意思是“单独海损不赔”，其实质含义指平安险只承担意外事故和自然灾害引起的货物全损和特定意外事故引起的货物部分损失，不承担单纯自然灾害引起的货物的部分损失。

水渍险的英文是with particular average，字面意思是“单独海损可赔”，水渍险的赔偿范围，只是在平安险的承保范围的基础上增加了单纯自然灾害引起的单独海损。

一切险包括水渍险的范围，并增加承保由于一般外来原因造成的货物全部损失和部分损失，是三个主险中承保范围最大的一个险种。

◆ 知识点梳理

除了三个主险之外，还有附加险，如下表所示：

war risk	战争险
theft, pilferage and nondelivery (TPND)	盗窃提货不着险)
rain fresh water damage	(淡水雨淋险)
risk of shortage	短量险
risk of contamination	沾污险
risk of leakage	渗漏险
risk of clashing & breakage	碰损破碎险
risk of odour	串味险
damage caused by sweating and/or heating	受潮受热险
hook damage	钩损险
loss and/or damage caused by breakage of packing	包装破裂险
risk of rusting	锈损险
risk of mould	发霉险
strike, riots and civil commotion (s. r. c. c.)	罢工、暴动、民变险
risk of spontaneous combustion	自燃险
deterioration risk	腐烂变质险
inherent vice risk	内在缺陷险
risk of natural loss or normal loss	途耗或自然损耗险
aflatoxin risk	黄曲霉素险
parcel post risk	邮包险

了解了以上知识后，我们看一下以下典型的保险条款：

范例一：

Marine insurance policies or certificates in negotiable form, for 110% full CIF invoice covering the risks of war & W. A. as per the People's Insurance Co. of China dated January 1st, 1976, with extended cover up to Kuala Lumpur with claims payable in (at) Kuala Lumpur in the currency of draft (irrespective of percentage)

参考译文：

作为可议付格式的海运保险单或凭证按照到岸价的发票金额 110% 投保中国人民保险公司 1976 年 1 月 1 日的战争险和基本险，负责到吉隆坡为止。按照汇票所使用的货币在吉隆坡赔付（无免赔率）。

范例二：

Insurance policy or certificate covering w. a. (or f. p. a.) and war risks as per ocean marine cargo clause and ocean marine cargo war risk clauses of the People's Insurance Company of China dated 1/1/1981。

参考译文：

保险单或凭证根据中国人民保险公司 1981 年 1 月 1 日的海洋运输货物保险条款和海洋运输货物战争险条款投保水渍险（或平安险）和战争险。

范例三：

For each shipment, Seller shall arrange marine insurance in favor of Buyer, covering the Concentrate Oil from the port of loading until discharged at the discharge port, for 110% of the value finally established in accordance with this Agreement, on the following conditions:

——institute All Risks;

——institute Strikes Risks (Cargo);

——institute War Risks (Cargo).

参考译文：

对于每批货物，卖方应投保以买方为受益人的海运险，按照该协议中精油价值的 110%，从起运港直到在目的港卸货整个过程中投保以下险种：

——一切险；

——罢工险；

——战争险。

范例四：

This insurance must be valid for a period of 60 days after arrival of merchandise at inland destination.

参考译文：

本保险扩展到货物到达内地的目的地后 60 天有效。

范例五：

Including w. a. & risk of fire for 60 days in customs warehouse after discharge of the goods at port of destination subject to China insurance clause.

参考译文：

按照中国保险条款投保水渍险和火险，在目的港卸货后存入海关仓库 60 天为止。

◆ 知识点梳理

与保险条款相关的专业术语表达如下：

Insurer	保险人
Insured	被保险人
Insured value	保险价值
Insured amount	保险金额
Insurance premium	保险费
Policy	保险单
Insurance certificate	保险凭证
Beneficiary/in the favor of	受益人/以…为受益人
Irrespective of percentage	无免赔率

七、包装条款（Packing Clause）

包装条款（packing clause）是用来规定货物包装方式、包装材料、包装费用负担和运输标志等方面内容的条款。包装条款一般包括包装的种类和性质、包装材料、包装尺寸、包装费用和运输标志等内容。

范例一：

To be packed in new strong wooden case (s) /carton (s) suitable for long distance ocean transportation and well protected against damps, moisture, shock, rust and rough handling. The Seller shall be liable for any damage to the goods on account of improper packing and for any rust damage attributable to inadequate or improper protective measures taken by the Seller, and in such case or cases any and all losses and/or expenses incurred in consequence thereof shall be borne by the Seller.

参考译文：

需用坚固的新木箱或纸箱包装，适合长途海运，防湿、防潮、防震及粗暴搬运。由于包装不良所发生的损失，由于采用不充分或不妥善的防护措施而造成的任何损坏，卖方应负担由此而产生的一切费用和/或损失。

范例二：

Goods must be packed with sturdy wooden boxes or cartons that are suitable for long-distance shipping / mailing / air transportation and adaptable to climate change, and have good moisture and earthquake resistance. In case any damage or loss are caused due to poor packaging or improper protective measures, the seller shall compensate all the losses resulted therefrom.

The packing box shall be accompanied with maintenance manual and operation instructions.

参考译文：

货物须采用坚固的木箱或纸箱包装，以宜于长途海运/邮寄/空运及适应气候的变化，并具备良好的防潮抗震能力。由于包装不良引起的货物损伤或由于防护措施不善而引起的货物损失，卖方应赔偿由此而造成的全部损失费用。

包装箱内应附有完整的维修保养、操作使用说明书。

范例三：

Shipping mark: The seller shall mark the box number, gross weight, net weight, size, contract number, port of destination, consignee number with non-fading paint on each container, and write "moisture-proof", "handle with care", "this face up" etc. words.

参考译文：

装运标记：卖方应在每个货箱上用不褪色油漆标明箱号、毛重、净重、尺寸、合同号、目的港、收货人编号，并书以"防潮"、"小心轻放"、"此面向上"等字样。

对于一些对包装要求不高的货物，装运条款就比较简单，如下例：

范例四：

Packing：1PC/POLYBAG，45 PCS/Carton

Shipping Mark：A. B. C.

08SUG0001

OSLO

C/NO. ：1-UP

参考译文：

包装：1 件/塑料袋，45 袋/箱

装运标记：A. B. C.

08SUG0001

奥斯陆

编号：1-UP

◆ 附包装中常见英文表述：

（1）识别标志：

箱（包）号：Case#

重量（毛）：Weight（Gross）

重量（净）：Weight（Net）

重量（法定）：Weight（Legal）

体积标志：Measurement Mark

表示为：Long × Wide × High 或 L × W × H

批号：Lon No. 或 batch No.

尺寸 cm：Dimensions in cm

数量：Quantity 或 qty

颜色：Colour

规格：Specification 或 spec

原产国标志：Country Of Origin

收货人：Consignee

发货人：Consignor

发运人：Shipper

由……到……：From……To……

经由：Via

港：Port

站：Station

目的地：Destination

空皮退到：When Empty，Return To

货号：Article No.

小心轻放——FRAGILE

向上——THIS END UP

（2）装箱标志（操作位置）

由此起吊（此处悬索或挂绳位置）：Sling Here；Lift Here；Heave Here

由此吊起（起吊点）：Haul

从此提起（起锚位置）：Heaver Here

挂绳位置：Sling Here；Points Of Slinging

从此开启（此处打开）：Open Here

先开顶部：Remove Top First Cut Straps

暗室开启：Open In Dark Room

用滚子搬运：Use Rollers

不可滚动：Use No Rollers

夹紧位置：Clamping Position

八、检验和索赔条款（Inspection and Claims）

检验和索赔条款往往是同时出现的，在检验中如发现产品不符的情况，买方可提出索赔要求或者其他补救措施。检验和索赔条款中并没有涉及很多的专业知识，特介绍一些范例如下：

范例一：

The manufacturer shall before making delivery, make a precise and comprehensive inspection of the goods as regards their quality, specifications, performance and quantity/weight, and issue certificates certifying that the goods are in conformity with the stipulations of this Contract. The certificates shall form an integral part of the documents to be presented to the paying bank for negotiation/collection of payment but shall not be considered as final in respect of quality, specifications, performance and quality/weight. Particulars and results of this test carried out by the manufacturer must be shown in a statement to be attached to the said Quality Certificate.

参考译文：

在交货以前，生产商应就订货的质量、规格、重量作出准确和全面的检验，并出具货物和本合同规定相符的证明书，该证书为议付/托收货款而应上交银行的单据的组成部分，但不得作为认定货物的质量、规格和重量的最后依据。生产商应将记载检测细节和结果的书面报告附在质量证明书内。

范例二：

After arrival of the goods at the port of destination, the Buyer shall apply to the China Commodity Inspection Bureau (hereinafter called the Bureau) for a preliminary inspection of the goods in respect of their quality, specifications and quantity/weight. If any discrepancies are found by the Bureau regarding the specifications or the quantity/weight or both, except those for which either the insurance company or the shipping company is responsible, the Buyer shall, within 120 days after discharge of the goods at the port of destination, have the right either to reject the goods or to claim against the Seller on the strength of the inspection certificate issued by the Bureau.

参考译文：

货物到达口岸后，买方应向中国商品检验局（以下简称商检局）申请就货物的质量、规格和重量进行初步检验。如发现到货到规格或重量与合同不符，除应由保险公司或船运公司负责外，买方于货物在到货口岸卸货后 120 天内凭商检局出具之检验证书有权拒收货物或向卖方索赔。

范例三：

Within the guarantee period stipulated in Clause 14 hereof, <u>should</u> the quality and/or the specifications of the goods to be found not in conformity with the contracted stipulations, or <u>should</u> the goods prove defective for any reasons, including latent defect of the use of unsuitable materials, the Buyer shall arrange for an inspection to be carried out by the Bureau and have the right to claim against the Seller on the strength of the inspection certificate issued by the Burau.

参考译文：

在合同第 14 条规定的保证期限内，如发现货物的质量及/或规格与本合同规定不符或发现货物无论任何原因引起的缺陷，包括潜在的缺陷或使用不良的原料，买方应申请商检局检验，并有权根据商检局签发的证书向卖方索赔。

注：上句中连续出现两个 should…条件句，这在法律英语中非常常见。在

这样的句型中，should 一般出现在句首，后面的动词用原形，没有时态等变化，句子为陈述句，并非疑问句。我们在第一章第二节专门探讨了这个问题。再比如例句：Should all or part of the contract be unable to be fulfilled owing to the fault of one party, the breaching party shall bear the responsibilities thus caused. Should it be the fault of both parties, they shall bear their respective responsibilities according to actual situations.

范例四：

Any and all claims shall be regarded as accepted if the Seller fail to reply within 30 days after receipt of the Buyer's claim.

参考译文：

卖方收到买方索赔通知后，如果在三十日内不答复，应视为卖方同意买方提供了一切索赔。

范例五：

Settlment of claims：

In case the Selleris liable for the discrepancies and a claim is made by the Buyer within the period of claim or quality guarantee period as stipulated in Clause 15 and 16 of this Contract, the Seller shall settle the claim upon the agreement of the Buyer in the following ways：

1. Agree to the rejection of the goods and refund to the Buyer the value of the goods so rejected in the same currency as contracted herein, and to bear all direct losses and expenses in connection therewith, including interest accrued, banking charges, freight, insurance premium, insepection charges, storage, stevedore charges and all other necessary expenses required for the custody and protection of the rejected goods.

2. Devaluate the goods according to the degree of inferiority, extent of damage and amount of losses sustained by the Buyer.

3. Replace the defective goods with new ones which conform to the specifications, quality and performance as stipulated in this Contract, and bear all expenses incurred and direct losses sustained by the Buyer. The Seller shall, at the same

time, guarantee the quality of the replacement goods for a further period of 12 months as specified in Clause 15 of this Contract.

参考译文：

索赔解决方法：

如货物不符合应由卖方负责，且买方按照本合同第 15 条和第 16 条的规定在索赔期限或质量保证期限内提出索赔，卖方在取得买方同意后，应按下列方式理赔：

1. 同意买方退货，并将退货金额以成交原币返还买方，并承担因退货而发生的一切直接损失和费用，包括利息、银行费用、运费、保险费、商检费、仓租费、码头装卸费以及为保管退货而发生的一切其他必要费用。

2. 按照货物的疵劣程度、损坏的范围和买方所遭受的损失，将货物贬值。

3. 调换有瑕疵的货物，换货必须全新并符合本合同规定的规格和质量。卖方应负担因此而发生的一切费用和买方遭受的一切直接损失。对换货的质量，卖方仍应按本合同第 15 条的约定，保证十二个月。

◆ 知识点梳理

在有关检验和索赔条款中，常见的表达句式有：

货物与合同相符 The goods are <u>in conformity with</u> the stipulations of this Contract
如发现货物规格、数量/重量等方面有不符 In case/if any <u>discrepancies</u> are found <u>regarding</u> the specifications or the quantity/weight…
如发现货物质量/规格与合同约定不符 Should the quality and/or the specifications of the goods to be found <u>not in conformity with</u> the contracted stipulations
Losses sustained/incurred by the Buyer 买方所遭受的损失
承担买方所遭受的费用和直接损失 Bear all expenses incurred and direct losses sustained by the Buyer
卖方对买方遭受的损失负责 The Seller <u>is liable for</u> the losses sustained by the Buyer

第二节　OEM 合作协议

OEM，英文全称为 Original Equipment Manufacturer，中文含义是原始设备生产商，俗称定点生产，俗称代工（生产）。基本含义为品牌生产者不直接生产产品，而是利用自己掌握的关键核心技术负责设计和开发新产品，将生产环节外包（outsourcing）。

原始设备制造商具体的加工任务通过合同订购的方式委托同类产品的其他厂家生产，之后将所订产品低价买断，并直接贴上自己的品牌商标。这种委托他人生产的合作方式简称 OEM，承接加工任务的制造商被称为 OEM 厂商，其生产的产品被称为 OEM 产品。可见，定点生产属于加工贸易中的“代工生产”方式，在国际贸易中是以商品为载体的劳务出口。

OEM 合作协议中的常见条款涉及：总则、商标使用、产品质量保证、交付标准、知识产权、赔偿责任等。

一、总则（General Provisions）

范例一：

Whereas, XXX TECHNOLOGIES PRIVATE LIMITED, a company incorporated under the Companies Act, 1956 having its registered office at ________ (hereinafter referred to as “Party A”) and YYY CO., LTD, a company duly organized and existing under the laws of the People’s Republic of China having its registered office at Zhuhai, P. R. China (hereinafter referred to as “Party B”), had duly executed an OEM SUPPLY AGREEMENT (“Agreement”) dated 21st August 2019 on such terms and conditions as stipulated thereunder.

参考译文：

鉴于 XXX 科技私人有限公司，一依据《1956 年公司法案》成立的位于________的公司（以下简称甲方），与 YYY 有限责任公司，一家依据中华人民共和国法律成立的位于珠海的公司（以下简称乙方），依照以下条款于 2019 年 8 月 21 日正式签订 OEM 供应协议（本协议）。

范例二：

Cooperation Manner：Both Parties agree that Party A shall sell the products by OEM；Meanwhile，Party B shall develop，manufacture and provide，by OEM，products with the brand designated by Party A（the "products"）.

参考译文：

双方同意甲方以 OEM 方式销售合作产品，乙方采用 OEM 方式研发、生产并提供合作产品，合作产品的商标由甲方指定。

二、商标使用（Use of Trademark）

范例一：

Party A warrants that the Brand and Trademark do not infringe on any intellectual property right of any third party. Otherwise，Party A shall indemnify Party B for any losses and damages resulting from such infringement（including but not limited to attorney fee，any penalty，damages or compensation）.

参考译文：

甲方保证其提供的品牌和商标等不侵犯任何人的权利，若乙方因品牌和商标侵权而造成的一切损失（包括但不限于律师费、违约金、赔偿金或者补偿金等），甲方应予以赔偿。

范例二：

Party B undertakes not to use the Trademark in any way without the expressed approval of Party A. The Trademark can only be used in products as approved by parties.

参考译文：

乙方承诺按双方约定的范围和方式使用甲方提供的商标。未取得甲方明确同意的情况下，不以任何方式使用商标。

范例三：

Party A shall provide Party B with the corresponding brand symbol，brand logo image and other relevant brand and/or design. The cost of putting the brand on the products shall be borne by Party B.

参考译文：

甲方应将相应的商标、商标标识设计，以及其他相关的商标或设计提供给乙方；将商标印制在产品上的费用由乙方承担。

三、产品质量保证（Product Quality Control）

范例一：

Party B undertakes to perform all the tests and/or approval tests before shipment that are necessary in order to establish that the Products comply with the technical specifications, as agreed between the Parties. Party B shall ensure each Product or batch of Products shall meet specification and where applicable is tested before delivery and supplied with a certificate of conformance to Specification. If Party B persistently fails to meet the required Specification, then Party A reserves the right to amend this contract. Alternatively, Party A may also,

· claim damages and /or expenses incurred by Party A relating to poor quality; or

· terminate this Agreement with immediate effect of persistent poor quality.

参考译文：

乙方承诺在产品装运之前对产品进行必要的检测，以使产品符合双方约定的技术标准。乙方应确保每个产品或每批产品符合规格要求，并在必要时进行检验并签发符合规格要求的检验证书。如果乙方持续未能满足所要求的规格，甲方则保留修订协议的权利，或者，甲方也有权采取以下行动：

·对于低劣质量导致甲方遭受的损失，甲方有权要求索赔；或者

·在产品质量持续低劣的情况下，立即终止本协议。

范例二：

Party B hereby guarantees that the products provided to Party A will comply with the quality standards provided in this agreement, or as maybe agreed upon in writing by both parties. In case the liability arising from product's quality is caused by Party A's directions, Party B will not be liable for the damages.

参考译文：

乙方承诺提供给甲方的产品符合本协议约定的质量标准或双方书面同意的标准；如产品的质量责任是由甲方的指示造成的，乙方不承担相关赔偿责任。

范例三：

Party B warrants that the Products and all parts including accessories thereof shall be free from defects in design, materials and workmanship and shall conform to the specification for Twelve (12) Months from the date of shipment to Party A. Regarding the accessories, the warranty policies of the original accessories suppliers shall apply which shall be for a minimum period of Six (6) Months.

参考译文：

乙方保证产品及其所有零件（包括附件）在设计、材料和工艺上均无瑕疵，并应符合从运往甲方之日起十二（12）个月的规范。关于附件，适用原始配件供应商的保修政策，即保修期至少为六（6）个月。

范例四：

Party A is entitled to appoint its technical representatives to participate in the quality control of the Products, and has the right to inspect the testing equipment, production process and quality control of the materials and parts related to the Products from time to time.

参考译文：

甲方有权委派其技术代表共同参与产品的质量控制，同时有权不定期检查与定牌产品相关的检测设备、生产过程及材料、零部件的质量控制等。

范例五：

In the event of any change in the design, specifications, raw materials and components of Party B's production of the Products, Party A's written consent shall be obtained in advance; in case Party A proposes any change hereof, Party B shall notify Party B in writing and the matter shall be discussed by both parties.

参考译文：

乙方生产定牌产品在设计、规格、原材料及部件等方面如有变更，须先征得甲方的书面同意；如果甲方提出任何变更要求，须书面通知乙方，并由双方协商，共同决定。

范例六：

Party B must choose raw materials in accordance with the provisions of the contract, and accept the testing from Party A. In case any quality problems of the Products arise because Party B conceals the defects of raw materials or uses the raw materials that is not in conformity with the contract stipulations, Party A shall have the right to request re-work, repair, price reduction or refund.

参考译文：

乙方必须依照合同规定选用原材料，并接受甲方检验。乙方隐瞒原材料的缺陷或者使用不符合合同规定的原材料而影响定做质量时，甲方有权要求重作、修理、减少价款或退货。

四、交付标准（Delivery Standards）

范例一：

The Product shall be packed in a manner suitable for transportation.

Each and every Product shall be marked with the product number and model designation and other markings as requested by Party A. The data label shall also give the production date (month and year) and the serial number of the Product according to the specifications given by Party A to Party B. Party B shall provide end to end traceability for the Products including spare parts (if applicable) supplied to Party A.

参考译文：

产品的包装应适合长途运输。

每个产品上应标识产品号码、产品型号及甲方所要求的其他标识。数据标签还应该依据甲方给乙方的规格要求标识出生产日期（年、月）及产品编号。同时，乙方还应该为供应给甲方的产品（包括零部件）提供端到端的追踪服务。

范例二：

Party B shall use reasonable commercial efforts to ship the Products on the delivery date specified in the contract. All deliveries shall be accompanied by the certificate of conformity, at no extra charge, which shall be in a specific format approved by Party A. Any requests for additional certification will be agreed in advance.

参考译文：

乙方应尽合理的商业努力以使在合同规定的交货日期装运产品。每批交付的货物均应附有合格证书（免费提供），合格证书应按甲方批准的特定格式制作。需要进行附加认证的，双方应提前协商确定。

五、知识产权（Intellectual Property）

范例一：

Party B agrees that all the Intellectual Property, arising from a contracted development work undertaken at the behest of Party A involving a change a design, electronics and/or software shall become the property of Party A either in its incomplete or completed form once the payment for the contracted job has been fully discharged by Party A.

Further Party B undertakes and ensures that Party A's Intellectual Property rights are not infringed, by any party/third party, in the process of developing work.

参考译文：

乙方同意，在甲方的指令下基于合同所开发的所有知识产权，包括设计、电子器件和/或者软件的变更，一旦甲方已经支付了所有的开发费用，都应属于甲方的财产，无论该等知识产权表现为非完整的或者完整的形式。

乙方进一步承诺并保证甲方的知识产权在开发过程中不被任何方/第三方侵犯。

范例二：

The intellectual property rights of the Trademark of the cooperative product belongs to Party A, and the liability and losses arising from trademark infringement shall be borne by Party A.

参考译文：

合作产品的商标的知识产权归甲方享有，因商标侵权所产生的责任及损失由甲方承担。

六、赔偿责任（Indemnification）

在 OEM 协议中，因代工的一方负责生产和产品质量控制等，且往往处于合同中较为弱势的一方，委托方往往会在协议中增加一些限制代工方的条款，督促代工一方切实履行产品质量保障义务，如下条款所示：

Party B agrees to defend, indemnify and hold Party A harmless against any liability, loss, expense, damage or cost arising out of personal or bodily injury or death or property damage caused directly by any defect in the products or parts thereof.

Party B agrees to indemnify and hold Party A harmless against any damages to persons and/or things, caused or that in any way derive from the activity of Party B's employees and/or of any other person employed by Party B in order to perform this Agreement.

Party B agrees to indemnify and hold Party A harmless against any claims/damages that may arise due to infringement of any Intellectual Property of any Party/third party in the process of purchase and maketing of Products of Party B by Party A.

Party B agrees to indemnify and hold Party A harmless against any claims/damages that may arise due to non-supply of spare parts of Products sold.

Party B agrees to indemnify Party A for breach of any the exclusivity right.

参考译文：

乙方同意，因产品或其部件的任何缺陷直接造成的人身或身体伤害、死亡或财产损失所引起的任何责任、损失、费用、损害或成本，为甲方辩护、作出赔偿并使之免受损害。

乙方同意，对于乙方的雇员和/或乙方雇用的任何其他人在履行本协议中以任何方式造成的对人身和/或财产损害，乙方对甲方作出赔偿并使之免受损害。

乙方同意，在甲方购买和销售乙方产品过程中因侵犯任何一方/第三方的任何知识产权而引起的任何索赔/损害，乙方对甲方作出赔偿并使之免受损害。

乙方同意，因所售定牌产品的备件供应不足而引起的任何索赔/损害，乙方对甲方作出赔偿并使之免受损害。

乙方同意，因违反任何专有权而对甲方作出赔偿。

◆ 知识点梳理

Original Equipment Manufacturer（OEM）	始设备制造商（贴牌生产）
Do not infringe on any intellectual property right of any third party	不侵犯任何第三方的知识产权
Indemnify sb. for any loss and damage resulting from infringement on the IRP of any third party	因侵犯任何第三方的知识产权而赔偿某人损失
Comply with the technical specifications	符合技术规格
Claim damages and expenses incurred from sb.	要求某人赔偿所产生的损失
Free from defects in design，materials and workmanship	在设计、材料和工艺方面均无瑕疵
In case any quality problems arise	如出现质量问题
Request re-work，repair，price reduction or refund	要求重作、修理、减少价款或退货
Use reasonable commercial efforts to	尽合理的商业努力
Certificate of conformity	合格证书
At the behest of……	在……的指令下
The liability and losses arising from trademark infringement shall be borne by……	因商标侵权所产生的责任及损失由……承担
Indemnify and hold ……harmless against any claims/damages	因任何索赔/损害，对……作出赔偿并使之免受损害

第三节 建设工程施工合同

建设工程施工合同（Engineering Works Contract）是指发包方（建设单位）和承包方（施工人）为完成商定的施工工程，明确相互权利、义务的协议。依照施工合同，施工单位应完成建设单位交给的施工任务，建设单位应按照规定提供必要条件并支付工程价款。建设工程施工合同是承包人进行工程建设施工，发包人支付价款的合同，是建设工程的主要合同，同时也是工程建设质量控制、进度控制、投资控制的主要依据。施工合同的当事人是发包方和承包方，双方是平等的民事主体。

建设工程施工合同中甲方、乙方一般分别指发包方（contract letting party）和承包方（contractor）。在一个标准的建设施工合同中，常见的专有条款涵盖：工程概括、工程工期、工程价款、付款方式、工程质量、竣工验收、违约责任等。

一、工程概况条款（Work Overview）

工程概括条款下主要包含工程名称、工程地点、承包方式、承包内容、工期等。如：

范例一：

Work Overview：

1. Name of project：Phase II Standard Workshop Renovation and Construction Project of Company A.

2. Location of project：________________________________

3. Contracting Means：Overall contracting，including contracting of materials and labor，quality，safety and schedule.

4. Contracting contents：include all works of demolishment and construction，which shall be subject to the attached Bills of Quantities.

参考译文：

工程概况：

1. 工程名称：A公司二期标准厂房改造施工工程

2. 工程地点：____

3. 承包方式：总承包（包工包料，包质量，包安全，包工期）

4. 承包内容：包括所有的拆除及施工工程，以附件《工程量清单》为准。

范例二：

Project contents:

A. Construction of network cabling systems of the new R & D center;

B. Construction of Data Center, mainly includes: data center decoration and electrical systems, air-conditioning systems, access control systems etc.

参考译文：

工程范围：

A. 新研发中心和新厂房的网络综合布线系统的施工；

B. 数据中心的建设，主要包含：数据中心的装饰工程、电气系统、空调系统、机房门禁系统等。

范例三：

Nature of contracting: Party B shall be responsible for both labor and materials of this project, and will be responsible for the quality, safety, and code of conduct during the project construction.

参考译文：

承包方式：乙方以包工包料，包工程质量、包安全、包文明施工的方式承包工程。

二、工程工期（Duration of Project）

Duration of Project: Commencement date: March 1, 2019

Completion date: October 30, 2019

Total number of days of construction: 243 days.

In case of the following circumstances, after the visa confirmation of on-site representative of Party A, the construction period can be postponed accordingly:

(1) In the course of construction, in case of power failure, water supply failure that lasts for more than 8 hours or more than 3 times of continuous intermittent water supply failure and power failure (more than 4 hours each time), affecting normal construction; or there is more than 2 days of water supply failure and power failure;

(2) Force majeure such as typhoon, heavy rain, and hurricane causes delays in construction;

(3) Other factors that are beyond the control of manpower causes delays in construction.

参考译文：

工程工期：开工日期：2019 年 3 月 1 日

竣工日期：2019 年 10 月 30 日

总工期天数：243 天。

如遇下列情况，经甲方现场代表签证确认后，工期可相应顺延：

(1) 在施工中如因停电、停水 8 小时以上或连续间歇性停水、停电 3 次以上；(每次连续 4 小时以上)，影响正常施工；或者停水停电 2 天以上；

(2) 因台风、暴雨、飓风等不可抗力的因素导致工期延期；

(3) 因人力不可抗拒的其他因素导致延误工期。

三、工程价款 (Project Cost)

建设工程合同常见的报价方式有：总价包干 (total price contracting)、单价包干 (unit price contracting)。总价包干也称为固定总价或者大包干，是指工程量和价格都包死了，不存在审计，完工直接结算。单价包干相当于据实结算，单价不变，工程量依据现场实际完成量据实计量。

范例一：

The total project price is RMB 20 million. This quotation is the total price contracting and covers materials and labor cost. In the event of fluctuation of the market price of materials, labor cost or changes in national policy, the total price will not be adjusted.

参考译文：

工程总价为人民币2000万元。该报价为固定总价。承包人包工包料，即使市场材料价格、人工价格或国家政策变化，固定总价不做任何调整。

范例二：

Contract price: The construction costs of this contract is RMB 20 million.

If the construction content or materials are changed, the corresponding project costs will be adjusted according to the actual costs incurred.

参考译文：

合同价款：本合同工程造价为人民币为2000万元。

若变更施工内容或材料等，变更部分对应的工程款按实际发生另计。

范例三：

Project price: The calculation method of the project price is: the unit price is ________*yuan* /m^2 (tax included). The price includes the direct cost, indirect cost, construction cost and supervision cost incurred by Party B to complete the qualified project. The specific area is subject to the construction drawings.

The unit price is the price for settlement of project cost, and no adjustment is made during the validity period of this contract.

参考译文：

工程价款：工程款计价办法为：单价包干人民币________元/m^2（含税），该包干价含乙方为完成本合格工程承包范围的直接费用、间接费用、施工措施费用及监理费用等，具体面积以施工图纸为准。

单价包干为结算单价，在本合同有效期内不作调整。

范例四：

Project cost: Total project cost is ____________ yuan (CNY). Detailed contract price list is shown in attached quotation list.

In the detailed design and construction process, if the project quantity changes, project cost will be adjusted according to the contract unit price; if the material is changed, the project cost will be adjusted according to the supplemental agreement agreed by both parties.

参考译文：

工程造价

合同工程总造价为￥ ________ 元（CNY）。详细合同价格表见附件报价清单。

在详细设计和施工过程中，若工程量发生变化，按合同单价相应调整工程造价；若材质发生变化，按双方商定的补充协议调整工程造价。

范例五：

The total contract amount is RMB ________, which is fixed total price contract.

This contract price includes the cost of equipment and materials, labor cost, machinery cost, management cost, profit, tax, government charges, insurance, transportation, service fee, and all other cost for the completion of the project, as well as system testing, installation, and commsioning costs.

参考译文：

本合同价格为人民币________，为固定总价合同。

本合同价款包括设备材料费、人工费、机械费、管理费、利润、税金、政府费用、保险费、运输费、服务费，及为完成本工程所发生的其他费用，还包括了设备检测、安装调试等费用。

四、付款方式（Methods of Payment）

Payment of project cost: project advance payment of 30% of the total project cost will be paid within 5 days after the contract is signed; 40% of the project cost will be paid upon the completion of project main structure; 25% of the project cost will be paid upon acceptance of the project; the remaining 5% is used as the quality guarantee deposit and will be paid in a lump sum within 5 days after the expiration of the warranty.

参考译文：

工程合同款支付：合同签订后 5 日内支付工程款 30% 的预付款；主体工程完成，支付工程款的 40%；工程验收合格后支付工程款的 25%；剩余 5%

作为质保金，五年质保期满后 5 日内一次性付清。

五、工程质量（Quality of Project）

范例一：

The project quality standard is "qualified" and meets the requirements of engineering construction drawings and engineering technical specifications. The inspection agency shall be designated by Party ________ to inspect the quality of the project, and the inspection fee shall be borne by Party ________.

参考译文：

工程质量等级为"合格"，并且符合工程施工图纸及工程技术规范要求。由________方指定检测单位对工程质量进行检测，检测费由________方承担。

范例二：

The quality of the project must comply with the requirements of the current national quality acceptance specifications and standards for engineering construction.

If the quality of the project does not meet the contractual standards due to the contract letting party's responsibility, the contract letting party shall bear the increased costs and/or delays of the construction period and pay the contractor a reasonable profit.

If the quality of the project does not meet the contracted standards due to the contractor's responsibility, the contract letting party has the right to request the contractor to repair, rework or rebuild until the quality of the project meets the contracted standards, and the contractor shall bear the additional costs and/or delayed construction period.

参考译文：

工程质量必须符合现行国家有关工程施工之质量验收规范和标准的要求。

因发包人原因造成工程质量未达到合同约定标准的，由发包人承担由此增加的费用和（或）延误的工期，并支付承包人合理的利润。

因承包人原因造成工程质量未达到合同约定标准的，发包人有权要求承包人修理或者返工、改建直至工程质量达到合同约定的标准为止，并由承包人承担由此增加的费用和（或）延误的工期。

范例三：

Quality of Project: the quality shall be "Excellent", and shall meet the requirements of this contract and the National Quality Standards, and shall by guaranteed to be accepted at the first attempt upon project completion. The scope of as-built acceptance includes, but not limited to: (1) concealed work; (2) itemized project; (3) reports of experiment; (4) reports of materials testing. In the event that project fails to be accepted at the first inspection and thus leads to delay in the start of the subsequent projects, Party B shall compensate Party A at the daily rate of 2‰ of the total contract price as penalty, but the total amount shall not exceed 5% of the total contract price.

参考译文：

工程质量：质量合格，达到本合同要求和国家质量验收标准，并确保竣工验收一次合格。验收内容包括但不限于：（1）隐蔽工程；（2）分项工程；（3）实验报告；（4）材料验收报告。如果由于验收未能一次通过而导致后续工程开工的延迟，乙方将按照每日工程总额的2‰金额赔偿给甲方作为罚金，但最多不得超过工程总价款的5%。

六、竣工验收（Acceptance）

After the completion of the project, upon the contractor's application for acceptance, it shall proceed in accordance with the following procedures:

(1) After the contractor submits the application report for acceptance to the supervisor, the supervisor shall complete the review and submit it to the contractor within 14 days after receiving the application report. If the supervisor considers that the conditions for acceptance have not been met, the contractor shall be notified of the work contents to be completed by the contractor before the acceptance inspection. The contractor shall submit the completion acceptance application report again after completing all the work contents notified by the supervisor.

参考译文：

工程竣工后，承包人申请竣工验收的，应当按照以下程序进行：

（1）承包人向监理人报送竣工验收申请报告，监理人应在收到竣工验收申请报告后 14 天内完成审查并报送发包人。监理人审查后认为尚不具备验收条件的，应通知承包人在竣工验收前承包人还需完成的工作内容，承包人应在完成监理人通知的全部工作内容后，再次提交竣工验收申请报告。

（2）If the supervisor considers that the conditions for acceptance have been met，the application for acceptance shall be submitted to the contract letting party. The contract letting party shall complete the review within 28 days after receiving the application report for acceptance，and shall organize the supervisor，contractor，designer and surveyor and other relevant units for the completion acceptance.

参考译文：

（2）监理人审查后认为已具备竣工验收条件的，应将竣工验收申请报告提交发包人，发包人应在收到经监理人审核的竣工验收申请报告后 28 天内审核完毕并组织监理人、承包人、设计人、勘察人等相关单位完成竣工验收。

（3）If the completion acceptance is qualified，the contract letting party shall issue a project acceptance certificate to the contractor within 14 days after the acceptance is passed.

参考译文：

（3）竣工验收合格的，发包人应在验收合格后 14 天内向承包人签发工程接收证书。

（4）In case the contract letting party fails to organize the acceptance within 28 days after receiving the application for acceptance submitted by the contractor，or fails to sign the acceptance conclusion after acceptance while does not give any opinion，it shall be deemed that the project has passed the completion acceptance.

参考译文：

（4）发包人在收到承包人递交的竣工验收申请报告后 28 天内无正当理由不组织验收，或者验收后不签署验收结论又不提出意见的，视为竣工验收合格。

七、违约责任（Liability for Breach of Contract）

范例一：

In case Party B fails to complete the work on time, it shall compensate Party A at the daily rate of 3‰ of the total contract price as penalty (directly deducted from the project cost); the unreasonable delay of 15 days or more shall be regarded as a fundamental breach of contract. Party A has the right to terminate this contract. In addition to the full refund of the construction amount paid by Party A, Party B shall also pay Party A penalty of 20% of the total construction cost.

参考译文：

乙方未能按时竣工的，每延期一日应按工程总价款的千分之三向甲方支付违约金（从工程款中直接扣除）；无故延期 15 日以上视为根本性违约，甲方有权解除本合同，乙方除应全额退还甲方已支付的工程款外，还应向甲方支付工程总价款的 20% 的违约金。

范例二：

In case quality problem occurs in the project, it shall be regarded as a serious breach of contract by Party B. Depending on the seriousness of the problem, Party B shall pay Party A penalty of 10% – 30% of the construction cost (can be directly deducted from the project cost). In addition, Party B shall compensate for the losses caused to Party A.

参考译文：

工程出现质量问题视为乙方严重违约，视情节轻重乙方应按工程款的 10% –30% 向甲方支付违约金（可从工程款中直接扣除），此外应赔偿因此给甲方造成的损失。

范例三：

In case one party rescinds or terminates this contract arbitrarily, the party in breach shall pay the non-breach party liquidated damages of 20% of the construction cost.

参考译文：

协议一方擅自解除或终止本合同的，违约方应按工程款的 20% 向守约方支付违约金。

范例四：

The construction project shall be completed independently by Party B. Party B is not allowed to use affiliated construction team, subcontract the project wholly or partly, or illegally complete the construction. Otherwise, Party B constitutes a fundamental breach of contract. Party A has the right to unilaterally terminate the contract and has the right to seek recourse from Party B liquidated damages of 30% of the total contract price.

参考译文：

本工程应由乙方独立完成施工，不得使用挂靠施工队伍，不得把工程分包、转包、乙方不得违法施工，否则，乙方构成根本违约，甲方有权单方解除合同，并有权向乙方追索合同总价 30% 的违约金。

◆ 知识点梳理

合同总造价	Total project cost
报价清单	Quotation list
工程量清单	Bills of quantities
工程工期	Duration of project
总价包干	Total price contracting
固定总价合同	Fixed price contract
单价包干	Unit price contracting
项目预付款	Project advance payment
质保金	Quality guarantee deposit
合同发包方	Contract letting party
合同承包方	Contractor
监理方	Supervisor
从工程款中扣除	Deduct from the project cost
竣工验收报告	Completion acceptance report

续表

合同根本违约	Fundamental breach of contract, material breach of contract
单方解除合同	Unilaterally terminate the contract
擅自解除或终止本合同	Rescind or terminate this contract arbitrarily
向……追索违约金	Seek recourse from ……liquidated damages
分项工程	Itemized project
隐蔽工程	Concealed project
转包	Subcontract the project wholly
分包	Subcontract the project partly
守约方	Non-breach party
违约方	Party in breach
按照每日工程总额的2‰金额赔偿……作为罚金	Compensate …… at the daily rate of 2‰ of the total contract price as penalty

第三章 服务类涉外合同法律文书

第二章介绍了有形商品相关的涉外合同法律文书，但在国际贸易中，还有相当一部分交易的标的是无形商品，比如技术咨询、管理咨询、法律服务、会计事务所提供的审计服务、租赁服务等。在此，本章将会探讨两类常见的服务类涉外合同法律文书，即，咨询服务协议和租赁协议。

第一节 咨询服务协议（Consulting Services Agreement）

咨询服务协议（Consulting Services Agreement）是顾问方利用知识、技术、经验和信息为委托方完成咨询报告、解答技术问题、提供决策的参考，是用于约定客户与顾问之间服务条款的合同，也称咨询合同（Consulting Contract）、商业咨询协议（Business Consulting Agreement）。

常见的咨询服务种类如下表所示：

心理咨询	Psychological counseling
生涯规划咨询	Counseling on career planning
就业咨询	Vocational counseling
留学咨询	Overseas education consulting
财务/金融咨询	Financial consulting
物流咨询	Logistics consulting
法律咨询	Legal consulting
企业管理咨询	Business management consulting
营销咨询	Marketing consulting

一份咨询服务协议中主要包括以下特殊条款：咨询内容、咨询费、服务的交付、保密义务、技术咨询报告的归属等。

一、咨询内容（Contents of Consultancy）

范例一：

Whereas Client desires to obtain the management consultancy service from Consultant and Consultant has agreed to perform such services, the two parties hereby reach the agreement as follows.

参考译文：

委托方希望获得咨询方提供的管理咨询服务，而咨询方愿意提供此项服务，双方达成以下协议。

范例二：

The Scope, Time Schedule and Staffing of the Technical Services are defined below.

参考译文：

技术服务的范围、进度安排和人员安排详见下面所述。

范例三：

Party B shall, at its own cost and expense, provide all equipment, tools and other materials necessary for the provision of the Services. If any of the Services are to be performed on Party A's premises, Party B shall comply with all applicable policies of Party A as provided in writing to Party B.

参考译文：

乙方应自费提供该服务所必需的所有设备、工具和其他资料；如果任何服务需要在甲公司的场所履行，乙方应遵守公司的所有适用的各类政策，甲方应以书面形式将该等政策提供给乙方。

需要注意的是，咨询服务协议中，购买咨询服务一方可称为委托方、顾客、公司等，英文表达为“Client”（Customer 一般适用于有形商品中的顾客）或“Company”；提供咨询服务一方可称为咨询方，用“Consultant”或者“Counselor”表示。

二、服务费（Service Fees）

范例一：

As full compensation for the Services and the rights granted to Party A under this Agreement, Party A shall pay to Party B a fixed fee in the amount of 50,000 *yuan* (the "Service Fee").

参考译文：

作为本协议项下提供给甲方的服务和权利的全部报酬，甲方应向乙方支付一笔50,000元人民币的固定费用（"服务费"）。

范例二：

The total contract price is ______ (say ______ only) in ______ (currency). The breakdown prices of the abovementioned total contract price are as follows:

Contract Price for Item 1: ________ (say ________ only) in ________ (currency);

Contract Price for Item 2: ________ (say ________ only) in ________ (currency);

Contract Price for Item 3: ________ (say ________ only) in ________ (currency).

参考译文：

本合同总价为________（币种）________（大写：________）。各分项的价格如下：

分项一的合同价为________（币种）________（大写：）；

分项二的合同价为________（币种）________（大写：）；

分项二的合同价为________（币种）________（大写：）。

范例三：

The total contract price will include all the service and technology provided by Consultant. The total contract price shall be firm and fixed and shall not fluctuate with any inflation. The total contract price shall include all charges and expenses incurred by Consultant in performing his obligations both in his own country and in the

Client's country and includes the expenses incurred in sending the Technical Documentation to Client's office by all kinds of forms.

In the event of Force Majeure as defined in the Contract, the total contract price shall be readjusted through friendly negotiations between the parties. If Client requires services not contemplated in the Scope of Services the parties shall friendly discuss an amendment to the total contract price. Any such amendment shall be in writing countersigned by both parties. This document shall then form integral part of the Contract.

参考译文：

本合同总价包括咨询方所提供的所有服务和技术费用，为固定不变价格，且不随通货膨胀的影响而波动。合同总价包括咨询方在其本国和委托方国家因履行本合同义务所发生的一切费用和支出和以各种方式寄送技术资料到委托方办公室所发生的费用。

如发生本合同规定的不可抗力，合同总价可经双方友好协商予以调整。如果委托方所要求的服务超出了本合同规定的范围，双方应协商修改本合同总价，任何修改均需双方书面签署，并构成本合同不可分割的部分。

范例四：

Party B shall submit an invoice in the full amount of the Service Fee upon completion of the Services.

参考译文：

乙方应在服务完成后提交全额的服务费发票。

范例五：

Party A shall pay all Service Fees within twenty (20) days after the issuance of the invoice.

参考译文：

甲方应在发票开具后的二十（20）日内支付所有服务费。

范例六：

For avoidance of doubt, the Service Fees shall include VAT, surcharges, duties or similar taxes imposed by any governmental authority.

参考译文：

为避免疑义，服务费包含任何政府部门征收的增值税、附加税、关税或类似的税费。

范例七：

All payments to be made by Client to Consultant under the present Contract shall be made by telegraphic transfer (TT).

参考译文：

委托方向咨询方的所有付款均通过委托方所在地的________银行以电汇方式支付到________银行咨询方的账户上。

范例八：

Client shall make all payments by wire transfer to Consultant's bank account.

Bank charges levied by the sending bank shall be borne by the Client and the bank charges levied by any other bank participating in the transaction (correspondent or beneficiary bank) shall be borne by the Consultant.

参考译文：

客户应通过电汇将所有款项支付到顾问的银行账户。

汇款银行收取的银行手续费应由客户承担，参与交易的任何其他银行（代理行或受益人银行）收取的银行手续费应由顾问承担。

◆ 知识点梳理

有关服务费的相关表达归纳如下：

Fixed fee	固定费用
Price is firm and fixed and shall not fluctuate with any inflation	价格固定不变，且不随通货膨胀的影响而波动
Breakdown price	分项价格
All charges and expenses	所有的费用
Pay fees in installments	分期支付费用
Charges levied by the bank	银行收取的费用

续表

The Service Fees shall include VAT, surcharges, duties or similar taxes imposed by……	服务费包括增值税、附加税、关税或者……征收的类似的税赋

三、服务的交付（Delivery of Service）

范例一：

The deadline for the delivery of the technical service report is ________.

参考译文：

交付技术咨询报告的最后期限为：________。

范例二：

Consultant will inform Client by Fax when the technical service reports are air-mailed to Client indicating the date and number of airway bill. Client will inform Consultant when the Technical service reports have been received.

参考译文：

咨询方在航空邮寄上述资料时应以传真方式将邮寄日期和航空提单号通知委托方。委托方收到上述技术咨询报告后应及时通知咨询方。

四、保密（Confidentiality）

范例一：

All data assembled, developed, compiled, reproduced, studied, and prepared in connection with the work done hereunder and furnished to Consultant by Client shall be considered confidential and shall not be divulged to any person, firm or corporation other than Client or its designated representatives. This Clause shall remain binding on Consultant notwithstanding the termination of the Contract for any reason.

参考译文：

由委托方收集的、开发的、整理的、复制的、研究的和准备的与本合同项下工作有关的所有资料在提供给咨询方时，均被视为保密的，不得泄露给除委托方或其指定的代表之外的任何人、企业或公司，不管本合同因何种原因终止，本条款一直约束咨询方。

范例二：

Within the validity period of Contract, both parties shall take proper measures to keep the materials or information under this contract strictly confidential. The other party shall not disclose or divulge to any third party without prior written consent of one party.

参考译文：

合同有效期内，双方应采取适当措施对本合同项下的任何资料或信息予以严格保密，未经一方的书面同意，另一方不得泄露给任何第三方。

范例三：

Either party shall be obliged to keep confidential any secret information of the other party which either party and its personnel may obtain or be accessible in the course of the performance of Contract. Either party shall not make use of or disclose such secret information obtained from the other party without prior written permission issued by the other party.

参考译文：

一方和其技术人员在履行合同过程中所获得或接触到的任何保密信息，另一方有义务予以保密，未经其书面同意，任何一方不得使用或泄露从他方获得的上述保密信息。

◆ 知识点梳理

有关保密的表达归纳如下：

· All data assembled, developed, compiled, reproduced, studied, and prepared in connection with the work done hereunder shall be considered confidential and shall not be divulged to ……

· both parties shall take proper measures to keep the materials or information confidential……

· not disclose or divulge to any third party……

· keep confidential any secret information of the other party

五、技术服务报告的归属（Ownership of Technical Service Report）

范例一：

Final version of the technical service report submitted to Client and all relevant data such as maps, plans and supporting material compiled in performing the Scope of Services, shall be the property of Client. Such materials shall be sorted and indexed by Consultant prior to transmission to Client.

参考译文：

所有提交给委托方的技术咨询报告及相关的资料的最后文本，包括为履行技术咨询服务范围所编制的图纸、计划和证明资料等，都属于委托方的财产，咨询方在提交给委托方之前应将上述资料进行整理归类和编制索引。

范例二：

Consultant shall be permitted to retain copies thereof, provided however that such materials, including the material furnished by Client as stated in Article 5 of this Contract, shall not be used by Consultant for purposes not related with this Project without the prior written approval of Client.

参考译文：

咨询方可保存上述资料的复印件，包括本合同第五条所指的委托方提供的资料，但未经委托方的书面同意，咨询方不得将上述资料用于与本咨询项目之外的任何项目。

◆ 知识点梳理

· Final version of the technical service report shall be the property of Client 技术咨询报告的最后文本属于委托方的财产

· Be sorted and indexed 进行整理归类和编制索引

第二节　租赁协议（Lease Agreement）

租赁协议（Lease Agreement/tenancy agreement/rental agreement），也称租赁合同（Lease Contract），租赁的对象包括不动产、动产等，而不动产租赁又

包括住宅租赁和商铺租赁。本节将主要围绕不动产租赁展开。

无论对于住宅租赁还是商铺租赁，都会涉及以下条款：租赁标的、租期、租金、水电费与物业费的承担、押金、维护与维修等。

一、租赁标的（Subject Matter of Leasing）

范例一：

Party A hereby agrees to lease its property located at ____________________ in good and tenantable condition to Party B for residential use.

The leased property shall be used by Part B for residential purpose.

参考译文：

甲方同意将其所有的位于____________________的房屋在良好及可租赁的状态下租给乙方为居住使用。

乙方应将出租房屋用作住宅用房。

范例二：

The premises to be leased is a shop located at ________________ (the "Premises"), with an area of ________ square meters.

参考译文：

拟租赁物业（"物业"）是位于________________的商铺。房屋面积为________平方米。

范例三：

Party A will lease to Party B the premises and attached facilities owned by itself which is located at ________________ and they must be in good condition for conducting business.

The registered size of the leased premises is ________________ square meters (gross size).

参考译文：

甲方将其所有的位于________________的房屋及其附属设施在良好的可经营商业的状态下出租给乙方使用。

出租房屋的登记面积为________平方米（建筑面积）。

二、租金（Rental）

范例一：

The rental will be ________ RMB per month. Party B will pay the rental to Party A in the form of remittance.

参考译文：

双方商定租金为每月________元整。乙方以汇款的形式支付给甲方。

范例二：

Payment of rental will be paid in monthly installments. The first installment will be paid before ________（date）. Each successive installment will be paid before ________（date）each month. Party B will pay the rental before using the premises and attached facilities, and Party A will issue a written receipt after receiving the payment.

参考译文：

租金按月分期支付。第一期租金于________（日期）以前付清；以后每期租金于每月的________日以前缴纳。乙方先付后住，甲方收到租金后予书面签收。

范例三：

The rent for the leased property as agreed to by both parties is RMB ________ Yuan per month, excluding property management fee and unities such as water, electricity, gas etc.

参考译文：

双方谈定的租赁物业租金为每月________人民币，租金不包括物业费和公用设施费，如水费、电费、燃气费等。

范例四：

During the term of tenancy, Party B is responsible for paying the charges in relation to water, electricity, gas, telephone charges on the basis of the actual consumption thereof by Party B. Such charges shall be paid when due according to the invoice received by Party B from the management company or relevant authority every month.

参考译文：

乙方应承担租赁期内实际使用而产生的水、电、液化气费、电话费，并按月自行如期交纳所属管理公司或有关机构。

范例五：

Utility Fee: The Tenant shall pay the utility fee, including without limitation Water, Electricity, Telecommunications and Air Conditioning that occurs in the shop.

参考译文：

公用事业费：租赁期内，该店铺产生的公用事业费，包括但不限于水、电、通讯及空调费用等均由乙方承担。

范例六：

In case the late payment is more than 10 working days, Party B will pay 0.5 percent of monthly rental as overdue fine every day; if the rental is 15 days overdue, party B will be deemed that it has quitted the lease automatically and therefore constitutes a material breach the contract. In this case, Party A has the right to pursue the liabilities of Party B.

参考译文：

如乙方逾期支付租金超过十个工作日，则每天以月租金的 0.5% 支付滞纳金；如乙方逾期支付租金超过十五天，则视为乙方自动退租，构成重大违约，甲方有权收回房屋，并追究乙方违约责任。

◆ 知识点梳理

有关租金及相关费用的表达归纳如下：

租金	Rental, rent
物业费	Property management fee
水、电、气费	Utilities
滞纳金	Overdue fine
按月支付租金	Pay rent in monthly installments

三、租期（Term of Lease）

范例一：

The term of lease will be from ________ （date）to ________ （date）. Party A will empty the premises and provide it to Party B for use before ________ （date）.

参考译文：

租赁期限自________（日期）起至________（日期）止，为期________年，甲方应于________（日期）前将房屋腾空并交付乙方使用。

范例二：

The tenancy shall be for a term of ________years, commencing on ________ （date）and expiring on ________ （date）.

参考译文：

租期为________年，自________（日期）起至________（日期）止。

四、押金（Security Deposit）

范例一：

In order to guarantee the safety and good conditions of the premises and attached facilities and account of relevant fees are settled on schedule during the lease term, party B will pay ________ RMB to party A as a deposit before ________ （date）. Party A will issue a written receipt after receiving the deposit.

参考译文：

为确保房屋及其附属设施之安全与完好，及租赁期内相关费用之如期结算，乙方同意于________（日期）前支付给甲方押金________元整。甲方在收到押金后予以书面签收。

范例二：

To ensure the protection and good condition of the leased property and the related facilities as well as the prompt payment and settlement of all related charges during the term of tenancy, Party B agrees to pay to Party A within 10 days of the execution of this agreement a security of RMB ________ for Party B's obligations hereunder.

参考译文：

为确保出租房屋及其设施之安全并完好及租赁期内相关费用之如期结算，乙方同意于签订合同10天内支付给甲方租赁押金计人民币________作为乙方确保合同履行之保证金。

范例三：

In case party B breaches this contract, party A has right to deduct the default fine, compensation for damage or any other expenses from the deposit. In case the deposit is not sufficient to cover such items, Party B shall make up the insufficiency within ten days after receiving the written notice of payment from Party A.

参考译文：

因乙方违反本合同的规定而产生的违约金、损坏赔偿金和其他相关费用，甲方可在押金中抵扣，不足部分乙方必须在接到甲方付款通知后十日内补足。

范例四：

Unless otherwise provided for by this contract, Party A will return full amount of the deposit without interest on the day when this contract expires, and Party B has cleared the premises and paid all due rental and other expenses.

参考译文：

除合同另有约定外，甲方应于租赁关系解除且乙方腾退房屋并付清所有应付费用后的当天将押金全额无息退还乙方。

五、维护与维修（Maintenance & Repair）

范例一：

In case the premise and attached facilities are damaged by quality problems, natural loss, force majeure or accidents, Party A will be responsible for repair and bearing the relevant expenses. If Party A can' t repair the damaged facilities within two weeks which influences Party B's normal use of the facilities, Party B has the right to terminate the contract and ask for return of the deposit.

参考译文：

房屋设施如因质量原因、自然损耗、不可抗力或意外事件而受到损坏，甲方有修缮并承担相关费用的责任。如甲方未在两周内修复该损坏物，以致乙方无法正常使用房屋设施，乙方有权终止该合约，并要求退还押金。

范例二：

Tenant shall not make any alteration, addition, expansion, or improvement to the Property without first obtaining Landlord's written consent.

参考译文：

未经房东书面同意，承租人不得对房屋进行任何改动、增添、扩建或改进。

范例三：

Party B shall treat the leased property with care. If as a result of Party B's negligence or misconduct, the leased property and the related facilities and accessories suffer any damage (except for fair wear and tear), Party B shall be liable to Party A for the damages.

参考译文：

乙方应爱护使用出租房屋，如因乙方的过失或过错致使房屋设施及屋内用具和饰品受到损坏（正常损耗除外），乙方应负赔偿责任。

范例四：

Party B shall use the leased property legally as agreed in this Agreement and may not change such use arbitrarily, nor store any dangerous items in the leased property which are prohibited by the laws of the People's Republic of China. In case any damage occurs, Party B shall be liable for any damages or losses resulted therefrom.

参考译文：

乙方应按本合同的约定合法使用出租房屋，不得擅自改变使用性质，不应存放中华人民共和国法律下所禁止的危险物品，如因此发生损害，乙方应承担全部责任。

◆ 知识点梳理

有关房屋租赁合同中涉及的术语表达汇总如下：

房东	Landlord/landlady
租客	Tenant
租金	Rent/rental
租期	Term of lease/tenancy
押金/保证金	Deposit/security deposit
租赁房屋	Leased premises/property
腾退房屋	Clear/empty premises
处于良好和可租赁的状态	In good and tenantable condition
保持房屋内地面和所有电器、固定装置和家具保持清洁、卫生和良好的状态	Keep the Premises, including the grounds and all appliances, fixtures and furnishings, in clean, sanitary and good conditions
从押金中抵扣违约金、损坏赔偿金和其它相关费用	Deduct the default fine, compensation for damages or any other expenses from the deposit
对房屋进行任何改动、增添、扩建或改进	Make any alteration, addition, expansion or improvement to the Property

第四章　知识产权类涉外合同

根据中国相关法律，知识产权（Intellectual Property）是指权利人依法就作品；发明、实用新型、外观设计；商标；地理标志；商业秘密；集成电路布局设计；植物新品种；法律规定的其他客体享有的专有的权利。

商业竞争中，掌握核心技术的企业必然拥有竞争优势。而科技的竞争归根到底就是知识产权的竞争。国外知识产权立法已经有 300 多年的历史，英国是世界上最早颁布法律来保护知识产权的国家，其于1623 年颁布的《垄断权条例》是世界上第一部正式而完整的专利法，1709 年颁布的《安娜女王法令》是世界上第一部具有现代意义的著作权法。这两部法律的颁布为英国奠定了世界知识产权保护制度鼻祖的地位，也对后来资本主义各国的知识产权立法产生了重大影响。而在中国，知识产权方面的立法要晚很多，中国于 1982 年颁布了《商标法》，1984 年颁布了《专利法》，1990 年颁布了《著作权法》，1993 年颁布了《反不正当竞争法》。由此可见，中国的知识产权立法仅仅有 30 多年的历史，立法还不够完善，知识产权保护力度也有待加强，这也造成很多中国企业在“走出去”过程中面对很多问题。

因此，我们有必要了解与知识产权相关的文书写作，本章将主要讨论三类知识产权类涉外合同，包括知识产权许可协议、特许经营协议和保密协议。

第一节　知识产权许可协议（Intellectual Property License Agreement）

知识产权许可协议（Intellectual Property License Agreement），是知识产权人在把如专利、商标、著作权等自己所有的知识产权许可给他人使用时订立的协议，是一种债权与债务关系的协议。根据具体知识产权的形态，知识产权可以划分为专利权、商标权、商业秘密权、著作权等，而专利权、商标权、商业秘密权又统一被称为工业产权。因此，知识产权许可包括专利权许可、商标权许可、著作权许可、商业秘密许可等形式。

而根据许可范围的不同，可分为以下三种许可：

1. Exclusive license 独占许可

The Licensor grants the Licensee an exclusive license of the Rights for the Territory for the duration of this Agreement. The Licensor shall not, subject as provided below, actively sell the Products in the Territory nor appoint other licensees for the Territory（独占许可，又称为独家许可，是指在一定期限和一定的区域范围内，被许可方对许可使用的知识财产享有独占使用权，许可人不得许可第三人在该时间、地区使用此知识财产，也不得将此知识财产转让，并且许可人自己也不得实施知识产权的许可）。

2. Sole license 排他许可

The Licensor grants the Licensee a sole license of the Rights for the Territory and for the duration of this Agreement. The Licensor shall not, subject as provided below appoint other licensees for the Territory, but may itself manufacture and sell the Products in the Territory（排他许可，是指在一定期限和一定的区域内，被许可方对许可使用的知识财产享有排他使用权，仅许可人和被许可人可以在该时间、地区使用此知识财产的许可）。

3. Non-exclusive license 普通许可

It leaves the licensor free to compete or appoint other licensees in the territory without restriction（普通许可，是指在一定期限和一定区域内，许可人除许可给被许可人使用外，还可以自己继续使用，并且可以将知识财产许可给其他人使用的许可合同）。

除了以上三种许可方式之外，还有一种政府介入的强制许可（Compulsory License），具体是指：A compulsory license is to work a patent or use a copyright without the consent of the owner but based on a license that is issued by a government. They arise when the owner of the intellectual property, in particular patents or copyrights, refuses or is unable to work the property in a particular country within a certain period of time（强制许可，是指国务院专利行政部门依照专利法规定，不经专利权人同意，直接允许其他单位或个人实施其发明创造的一种许可方

式，又称非自愿许可）。可见，强制许可是为防止滥用专利垄断权、保护社会公共利益的重要武器，历来是各国专利制度的重要组成部分。

一、许可授予条款（Grant of License）

许可授予条款，英文中可写作 License，Grant，License Grant 或 Grant of License，一般是知识产权许可协议（除序言条款、定义条款外）正文中的第一条。请看下例：

范例一：

For the term of validity of this Agreement, ________ and its Affiliates, as Licensor, grant to Company and Affiliates of Company, as Licensee, a non-exclusive, indivisible, non-transferable, royalty-free license in the Territories, without the right to sublicense.

参考译文：

在本协议有效期内，作为许可人的________及其关联公司，授予作为被许可人的公司及其关联公司，在区域内非独占、不可分、不可转让、不可转许可、免费的许可。

范例二：

The Licensor shall grant the Licensee a non-exclusive license for the Licensed Process and Equipment, for use in plants and locations within the geographical area named in Appendix 3, and the Licensee shall use the patents and know-how in accordance with the conditions specified in this Agreement

参考译文：

许可方授予被许可方许可工艺和设备的普通许可，供其在附件 3 指定地理区域内的工厂和地点使用，被许可方应根据本协议规定的条件使用专利和专有技术。

范例三：

The Licensee is not authorized to use the Licensed Process and Equipment for any other purpose than specifically defined in Article 2.

参考译文：

除第2条具体规定的目的外，被许可方无权将许可工艺和设备用于其他任何目的。

范例四：

Licensor agrees to grant Licensee the sole license and right to design, manufacture, use, sell and export the Contract Products in ________.

参考译文：

许可方同意授予被许可方在________国设计、生产、使用、销售和出口合同产品的独占许可权。

除了授予许可本身外，有的许可还要求对许可技术的改良也授予许可，如下例所示：

范例五：

In addition to the license granted, the Licensor shall grant the Licensee Non-exclusive licenses relating to improvements to the licensed products provided (that) these have been made by the Licensor during the term of this Agreement. This shall not lead to an increase in the royalties.

参考译文：

除授予的许可外，许可方还应向被许可方授予关于许可产品改良的非独家许可，但条件是该等改良应是许可方在本协议期限内作出。授予该等非独家许可不得提高许可费。

注：本句中 provided（that）…句型经常出现在法律文本中，表达一种条件或者假设。

◆ 知识点梳理

1. 许可授予条款写作句式

（1）Subject to the terms and conditions of this Agreement, Licensor hereby grants to Licensee a… license to do…

（2）The Licensor shall grant the Licensee a Non-exclusive license for the Licensed Process and Equipment

（3）Licensor agrees to grant Licensee the sole license to…

2. 许可类型

许可类型较多，例如非独家许可、不可分割许可、不可转让许可、免使用费许可等。常用许可类型英文表达如下：

独占许可	Exclusive license
排他许可	Sole license
非独家许可/非排他性许可、普通许可	Non-exclusive license
强制许可	Compulsory license
不可分割许可	Indivisible license
不可转让许可	Non-transferable license Non-assignable license
不可转许可的许可	Non-sublicensable license
不可转许可	Without the right to sublicense; licensee shall not sublicense the rights granted
许可使用费	Royalty, royalties
免许可费的许可	Royalty-free license

3. 许可标的

许可标的包括但不仅限于发明专利、实用新型专利、外观设计专利、非专利技术、商业秘密、著作权、商标权、服务标识和其他知识产权等。常用许可标的英文表达如下：

发明专利	invention patent
实用新型专利	utility model
外观设计专利	design patent
非专利技术	nonpatented technology
商业秘密	trade secret
著作权	copyright
商标权	trademark
服务标识	service mark

二、许可费用（Royalties）

许可费用条款是知识产权许可协议中一项重要的条款，除了许可费之外，知识产权许可协议中涉及的其他费用条款的表达如下：

许可费	Royalties/license fees
维护费	Maintenance fees
增值税	VAT（value added tax）
关税	Customs duties
运费	Freight
包装费	Packing expenses
保险费	Insurance premium
商业折扣	Commercial discounts
佣金	Commissions

范例一：

Royalty at the rate of ________ percent shall be calculated in terms of "Net Selling Price" after the contract products are sold in this year; the contract products which not sold shall not be included. "Net Selling Price" means the remaining sum of the selling commercial invoice price after deducting the packing expenses, transportation expenses, insurance premium, commissions, commercial discounts, taxes and expenses for bought out elements and parts etc.

参考译文：

特许权使用费率为________%，应按本年销售的合同产品的净售价计算；未售出的合同产品不包括在内。"净销售价"是指合同产品的销售发票价格扣除包装费、运输费、保险费、佣金、商业折扣、税费、外购件等费用后的余额。

范例二：

Royalty fee and other cost of the Contract shall be paid in dollar（$）. Licensee shall pay Licensor a lump-sum royalty fee of ________, which is due and payable ________ days from the date when the Contract takes effect.

参考译文：

本合同涉及的专利实施许可费等计价的货币为美元（$）。合同总价金额为________，采用一次性总付方式，合同生效之日起________日内，被许可方应将专利实施许可费全部汇至许可方账号。

范例三：

To cover the obligations of the Licensor including supplying sets of equipment as specified in Appendix 4, including spare parts, the Licensee shall pay a one-off license fee of RMB 300,000 per set of equipment delivered to the Licensee.

参考译文：

许可方的义务包括供应附件 4 规定的各套设备（包括备件），作为交换，被许可方每收到一套设备，均应一次性支付许可方人民币 300,000 元。

范例四：

The license fee is a net payment.

Any taxes, fees or charges of whatever nature levied now or in the future in the Licensed Area according Appendix 4 are excluded from this license fee and shall be borne and paid directly by the Licensee.

参考译文：

许可费为支付净额。

当前或将来根据附件 4 在许可区域征收的任何性质的税收、费用或收费均不包括在许可费内，应由被许可方承担并直接缴纳。

范例五：

In consideration of the rights granted to Licensee by this Agreement, Licensee shall pay to Licensor the Royalties listed in Annex 5.

参考译文：

作为本协议中向被许可人授予权利的对价，被许可人应向许可人支付附件五所列明的许可费。

范例六：

Licensee shall pay such fees to Licensor within sixty (60) days of Licensor's issuance of invoices in respect thereof.

参考译文：

被许可人应在许可人出具相关发票的六十（60）日内向许可人支付该等费用。

范例七：

Royalty fee stipulated in Section 3 to the Contract shall be effected by Licensee to Licensor through the Bank ________, and payment shall be settled in ________.

参考译文：

本合同第三条中规定的专利实施许可费，被许可方将通过________银行支付给许可方，支付中使用的货币为________。

范例八：

Licensor shall issue the related documents. The Royalty fee shall be paid by Licensee to Licensor within 30 (thirty) days after Licensee has received the following documents which are provided by Licensor and found them in conformity with the stipulations of the Contract.

参考译文：

许可方应开具相关的单据。在被许可方收到许可方开具有关单据后三十天内经审核与合同规定无误，即支付专利实施许可费给许可方。

范例九：

Licensee shall have the right to deduct from any of the abovementioned payment the penalties and/or compensations which Licensor shall pay in accordance with the stipulations of the Contract.

参考译文：

按本合同规定，如许可方需要向被许可方支付违约金或赔偿金时，被许可方有权从上述支付中直接扣除。

◆ 知识点梳理

有关许可费的支付方法，主要有以下几种支付方式

一次性付款	Pay in a lump sum/one-off payment
分期付款	Pay in installments /periodic payment
滑动费率	Sliding royalties based on performance
首期付款	Down payment

三、不侵权承诺（Non-infringement Commitment）

在知识产权许可协议中，许可人一般会作出所许可的知识产权不侵犯第三方知识产权的声明，确保权利无瑕疵，如：

范例一：

Licensor guarantees that it is the legitimate owner of the Patent according to the stipulations of the Contract, and that it is lawfully in a position to transfer the Patent to Licensee. In the case of accusation of infringing the rights of a third party, Licensor shall be responsible for the matter and bear all the legal and economic liabilities arising therefrom.

参考译文：

许可方保证，它是依本合同条款转让给接受方的专利权的合法所有人，在法律上享有向接受方转让专利权的权利。若发生侵犯任何第三者权利的事件，则许可方应对侵权事件负责，并承担由此而产生的全部法律和经济责任。

范例二：

Licensor warrants that it has authority to enter into this Agreement and that it owns the patent right of the Utility Model, free and clear of any adverse claim, lien, charge or encumbrance of any sort.

参考译文：

许可方保证其有权签订本协议并且拥有该实用新型专利权，且该专利不具有任何异议、留置、抵押或权利负担。

范例三：

So far as the assignor is aware, no third party has any right, title or interest in the Assigned IP, and it is not aware of any lawful basis of objection or revocation of the assignment of the Assigned IP hereunder.

参考译文：

据让与人所知，不存在任何第三方对拟转让的知识产权拥有任何权利、所有权或利益，并且让与人不知晓任何针对本协议中拟转让的知识产权的驳回或撤销的合法依据的存在。

范例四：

Licensor represents and warrants that Licensor has the right and authority to grant the licenses granted to Licensee in this Agreement and that this License do not and will not infringe on the IP of any third party.

参考译文：

许可人陈述并保证许可人有权授予本协议中授予被许可人的许可，并且本许可现在不会、将来也不会侵犯任何第三方的知识产权。

范例五：

Licensor will indemnify, defend and hold Licensees and the persons and entities described in Article 2 hereof harmless from any claim that Licensees or their use of the XXX Marks in the Territory of this agreement is an infringement of a third party's trademark.

参考译文：

如果被许可人或本协议第二条规定的个人和实体因在合同规定的领土内使用 XXX 标志侵犯第三方商标权，许可人将对之作出赔偿、为之辩护并使之免受任何因此引致的赔偿责任。

范例六：

The Licensor indemnifies the Licensee from any and all liabilities including consequential damages arising from any use of the Licensed Process and Equipment.

参考译文：

关于任何及一切责任，许可方均对被许可方作出赔偿，包括因对许可工艺和设备进行任何使用而产生的衍生性损害。

范例七：

Assignor undertakes to indemnify Assignee on demand against all liabilities, damages and losses, including any direct, indirect or consequential losses, loss of profit, loss of reputation, together with all related costs which may be suffered or incurred by Assignee and which arise directly or indirectly in connection with the following circumstances.

参考译文：

让与人承诺，一经要求，立即就受让人可能遭受或发生的，由以下情形所直接或间接引起的所有责任、损害和损失，包括任何直接或间接损失、利润损失、声誉损失，以及所有相关费用，赔偿受让人。

范例八：

Licensor shall at all times during the term of this Agreement and thereafter indemnify, defend, and hold Licensee, its directors, officers, employees, and affiliates harmless against all claims, proceedings, demands, and liabilities of any kind whatsoever, including but not limited to legal expenses and reasonable attorneys´ fees, arising out of any breach of any representation, warranty, or covenant expressly made by Licensor in this Agreement.

参考译文：

在本协议有效期内，许可人应就因其违反其在本协议中明确作出的声明、保证或承诺而造成的任何类型的索赔、诉讼、要求和法律责任，包括但不限于诉讼费和合理的律师费，对被许可人及其董事、高级管理人员、雇员和关联公司作出赔偿、为之抗辩并使之免受此类损害。

◆ 知识点梳理

1. 有关不侵权声明主要有以下句式：

（1）Licensor guarantees that it is the legitimate owner of the Patent…

（2）Licensor represents and warrants that…

(3) Licensor represents and warrants that Licensor has the legal right to grant the License.

(4) Licensor represents and warrants that it has the right and authority to enter into this Agreement.

2. 有关侵权后的赔偿责任有如下句式：

(1) Licensor shall indemnify, defend and hold Licensee harmless from/against all claims/liabilities arising out of…/arising from…/resulting from. . .

许可人将对……所导致的索赔/责任对被许可人作出赔偿、为之抗辩并使之免受损害

(2) Licensor agrees to defend Licensee against any such Infringement Claim…

(3) Indemnify Assignee against all liabilities, damages and losses, including any direct, indirect or consequential losses, loss of profit, loss of reputation, together with all related costs which may be suffered or incurred by Assignee

就受让人可能遭受的所有责任、损害和损失，包括任何直接或间接损失、利润损失、声誉损失，以及所有相关费用，赔偿受让人

3. 知识产权侵权中的常用表达如下：

侵犯专利权、著作权或商标权	An infringement of any patent, copyright or trademark
诉讼、索赔、法律程序、要求、法律责任	Suits, claims, proceedings, demands and liabilities
诉讼费、合理的律师费、和解金额以及任何损害赔偿金	Litigation costs, reasonable attorney's fees, settlement payments and any damages

四、技术服务和培训（Technical Service and Training）

范例一：

During the validity period of the Contract, Licensor shall send a specialist to Licensee's factory to explain the drawings and technical documents and to provide technical service in designing, manufacturing, adjustment, inspection and maintenance of the Contracted Product so as to enable Licensee to use, as fast as possible, home-made raw material and components without affecting the properties of the Products so manufactured.

参考译文：

许可方在合同有效期内派遣一名技术专家到被许可方，对合同产品的图纸和技术资料进行解释，并就产品设计、制造、调试和检验，以及维修等方面进行技术指导，以使被许可方在保证合同产品性能的情况下，能尽快采用国产的材料和元器件，实现合同产品的生产。

范例二：

The Licensed Process and Equipment may only be applied according to the Licensors Training Manual by trained and certified personnel. The goal of the training is that the Licensee gains the ability to ________ at the Licensed Areas without any assistance from the Licensor.

参考译文：

许可工艺和设备只能由经过培训和认证的人员按照许可方培训手册的要求使用。培训目标是被许可方无须许可方任何协助即能够在许可区域进行________。

范例三：

Training cost and expenditures incurred by Licensor are to be borne by the Licensee.

参考译文：

许可方产生的培训费用和开支由被许可方承担。

五、回授条款（Grant-back Clause）

回授条款（grand-back clauses）是指专利权人以许可为条件，要求被许可人必须将基于该专利而作出的改进或发明专利，授权给许可人。

回授条款是否构成专利权滥用，须考虑相关市场中竞争产品存在与否，独占或非独占许可，是否对竞争有不利影响，以及对被许可人发明意愿的影响等。如果该回授条款为非独占许可，通常有促进竞争的效果，因为这可让被许可人和许可人分担风险，并且让许可人得以再利用回授的技术进行更进一步研发。而独占回授条款则让被许可人就其改进的技术非但不得许可他人使用，连自身都无法使用，因此容易减少被许可人从事改进发明的动力，造成限制竞争的效果。回授条款可能减少被许可人发展有价值的改进专利的动力，并且可能集中和扩张许可人的垄断地位，因为许可人可以通过基础专利来控制所有的改进专利。因此，独占回授条款构成专利权滥用。

Assignee hereby grants to Assignor a fully paid-up, royalty-free, worldwide, irrevocable, Non-exclusive, Non-transferable and Non-sublicensable licence to use, reproduce, modify, execute, perform, distribute, display and make use of the Assigned IP, and to make, use, sell, lease, or import products, services, processes, methods, and materials embodying or deriving from the Assigned IP in the course of Assignor's own business.

参考译文：

受让人特此授予让与人已付清对价的、免特许权使用费的、全球范围内的、不可撤销的、非独占性的、不可转让的和不可转许可的许可，以使用、复制、修改、实施、履行、分发、展示和利用拟转让的知识产权，并在让与人的自有业务过程中生产、使用、出售、出租或进口包含或源自拟转让的知识产权的产品、服务、流程、方法和材料。

◆ 知识点梳理

有关知识产权转让中出现的各方当事人的表达归纳如下：

许可人	Licensor
被许可人	Licensee
让与人	Assignor
受让人	Assignee
转让人	Transferor
承让人	Transferee

法律知识点补充：目前在世界上有关知识产权的两个公约分别是：《巴黎公约》（International Convention for the Protection of Industrial Property, the Paris Convention）和《伯尔尼公约》（The Berne Convention for the Protection of Literary and Artistic Works, the Berne Convention）。《巴黎公约》主要保护的对象是工业产权，如专利权、商标权、商业秘密，而《伯尔尼公约》主要保护文学

艺术领域的著作权。除此之外，WTO 发布了《与贸易有关的知识产权协议》(Agreement on Trade-Related Aspects of Intellectual Property Rights ，TRIPS Agreement)，以上共同组成了国际上的知识产权保护框架。

第二节 特许经营协议

特许经营（Franchising）是企业在境外从事商业活动的一种重要的经营方式，特许权使用人可以利用特许人已经建立的品牌优势从而迅速占领市场并取得优势地位，很多知名品牌，如可口可乐、麦当劳、肯德基等均采用特许经营模式。

特许经营协议（Franchise Agreement）指拥有注册商标、企业标志、专利、专有技术等经营资源的企业，以协议形式将其拥有的经营资源许可其他经营者（被特许人）使用，被特许人按照合同约定在统一的经营模式下开展经营，并向特许人支付特许经营费用的经营活动。特许经营协议和知识产权转让协议本质上都是权利人将自己拥有的知识产权许可给他人使用，因此，特许经营协议可以被视为是知识产权转让协议的一种特殊形式，只是在主体的称呼方面有所差异，即，许可人（licensor）是特许人（franchisor），而被许可人（licensee）是特许权使用人（franchisee）。

特许经营协议中常见专业术语如下：

Franchisor	特许人、特许权人、授予特许者、特许权拥有人
Franchisee	特许经营人、特许权使用人、加盟人
Royalty, royalties	特许费、特许权使用费
Initial fee, franchise fee	加盟费

三种常见的特许经营模式有：

Distributorship franchise	A manufacturer licenses a dealer to sell its products, for example, automobile dealership.
Chain-style franchise	An arrangement in which a franchise operates under a franchiser's trade name and is identified as a part of the franchiser's business chain, for example, most of the foreign fast food restaurants, such as KFC, Pizza Hut etc.

续表

Manufacturing or processing plant franchise	A franchiser provides the franchisee with the formula or the essential ingredients to make a popular product, such as Coca Cola.

一、序言条款（Preamble）

特许经营协议的序言条款往往会写明许可方所拥有的权利、其希望许可权利的意愿，以及特许经营人希望获得这项权利的意愿，如：

范例一：

THISMASTER FRANCHISE AGREEMENT is dated … and is made BETWEEN：

（1）（name of franchisor）［a company incorporated with limited liability under the laws of［　］and whose registered office is at（address），company registration number…（or as required）］　　（referred to in this agreement as the "franchiser"）；and

（2）（name of franchisee）［a company incorporated with limited liability under the laws of［　］and whose registered office is at（address），company registration number…（or as required）］（referred to in this agreement the "franchisee"）.

WHEREAS：

（A）The "franchiser" have developed the Concept and have established a reputation for the Business as（　　）of great distinction；

（B）The "franchiser" is the proprietor of the Marks，which are associated with high standards of quality and service，in the Territory；

（C）The "franchiser" wishes to expand its franchised network internationally and are therefore willing to grant the "franchisee" the master franchise right for the Business in the Territory；

（D）The "franchisee" desires the right during the continuance of this agreement to carry on the Business in the Territory.

NOW IT IS AGREED as follows：

参考译文：

该总特许经营协议签署于________（日期），在以下两方之间达成：

（1）（特许人名称）［根据［ ］法律注册的有限责任公司，其注册办事处位于（地址），公司注册号…（或根据要求）］（在该协议被称为“特许人”）；和

（2）（特许经营人名称）［根据［ ］法律注册的有限责任公司，其注册地址为（地址），公司注册号…（或根据要求）］（在本协议中被称为“特许经营人”）。

鉴于：

（A）特许人已经开发了“概念”，并在商业领域（插入详细信息）建立了很高的声誉；

（B）特许人是该领土的商标所有人，这些商标与高质量和高标准的服务有关；

（C）特许人希望在国际上扩展其特许经营网络，因此愿意授予特许经营人该地区业务的总特许经营权；

（D）特许经营人希望在本协议的延续期间有权在该领土开展业务。

现双方达成以下条款：

范例二：

WHEREAS, Franchisor and certain of its Affiliates own, operate and franchise [DESCRIPTION] throughout [COUNTRY] which, among other things, rent, sell and market [PRODUCT/SERVICE] to the [general public or Coporations or Government]; and

WHEREAS, Franchisor and certain of its Affiliates acquire, produce, license market and sell [PRODUCT/SERVICE]; and

WHEREAS, Franchisee is willing to purchase on a per Location basis a specified number of [PRODUCT/SERVICE]; and

WHEREAS, Franchisor is willing to provide various marketing, advertising and promotional services and activities in support of Franchisee;

NOW, THEREFORE, based on the above premises and in consideration of the covenants and agreements contained herein, and intending to be legally bound, the parties agree hereto as follows:

参考译文:

鉴于,特许人及其某些关联公司在［国家］拥有、经营和特许［特许权描述］,以及向［一般公众或公司或政府］出租、出售和销售［产品/服务］;和

鉴于,特许人及其某些关联公司获取、生产、许可市场并出售［产品/服务］;和

鉴于,特许经营人愿意在每个位置购买指定数量的［产品/服务］;和

鉴于,特许人愿意提供各种营销、广告和促销服务及活动以支持特许经营人;

因此,基于上述前提,并考虑到此处包含的约定和协议,并希望受到法律约束,双方兹达成以下协议:

二、特许授予条款(Grant of Franchise)

范例一:

Franchisor grants to Franchisee, and Franchisee accepts, a Non-exclusive license and franchise to operate ________ carrying the name of ________ at ________ (address) during the term of this Agreement. If Franchisor wants to operate another franchise of ________ with the same terms of this franchise, the Franchisee has the priority to be considered as the grantee.

参考译文:

特许人向特许经营者授予、特许经营者接受非专有许可和特许经营权,在本协议有效期内,在________(地址)以________名称经营________。如果特许经营者想以相同的特许经营条件经营另一家________特许经营店,则特许经营者有优先权。

范例二:

XXX COMPANY desires to grant FRANCHISEE a franchise to establish and operate a XXX SHOP at the ________, subject to the terms and conditions of this AGREEMENT, and conditioned upon FRANCHISEE's continual adherence and conformity to the SYSTEM STANDARDS.

参考译文：

根据本协议的条款，并在特许经营人持续遵守系统标准的前提下，XXX 公司希望授予特许经营人专营权，在________中建立和运营 XXX 商店 。

范例三：

We grant to you, during the Term and subject to the terms and conditions of this agreement, the Non-exclusive right within the Territory to carry on Your Master Franchise Business and use the Marks in accordance with this agreement.

参考译文：

我们在协议期限内并在不违反本协议条款的前提下，向您授予在该领土范围内开展您的特许经营并根据本协议使用商标的非专有权利。

范例四：

Subject to the provisions of this AGREEMENT, XXX hereby grants FRANCHISEE the personal, limited right and license (the "FRANCHISE") to, during the TERM, operate the SHOP, at the SHOP PREMISES, in association with the MARKS, and in compliance with the SYSTEM STANDARDS.

在遵守本协议条款的前提下，XXX 特此授予 FRANCHISEE 个人的、有限的权利和许可（以下简称"特许经营权"），以便在特许经营期间，在商店经营场地按照系统标准使用"商标"进行经营。

◆ 知识点梳理

授予特许经营权写作句式：

· Franchisor grants to Franchisee, and Franchisee accepts, a Non-exclusive license and franchise to……

· Subject to the terms and conditions of this AGREEMENT, and conditioned upon FRANCHISEE's continual adherence and conformity to the SYSTEM STANDARDS, XXX COMPANY desires to grant FRANCHISEE a franchise to……

· We grant to you, during the Term and subject to the terms and conditions of this agreement, the Non-exclusive right within the Territory to……

三、费用条款（Fees）

与知识产权许可协议相同，特许经营协议的核心条款也包括费用条款。主要的费用有：特许费（royalties）、加盟费/初始特许权费用（initial fee）、持续费用（continuing fee，一般基于业绩表现）及其他费用，如广告费（advertising fee）。

范例一：

Franchise Fee. In consideration of the grant of this franchise, Franchisee must pay to Franchisor a Non-refundable franchise fee of Renminbi 80,000 per annum for the Trademark throughout the term of this Agreement. The fee is due and payable within 10 days from the date of signing this Agreement, and on an annual basis thereafter throughout the term of this Agreement, on or before the date which is annual anniversary date of signing this Agreement.

参考译文：

加盟费。作为授予本特许经营的对价，在本协议的整个有效期内，特许经营人必须向特许人支付“商标”每年80,000人民币的不可退还的特许经营费。该费用应在签署本协议之日起10天内支付，并应在本协议期限后，以年为基础在签署本协议的周年日之日或之前支付。

范例二：

FRANCHISEE shall pay an initial franchise fee (the “FRANCHISE FEE”) to XXX COMPANY, for the right to enter into this AGREEMENT and in consideration of the FRANCHISE, in an amount determined as follows:

(a) If this AGREEMENT grants the Franchise to a New FRANCHISEE for a New XXX Shop, then the full amount of the FRANCHISE FEE is $30,000. The FRANCHISE FEE is due in two installments. The first installment, in the amount of $10,000, must be paid upon FRANCHISEE's signing of this AGREEMENT. The second installment, in the amount of $20,000, must be paid within 15 days following ABC COMPANY's designation of the SHOP PREMISES.

(b) If this AGREEMENT grants the Franchise to an Existing FRANCHISEE for a New XXX Shop, then the full amount of the FRANCHISE FEE is \$15,000. The FRANCHISE FEE is due in two installments. The first installment, in the amount of \$10,000, must be paid upon FRANCHISEE's signing of this AGREEMENT. The second installment, in the amount of \$5,000, must be paid within 15 days following ABC COMPANY's designation of the SHOP PREMISES.

参考译文：

特许经营人应向 XXX 公司支付加盟费（“特许费”），以获得签订本协议的权利，以及获得本特许经营权的对价，加盟费金额如下：

（a）如果本协议将特许经营权授予新的特许经营人以开设新的 XXX 商店，则加盟费总金额为 30,000 美元。加盟费分两期支付。在特许经营人签署本协议时应支付第一笔加盟费 10,000 美元。第二笔加盟费 20,000 美元必须在 XXX 公司指定商店经营场地后 15 日内支付。

（b）如果本协议将特许经营权授予现有的特许经营人以开设新的 XXX 商店，则特许费为 15,000 美元。加盟费分两期支付。在特许经营人签署本协议时应支付第一笔加盟费 10,000 美元。第二笔加盟费 5,000 美元必须在 XXX 公司指定商店经营场地后 15 日内支付。

范例三：

You must pay to us or our nominee from time to time, in pounds sterling or such other currency as we may require, the following sums without deduction or set-offs:

(1) immediately upon signing this agreement the Master Franchise Fee;

(2) a sum equivalent to [5]% of the initial payment paid to you by each of Your Unit Franchisees on entering into [his] franchise agreement, which payment shall be at a rate to be set by us;

(3) the Service Fee, payable each calendar month within [28 days] of the month end;

(4) within [10 days] of the date of an invoice presented to you by us, the costs of any advertising, promotional aids such as leaflets and other goods or services supplied to you by us during the period of that invoice;

(5) the cost of the Equipment and Materials invoiced to you by us;

(6) our legal costs in respect of the signing of this agreement.

The Service Fee shall be due and payable whether or not you have received the service fee due to you in respect of any outlet under the relevant franchise agreement.

参考译文：

您必须不时以英镑或我们可能要求的其他货币向我们或我们的代名人支付以下款项，且不得扣除或抵销：

(1) 签署本协议后，立即支付总特许经营费；

(2) 您的次特许经营者在签订特许经营协议时向您支付的加盟费的[5]%，该加盟费率应由我们确定；

(3) 服务费，应在月底的［28 天］内支付；

(4) 在我们向您提供发票之日起［10 天内］，在该发票期内由我们提供给您的任何广告支出、促销手段（例如传单）和供应其他商品或服务所产生的费用；

(5) 我们向您开具发票的设备和材料的费用；

(6) 我们签订本协议支出的律师费。

无论您是否已收到根据相关特许经营协议任何一家门店应付给您的服务费，服务费均应支付。

◆ 知识点梳理

初始费用条款写作句式：

· In consideration of the grant of this license, the Franchisee shall pay to the Franchisor a Non-recurring and Non-refundable initial franchise fee of ______(amount)______.

· FRANCHISEE shall pay an initial franchise fee (the "FRANCHISE FEE") to XXX COMPANY, for the right to enter into this AGREEMENT and in consideration of the FRANCHISE, in an amount determined as follows.

· The initial fee is due in two installments.

持续费用条款写作句式：

· In consideration of the grant of this license/the rights granted to the Franchisee, the Franchisee shall pay to the Franchisor on ______(date)______ during the term of the Agreement a Non-refundable royalty fee equal to ___(percent)___ of the Franchisee's Gross Revenue/ Gross Sales/Gross Profit.

· Franchisee must pay to Franchisor a Non-refundable franchise fee of Renminbi ___per annum for the Trademark___ throughout the term of this Agreement.

四、期限与续期（Term and Renewal）

范例一：

The term of the FRANCHISE (the "TERM") will commence on the "COMMENCEMENT DATE" determined under this Article 5, and will end on the EXPIRATION DATE determined under this Article 5; unless this AGREEMENT is sooner cancelled or terminated in accordance with its provisions.

参考译文：

本特许权的期限（"期限"）将从第5条确定的"生效日期"开始，到第5条确定的终止日期结束；除非根据本协议的规定该协议很快被取消或终止。

范例二：

The term of this Agreement shall commence on the date first set forth above and shall expire on the date that is five years after the Effective Date (the "Initial Term"). The term will automatically renew for an additional five-year period unless a party chooses not to renew it by submitting written notice to the other party at least three months prior to the expiration of the then current term.

参考译文：

本协议的有效期自上述日期开始，并于自生效日期起满五年（"初始期限"）到期。除非一方在当前期限届满前至少三个月书面通知另一方其无意续期，否则该期限到期后将自动续期五年。

范例三：

If, upon expiration of the initial term of the franchise:

Franchisee has, during the term of this Agreement, substantially complied with all its provisions; and either Franchisee maintains possession of and agrees to refurbish and decorate the premises of the ________, replace fixtures, equipment, signs, and otherwise modify the ________ in compliance with specifications and standards then applicable under new franchises for ________; or Franchisee is unable to maintain possession of the premises, or in the judgment of Franchisor the ________ should be relocated, and Franchisee secures substitute premises approved by Franchisor and agrees to develop substitute premises in compliance with specifications and standards then applicable under new franchises for ________,

then Franchisee has the right to renew the franchise for one additional term equal to the then-customary initial term granted under Franchisor's then-current form of standard franchise agreement. Franchisee must pay Franchisor, three months prior to the date of renewal, a renewal fee to be agreed between Franchisee and Franchisor. The Franchisee must execute a new Agreement, which may provide for a higher management fee and for greater expenditures than this Agreement.

参考译文：

如果在特许经营权的初始期限到期后：

在本协议有效期内，特许经营者已基本遵守其所有条款；且特许经营者拥有场地使用权并同意翻新和装修________的房屋，更换固定装置、设备、标牌，或以符合________的新授权下适用的规范和标准对________进行修改；或特许经营者无法获得该场所的使用权，或特许人认为________场地应该搬迁，且特许经营者找到了特许人认可的替代场所，并同意按照新特许经营中适用于________的规范和标准开发替代场所，

则特许经营者有权将特许权延续一个新的期限，该期限等于特许人的标准特许经营协议当时的惯常初始期限。特许经营者必须在续约之日前三个月向特许人支付特许费，特许费由特许人与特许经营人商定。特许经营者必须签署一个新的协议，该协议可能会规定比当前该协议更高的管理费和更多的支出。

范例四：

FRANCHISEE shall have the opportunity to continue the operation of the SHOP during a second 10-year term (the "RENEWAL TERM"), subject to and conditioned upon each and every one of the following provisions:

If FRANCHISEE desires to continue to operate the SHOP for the RENEWAL TERM, then FRANCHISEE must in writing, at least 180 days before the EXPIRATION DATE, but no more than 270 days before the EXPIRATION DATE, request that XXX COMPANY issue its then current standard form franchise agreement for renewal terms (a "RENEWAL AGREEMENT"), contemplating a single ten-year franchise term for the SHOP, at the SHOP PREMISES. FRANCHISEE acknowledges and agrees that terms of a RENEWAL AGREEMENT, including the amount of the ROYALTY payable during the RENEWAL TERM, may be substantially different from the terms of this AGREEMENT.

参考译文:

特许经营人应有机会在第二个 10 年期限(“续展期限”)内继续经营商店,但须遵守以下每一项规定:

如果特许经营人希望继续在续展期经营商店,则特许经营人必须至少在期限届满 180 日之前、但不超过 270 日之前,以书面形式要求 XXX 公司公布续展期间标准版本的特许经营协议(“续约协议”),该协议是有关在商店经营场地另一个十年期的特许经营权。特许经营人承认并同意续约协议的条款,包括在续约协议内支付的特许费,有可能与本特许经营协议的条款有很大差异。

范例五:

FRANCHISEE acknowledges and agrees that this AGREEMENT confers no right to continuation, renewal, or a subsequent franchise agreement on or after the EXPIRATION DATE.

参考译文:

特许经营人承认并同意,本协议不授予在到期日或之后续约或者续订新的特许经营协议的权利。

◆ 知识点梳理

有关期限及其相关表达如下:

初始期限	Initial term
续展期限	Renewal term
开始	Commence, begin, start
终止	End, expire
开始日	Commencement date
终止日	Expiration date
本协议生效日	The effective date of this agreement
不授予续期	Confer no right to continuation, renewal

◆ 知识点梳理

期限与续期条款写作句式如下：

· The term of this Agreement shall commence on the date first set forth above and shall expire on the date that is five years after the Effective Date.

· This Agreement shall remain in effect for an initial term of five years commencing on the Effective Date of this Agreement.

· The term of the FRANCHISE (the "TERM") will commence on the "COMMENCEMENT DATE" determined under this Article 5, and will end on the EXPIRATION DATE determined under this Article 5.

· Franchisee has the right to renew the franchise for one additional term equal to……

· The term will automatically renew for an additional ten (10) year period unless ……

· FRANCHISEE shall have the opportunity to continue the operation of the SHOP during a second 10-year term (the "RENEWAL TERM"), subject to and conditioned upon each and every one of the following provisions:

· FRANCHISEE acknowledges and agrees that this AGREEMENT confers no right to continuation, renewal, or a subsequent franchise agreement on or after the EXPIRATION DATE.

五、培训（Training）

范例一：

Before theinitial opening of the SHOP, XXX COMPANY shall, at no charge to FRANCHISEE, provide initial training for the DESIGNATED SHOP MANAGER and up to one additional person in accordance with Section 11.

参考译文：

在商店初次开业之前，XXX 公司应根据 11 节的规定，免费向指定的商店经理和最多一人提供初始培训。

范例二：

Opening assistance. Before and in connection with the initial opening of the SHOP, XXX COMPANY shall, at no charge, provide FRANCHISEE with such pre-opening and opening assistance and guidance as ABC COMPANY deems appropriate. If FRANCHISEE is a NEW FRANCHISEE, then the assistance provided by ABC COMPANY will include the physical presence of one or more ABC COMPANY representatives for a total of at least five person-days (based on an 8-hour work day) before, during, and/or just after the SHOP first opens for business.

参考译文：

开业协助。在商店首次开业之前和与开业相关的活动中，XXX 公司应免费向特许经营人提供 XXX 公司认为适当的开业前协助和开业帮助及指导。如果特许经营人是初次加盟，则 XXX 公司提供的协助还包括在商店首次开业前、期间或者之后，XXX 公司派驻一名以上代表驻场指导，总计至少五人日（基于每日 8 小时）。

范例三：

At a mutually convenient time agreed upon sufficiently in advance of the initial opening of the SHOP, XXX COMPANY shall, at no charge to FRANCHISEE, inspect the SHOP to determine that it reasonably conforms to the plans and specifications approved by XXX COMPANY.

参考译文：

在商店首次开业前双方充分商定的彼此方便的时间内，XXX 公司应免费检查特许经营人商店，确保其基本符合 XXX 公司批准的计划和规格。

范例四：

Ongoing Advice and Assistance. During the TERM, ABC COMPANY shall, at no charge, from time to time provide FRANCHISEE with such advisory assistance, information, techniques, data, and instructional materials concerning the sale of items from the SHOP, operation of the SHOP, marketing programs applicable to the SYSTEM, local marketing of the SHOP, and adherence to the SYSTEM STANDARDS as ABC COMPANY deems advisable.

参考译文：

持续的建议和协助。在特许期限内，XXX 公司应不时免费向特许经营人提供 XXX 公司认为适当的有关商店销售、运作、用于该系统的营销计划、商店的本地营销以及系统标准遵循等方面的咨询协助、信息、技术、数据和指导性材料。

范例五：

Remedial training. In lieu of declaring a default under this AGREEMENT, or terminating this AGREEMENT for material breach, XXX COMPANY shall have the absolute right to direct FRANCHISEE by NOTICE to have the DESIGNATED SHOP MANAGER attend training directed toward curing specific operational deficiencies. FRANCHISEE may be required to reimburse ABC COMPANY for the reasonable costs of remedial training provided by XXX COMPANY.

参考译文：

矫正培训。XXX 公司有绝对权力通知特许经营人指定的商店经理参加纠正特定操作缺陷的培训，而非宣布特许经营人违反本协议或因重大违约终止本协议。特许经营人有可能需要支付 XXX 公司因提供矫正培训所花费的合理费用。

◆ 知识点梳理

培训的几个阶段有：

初始培训	Initial training
开业前培训	Pre-opening training
最终检查	Final inspection
持续的建议和协助	Ongoing Advice and Assistance
矫正培训	Remedial training

第三节 保密协议（Non-Disclosure Agreement）

保密协议是指协议当事人之间就一方告知另一方的书面或口头信息，约定不得向任何第三方披露该等信息的协议。负有保密义务的当事人违反协议约定，将保密信息披露给第三方，将要承担民事责任甚至刑事责任。保密协议的英文可写为Confidential Agreement，Non-Disclosure Agreement或Secrecy Agreement。

保密协议可以是知识产权许可协议、特许经营协议、劳动合同等协议中的一个条款，也可以是单独的一个协议。保密协议一般包括保密信息、责任主体、保密期限、保密义务及违约责任等条款。

一、保密信息（Confidential Information）

范例一：

"Confidential Information" means any and all information whether commercial, marketing, technical, scientific or other information relating to the business of Seller or Target, including without limitation, know-how, data, processes, designs, photographs, drawings, specifications, software programs, and samples, which is marked with an indicator such as "Confidential" or "Proprietary", is disclosed in circumstances of confidence, or would be understood by the Parties, exercising reasonable business judgement, to be confidential. For the avoidance of doubt, the existence and contents of this Agreement shall also be considered Confidential Information, and Confidential Information disclosed by an agent, attorney, accountant or other advisor of a Party shall be deemed to be disclosed by such Party.

参考译文：

“保密信息”指在保密的情况下披露的或双方根据合理的商业判断应理解为保密资料的，标记有“保密”或“……所有”字样的，与卖方或目标公司业务相关的所有商业、营销、技术、科学或其他信息，包括但不限于专有技术、数据、工艺、设计、照片、图纸、技术参数、软件程序和样品等。为免存疑，本协议的存在及其内容也应视为保密信息，并且一方的代理、律师、会计师或其他顾问披露的保密信息也应视为由该方披露。

范例二：

Confidential information shall mean any and all information that concerns, either directly or indirectly, the Equipment as well as the enterprise, products, services, know-how, business activity, co-workers and counterparts of the Parties, regardless of whether it constitutes the secret of the enterprise (including information contained in agreements, commercial documents, and by-laws) and any and all other information, regardless of its nature and form (written, oral, electronic) that has or may be disclosed by one Party or on its behalf to the other Party in relation to or during the performance hereof, regardless of the form of transferring or obtaining such information.

参考译文：

机密信息是指与本设备以及企业、产品、服务、专有技术、业务活动、双方的同事和对口方直接或间接有关的任何和所有信息，无论它是否构成企业的秘密（包括协议、商业文档和章程中包含的信息）以及其他任何由一方或者一方代表向另一方就本协议或在履行本协议过程中向另一方披露的信息，无论其性质和形式（书面、口头、电子），也无论是以何种形式转让或者获取该种信息。

范例三：

“Confidential Information” shall mean and include any information and data of a commercially sensitive nature that is not generally known to the public, that is marked “confidential” or “proprietary”, or identified as confidential at the time of disclosure, or which by its nature or the circumstances surrounding its disclosure should reasonably be regarded as confidential (regardless of whether such information is specifically designated as confidential and regardless of whether such information is in written, oral, electronic, or other form), relating to the business, technology, research, manufacturing, marketing, products, samples, processes and/or customers or suppliers of a Party, disclosed by the Disclosing Party to the Receiving Party under this Agreement. Confidential Information shall also include the substance and contents of the Parties' discussions regarding and in furtherance of the Purpose, including but not limited to, the fact that the Parties have entered into this Agreement or exchanged Confidential Information pursuant to the terms and conditions hereof.

参考译文：

"保密信息"是指并包括任何不为公众所熟知的、具有商业敏感性的、已被标记为"机密"或"专有"或在披露时被标识为机密的信息和数据，或其性质或围绕其披露的情况应合理地视为与业务、技术有关的机密信息（无论此类信息是否被专门指定为机密，并且无论该信息是书面、口头、电子还是其他形式），且该信息是披露方根据本协议向接受方披露的与商业、技术、研究、制造、营销、产品、样品、过程和/或一方的客户或供应商相关。机密信息还应包括双方就该目的并为达成此目的而进行的讨论的实质和内容，包括但不限于双方已根据本协议的条款订立本协议或交换机密信息的事实。

范例四：

The term "Proprietary Information" shall mean information ofthe Disclosing Party, including but not limited to, trade secrets, proprietary, technical, developmental, operating, financial, performance, cost, know-how, process, client and prospect information, and all samples, models, reports, tables, data and prototypes containing or disclosing such information, that is (a) marked or accompanied by documents clearly and conspicuously designating the information as "confidential" or the equivalent, or (b) identified by the Disclosing Party in writing as confidential before, during or promptly after the disclosure. In addition, the term "Proprietary Information" shall be deemed to include any notes, analyses, compilations, interpretations, memoranda or other documents prepared by the Recipient or its Representatives which contain, reflect or are based upon, in whole or in part, any Proprietary Information of the Disclosing Party.

参考译文：

“专有信息”一词是指披露方的信息，包括但不限于商业秘密、专有信息、技术信息、开发信息、运营信息、财务信息、性能、成本、专有技术、流程、客户和潜在客户信息，以及包含或披露此类信息的所有样本、模型、报告、表格、数据和原型，即（a）清楚地标明或附有文档的文件，或明显标明该信息为“机密”或等同的信息，或（b）信息披露前、披露中或披露后，披露方以书面形式标记为“机密”的信息。另外，“专有信息”一词应视为包括收件人或其代表编写的任何注释、分析、汇编、解释、备忘录或其他文件，这些文件包含、反映或基于披露方任何全部或部分的专有信息。

◆ 知识点梳理

保密信息条款，往往会出现非常大量的并列结构，尽可能全面列明保密信息的范畴，以达到真正有效保护商业秘密的目的，这也体现了法律语言的精确性。如：

· including without limitation, know-how, data, processes, designs, photographs, drawings, specifications, software programs, and samples;

· including but not limited to, trade secrets, proprietary, technical, developmental, operating, financial, performance, cost, know-how, process, client and prospect information, and all samples, models, reports, tables, data and prototypes containing or disclosing such information;

· relating to the business, technology, research, manufacturing, marketing, products, samples, processes and/or customers or suppliers of a Party, disclosed by the Disclosing Party to the Receiving Party under this Agreement;

· Confidential information shall mean any and all information that concerns, either directly or indirectly, the Equipment as well as the enterprise, products, services, know-how, business activity, co-workers and counterparts of the Parties, regardless of whether it constitutes the secret of the enterprise.

二、保密义务（Confidentiality Obligation）

范例一：

The Recipient and its Representatives shall hold in confidence, and shall not disclose, any Proprietary Information of the Disclosing Party.

参考译文：

接收方及其代表应对披露方的任何专有信息保密，且不得泄露。

范例二：

From time to time prior to and during the Term, Seller has disclosed or may disclose Confidential Information to Buyer. Buyer shall, during the Term:

（a） maintain the confidentiality of Confidential Information;

（b） not use Confidential Information for any purposes other than in connection with the Purpose or the Proposed Acquisition; and

（c） not disclose any such Confidential Information to any person or entity, except to（i） its employees or employees of its affiliates, its agents, attorneys, accountants and other advisors who need to know such information to perform their responsibilities in connection with the Purpose or the Proposed Acquisition and who have signed written confidentiality agreements containing terms at least as stringent as the terms provided in this Clause2,（ii） authorized securities regulators or exchanges in accordance with applicable laws or the relevant rules of the securities exchange to which Buyer is subject, and（iii） officials in relevant government departments in accordance with applicable laws to which Buyer is subject（collectively "Permitted Disclosure Parties"）.

参考译文：

在本协议订立前以及在本协议期限内，卖方已经或者可能不时向买方披露的保密信息。在本协议期限内，买方应当：

（a）对保密信息予以保密；

（b）不得为除目的或拟议收购之外的其他目的使用保密信息；

（c）不得向任何人或任何实体披露该等保密信息，下述对象除外：（i）为履行其与目的或拟议收购有关的职责而确有必要知悉保密信息的买方雇员或其关联机构雇员、买方的代理、律师、会计师或其他顾问，且上述人员已签署保密协议，其中条款的严格程度不得低于本协议第 2 条的规定；（ii）根据买方所受约束的适用法律或相关证券交易所规则授权的证券监管机构或证券交易所；（iii）根据买方所受约束的适用法律规定的相关政府部门的官员（合称“经允许的披露对象”）。

范例三：

The Receiving Party shall retain all Confidential Information in a secure place with access limited to only such of the Receiving Party's employees or agents who have fulfilled the requirements specified in Section 2 above. The Receiving Party shall provide the same care to avoid disclosure or unauthorized use of the Confidential Information as it provides to protect its own similar confidential and/or proprietary information, but in no event less than reasonable care.

参考译文：

接收方应将所有机密信息保存在安全的地方，并且仅允许已满足上述第 2 节规定的接收方的员工或代理商进行访问。接收方应采取与保护其自身相似的机密和/或专有信息相同的谨慎措施，以避免泄露或未经授权使用机密信息，但在任何情况下，均不得少于合理的谨慎程度。

范例四：

During the term hereof and for the period for 5 years after the expiration, termination, notice of withdrawal from this Agreement, the Parties and their subcontractors as well as any and all third parties performing the activities for Party hereunder shall maintain the secrecy of confidential information they may become familiar with during or in relation to the performance hereof, except for information that has been announced to the public before by the other Party. Any and all transfer, disclosure, use, acquisition or offer to sell confidential information shall be allowed only by prior consent of the other Party given in writing or otherwise null and void.

参考译文：

在本协议有效期内，以及在本协议期满、终止、通知解除本协议后的 5

年内，双方及其分包商以及为该方开展活动的任何及所有第三方在履行本合同过程中或与履行本合同有关的信息均应保密，但另一方之前已向公众宣布的信息除外。任何和所有转让、披露、使用、获取或出售机密信息的提议，均应事先征得另一方书面同意，否则无效。

◆ 知识点梳理

保密义务条款常用表达：

对信息保密	· hold in confidence, and shall not disclose, any Proprietary Information of the Disclosing Party · keep Confidential Information secret and to handle it with the same level of diligence that it exercises to protect its own confidential information · maintain the confidentiality of Confidential Information · provide the same care to avoid disclosure or unauthorized use of the Confidential Information as it provides to protect its own similar confidential and/or proprietary information
仅为本目的使用或者复制保密信息	· not use Confidential Information for any purposes other than · reproduce Confidential Information only to the extent necessary to pursue the Purpose
仅向特定人员提供保密信息	· make Confidential Information only available to … · make available Confidential Information only to those persons within its organization · retain all Confidential Information in a secure place with access limited to only such of the Receiving Party's employees or agents
不得向第三方披露保密信息	· not disclose any such Confidential Information to any person or entity · not disclose Confidential Information to third parties by any means, nor make any unauthorized copies thereof

三、保密义务的豁免（Exemption from Confidentiality Obligation）

范例一：

The Confidentiality obligation shall not apply to information that:

(1) can be shown to be known by Buyer by written records made prior to disclosure by Seller;

(2) is trivial or obvious;

(3) is or becomes public knowledge otherwise than through Buyer's breach of

this Agreement; or

(4) was obtained by Buyer from a third party having no obligation of confidentiality with respect to such information.

参考译文：

保密义务不适用于以下信息：

(1) 能够通过在卖方向买方披露前制作的书面记录证明已被买方掌握的信息；

(2) 不重要的或显而易见的信息；

(3) 目前或将来非因买方违反本协议而被公众知悉的信息；

(4) 买方从对该信息无保密义务的第三方获得的信息。

范例二：

Information ceases to qualify as confidential under the following circumstances:

(1) is at the time of disclosure or which subsequently becomes freely available in the public domain not as a result of breach of this Agreement; or

(2) the Recipient can show is known to it at the time of disclosure; or

(3) is disclosed to the Recipient in good faith by a third party not bound by any duty of confidentiality.

参考译文：

在以下情况下，信息将不再具有保密性：

(1) 在披露之时或随后不因违反本协议而被大众周知；或者

(2) 接收方能够证明在披露方披露之前已经获知该信息；或者

(3) 接收方善意地从无保密义务的第三处获得的信息。

范例三：

Confidential Information does not include:

(1) Information that the Receiving Party can demonstrate by competent written documents is, as of the time that it is disclosed, or that later becomes, without breach of this Agreement, part of the public knowledge or literature; or

(2) Information that the Receiving Party can demonstrate by competent written documents is rightfully in the possession of the Receiving Party, or its affiliates or

subsidiaries, prior to and independently of the disclosure of same to the Receiving Party by the Disclosing Party; or

(3) Information that the Receiving Party can demonstrate by competent written documents is or has been independently developed by the Receiving Party or its affiliates or subsidiaries without reference or access to or use of Confidential Information, and without any other breach of this Agreement.

参考译文:

机密信息不包括:

(1) 接收方可以通过足够的书面文件证明在不违反本协议的情况下，该信息自披露之时或披露后成为公众知识或文献的一部分；或者

(2) 接收方可以通过足够的书面文件证明在披露前该信息由接收方、其关联公司或者子公司合法拥有，或者独立于该披露行为；或者

(3) 接收方可以通过足够的书面文件证明该信息由接收方、其关联公司或者子公司独立开发，且开发中未参考、获得或者使用该保密信息，且不存在其他违反和协议约定的情形。

◆ 知识点梳理

保密义务的豁免主要有以下情形:

信息已为公众知晓或者称为常识	· be already known to the general public · be available to the public at the time of disclosure · be in the public domain · become common knowledge
签署保密协议前，信息已被一方知晓	· be already known to Party B before the disclosure by Party A · be lawfully in Party B's possession before disclosure under this Agreement
从具有合法披露权利的第三方获取的信息	· be acquired legally from a third party who is entitled to disclose it · be disclosed to Party B by a third party who has the lawful right to disclose such information · disclosed to the Recipient in good faith by a third party not bound by any duty of confidentiality
依法院或政府机关的决定而需要披露保密信息	· by virtue of a decision of a court or of a governmental authority

续表

由接收方独立开发的信息	· independently developed by the Receiving Party or its affiliates or subsidiaries without reference or access to or use of Confidential Information
不重要的或显而易见的信息	· trivial or obvious information

四、保密信息的归还（Return of Confidential Information）

范例一：

The Recipient shall, upon the written request of the Disclosing Party, return to the Disclosing Party all Proprietary Information received by the Recipient hereunder (and all copies and reproductions thereof). In addition, upon any such request, the Recipient shall destroy all Proprietary Information prepared by the Recipient or its Representatives (and all copies thereof). Notwithstanding the return or destruction of the Proprietary Information, the Recipient and its Representatives will continue to be bound by their obligations of confidentiality and other obligations hereunder.

参考译文：

接收方应披露方的书面要求，将接收方根据本协议收到的所有专有信息（及其所有副本和复制品）退还给披露方。此外，应任何此类请求，接收方应销毁接收方或其代表制备的所有专有信息（及其所有副本）。尽管专有信息已经归还或者销毁，但接收方及其代表将继续受到其保密义务和本协议项下其他义务的约束。

范例二：

If the Parties terminate negotiations and discussions in connection with the Proposed Acquisition and do not proceed to completion of the Proposed Acquisition, then upon Seller's request at any time, whether before or after the expiration of the Term, Buyer shall:

(1) return to Seller, or at Seller's direction destroy, all materials (including any copies thereof) embodying the Confidential Information; and

（2） certify in writing to Seller, within [10] days after Seller's request, that all of such materials have been returned or destroyed.

参考译文：

如果双方终止与拟议收购相关的谈判和磋商，并且不再继续完成拟议收购的，经卖方随时（无论在协议期限届满之前或之后）提出要求的，买方应当：

（1）将所有含有保密信息的资料（包括所有复印件）归还于卖方，或根据卖方的指示销毁；以及

（2）在卖方提出请求后【10】天内，书面向卖方确认所有该等资料均已归还或销毁。

范例三：

Upon termination of Business Relationship or at the request of Party A, Party B shall without delay return to Party A any and all Confidential Information it has received from the latter. Party B shall provide Party A with written confirmation to the effect that it has returned the Confidential Information according to this Agreement.

参考译文：

在业务关系终止时或依甲方的要求，乙方应立即返还其从甲方接收的任何保密信息。乙方应向甲方书面确认其已根据本协议返还保密信息。

◆ 知识点梳理

保密信息归还条款写作句式：

· Upon the written request of the Disclosing Party, return to the Disclosing Party all Proprietary Information.

· Notwithstanding the return or destruction of the Proprietary Information, the Recipient and its Representatives will continue to be bound by their obligations of confidentiality.

· Upon termination of Business Relationship or at the request of Party A, Party B shall without delay return all Confidential Information.

· Upon Seller's request at any time, whether before or after the expiration of the Term, Buyer shall return to Seller, or at Seller's direction destroy, all materials embodying the Confidential Information.

· Certify in writing to Seller, within [10] days after Seller's request, that all of such materials have been returned or destroyed.

· Provide Party A with written confirmation to the effect that it has returned the Confidential Information

五、其他协议中的保密条款（Confidentiality Clauses in Others）

在涉及知识产权保护或者商业秘密保护的协议中，如知识产权许可协议、特许经营协议、劳动合同中，也经常会出现保密条款，特举例如下：

范例一：

FRANCHISEE acknowledges that XXX COMPANY will from time to time provide FRANCHISEE with information that is confidential in nature, and that if disclosed to third parties might adversely impact the ability of ABC COMPANY or SYSTEM franchisees to remain competitive. FRANCHISEE agrees that, unless otherwise determined by ABC COMPANY, the marketing strategies and programs developed by ABC COMPANY shall be treated as confidential until publicly disseminated in accordance with the instructions of ABC COMPANY. FRANCHISEE shall not disclose any confidential information to any person other than FRANCHISEE's employees as may be necessary to discharge FRANCHISEE's obligations hereunder, and FRANCHISEE agrees not to use any such confidential information for any purpose other than to discharge its obligations under this AGREEMENT.

参考译文：

特许经营人承认 XXX 公司将不时向特许经营人提供本质上机密的信息，并且，如果向第三方披露该信息，可能会对 XXX 公司或者该系统的特许经营人的竞争力产生不利影响。特许经营人同意，除非 XXX 公司另有决定，否则 XXX 公司制定的营销策略和项目应视为机密，直到根据 XXX 公司的指示公开发布为止。特许经营人不得向其员工以外的任何人透露任何机密信息，这对于特许经营人履行本协议的义务可能是必要的，并且特许经营人承诺除为了履行本协议所规定的义务外，不会将此机密信息用于其他任何目的。

范例二：

Franchisee shall not at any time, without franchisor's prior written consent, copy, duplicate, record or otherwise reproduce in any manner any part of the manuals, updates, supplements, or related materials, in whole or in part, or otherwise make the same available to any unauthorized person.

参考译文：

未经特许人事先书面同意，特许经营人不得在任何时候以任何方式对手册、更新文件、增补或相关材料的任何部分进行全部或者部分复印、复制、重写或以其他方式复制，或者以其他方式将上述材料提供给任何未经授权之人。

范例三：

The Licensee shall keep secret towards third parties all the technical specifications for the products under license entrusted to him by the Licensor as well as all the other experience (know-how) transferred to the Licensee except as required by the purpose of this Agreement.

参考译文：

对于许可方向其授予的许可项下产品的一切技术规范以及向被许可方转让的其他一切经验（专有技术），被许可均应予以保密，除非本协议另有要求。

范例四：

The Licensee shall impose this confidentiality obligation also on his employees and agents by means of appropriate measures and agreements. The Licensee shall be responsible for the observance of this confidentiality obligation by his employees, even after their possible departure from the company. The same applies for any third parties commissioned by the Licensee.

参考译文：

被许可方应通过妥当措施和协议，对其雇员和代理人设立该项保密义务。被许可方应负责其雇员遵守该项保密义务，甚至在雇员离开公司之后仍然承担该项责任。本项规定同样适用于被许可方委托的任何第三方。

第五章　用工类涉外合同法律文书

第一节　劳动合同（Employment Contract）

中国2008年颁布了《劳动合同法》，此后经过多次修订。《劳动合同法》是劳动力资源市场配置和劳动关系协调的法律手段，以稳定劳动关系为基本功能，是倾斜保护劳动者的一部兼具公法和私法性质的法律。

劳动合同作为劳动关系运行的法定平台，是依法治理劳动关系的法定纽带。在一个规范的劳动合同中，主要包括以下法定必备条款：

用人单位基本信息	Basic information of Employer
劳动者基本信息	Basic information of Employee
劳动合同期限	Term of Employment Contract
工作内容和工作地点	Duties and work place
工作时间和休息休假	Working hours and holidays
劳动报酬	Remuneration
社会保险	Social insurance
劳动保护	Labor protection
劳动条件和职业危害防护	Working conditions and control of occupational hazard

除了以上必备条款以外，劳动合同还包括以下约定条款：

试用期	Probation period
培训	Training
保守秘密	Confidentiality
竞业限制	Non-competition

续表

补充保险	Supplementary insurance
福利待遇	Welfare and fringe benefits

接下来我将介绍劳动合同中典型的条款，如：合同序言、合同期限、工作岗位和职责描述、工作时间和休息休假、工作报酬、工作条件和劳动保护、保密义务、劳动合同的终止等八大条款。竞业限制条款将作为单独的一节来介绍。

一、合同序言（Preamble）

范例一：

WHEREAS, the Company is a limited liability company duly incorporated in accordance with the laws of the People's Republic of China; and having its registered office at ________________________.

WHEREAS, the Employee is a Chinese citizen, specialized in law in higher education;

WHEREAS, The Employee wishes to perform the work described in the Terms of Reference below, and Company wishes to hire the Employee to perform such work;

NOW THEREFORE, the Company and the Employee, on the basis of their equal and friendly negotiation, agree to enter into this Agreement and establish the employment relationship in accordance with the *Employment Contract Law of the People's Republic of China* and other relevant laws and regulations.

参考译文：

鉴于，本公司是一家依据中华人民共和国法律设立的有限责任公司，注册地址在________________________。

鉴于，该员工为中国国籍，拥有高等学校法学专业背景；

鉴于，员工同意并且希望按本合同下述条款为公司提供服务、与公司建立劳动关系；公司亦同意聘用员工作为正式雇员；

因此，公司和员工本着平等友好协商一致的原则，根据《中华人民共和国劳动合同法》及其他相关法律法规同意签署该劳动合同，建立劳动关系。

范例二：

This Employment Contract is entered into by and between ________ (name) (hereinafter referred to as Employer) and ________ (name) (hereinafter referred to as Employee).

Employer hereby employs Employee and Employee hereby accepts to be employed by Employer to serve and perform the duties required of him/her in the job provided below.

参考译文：

此劳动合同由×××（以下简称雇主）和×××（以下简称雇员）缔结。

雇主雇用雇员，雇员接受雇主雇用并且履行其在以下提供的工作中所需的职责。

二、劳动合同期限（Term of Employment Contract）

根据中国的劳动合同法，劳动合同期限分为固定期限劳动合同和无固定期限劳动合同，其表述分别为：

固定期限劳动合同	Fixed-term employment contract
无固定期限劳动合同	Non-fixed term labor contract Open-ended employment contract
试用期	Probation period, probationary period

范例一：

The parties agree that this labor contract is Non-fixed term labor contract, starting from ________ (date), without probation period.

参考译文：

双方同意，本合同为无固定期限劳动合同，从________（日期）开始，无试用期。

范例二：

The employment term is three years, lasting from ______ (date) ______ to ______ (date) ______. After expiration of this term, renewal of the employment contract is subject to the agreement of both parties.

参考译文：

本合同的期限为3年，自________（日期）起至________（日期）止。合同到期后，双方可协商续签合同。

范例三：

The Contract will be valid from ________ (date) to ________ (date), a period lasting for [ ] years.

参考译文：

本合同的期限自________（日期）起至________（日期）止，共计____年。

范例四：

This contract will become effective as from ________________ and it will continue for an indefinite period until it has been cancelled.

参考译文：

本合同为无固定期限劳动合同，将从________________起生效，直至本合同被解除。

范例五：

The term of the employment contract and Probation Period is:

(1) Fixed period. The term of this Contract shall be ________ years, from ________ (date) to ________ (date) during which there shall be a probation period of ________ months, from ________ (date) to ________ (date).

(2) Unfixed period. The term of this Contract shall be calculated from the date of ________ (date), including the probation period of ________ months. This contract shall be terminated when the circumstances of statutory termination occur.

参考译文：

劳动合同的期限和试用期为：

（1）固定期限。本合同的期限为________年，从________（日期）到________（日期），其试用期为________个月，从________（日期）到________（日期）。

（2）不定期。本合同的期限应自________（日期）之日起算，包括试用期________个月。发生法定终止的情况时，本合同应当终止。

试用期条款如下例：

范例一：

The Employee's appointment is subject to a two (2) month's probationary period during which period the Employer may terminate the services of the Employee for any fair reason. The Employee may terminate the services with a written notice to the Employer.

参考译文：

劳动合同包含两（2）个月的试用期，在此期间雇主可以出于任何合理原因终止劳动合同。员工也可以在试用期间书面通知雇主终止劳动合同。

范例二：

It is understood and agreed that the first sixty (60) days of employment shall constitute a probationary period during which period the Employer may, in its absolute discretion, terminate the Employee's employment, for any fair reason.

参考译文：

双方知悉并同意聘用期的前六十（60）天为试用期，在此期间雇主可自行决定以任何合理理由终止劳动合同。

三、工作岗位和职责描述（Position and Job Description）

范例一：

According to the requirement of the Company's operation and business, the Company hereby engages the Employee as Senior Consultant with such duties, authority and responsibilities as are normally associated with and appropriate for such positions. The Employee hereby agrees to accept this position. The Employee will report to the person as designated by the Company.

参考译文：

根据公司业务要求，公司聘任员工担任高级咨询顾问，员工同意接受公司的聘任。员工直接向公司指定人员汇报工作。

范例二：

The Employer agrees to employ ________ as Sales Representative, located in ________ (location).

参考译文：

甲方聘任________担任________（区域）销售代表。

范例三：

________ will be appointed as the position of Chief Executive Officer and will report to the Board of Directors.

参考译文：

________将被聘任为首席执行官，并对董事会负责。

范例四：

Duties:

(1) Develop new customers in Netherland and Belgium;

(2) Maintain and further develop the customers which the Employee and China support team developed in 2018, such as ________ .

参考译文：

岗位职责：

(1) 开发荷兰和比利时区域的新客户；

(2) 维护和进一步开发乙方及中国支持团队在 2018 年开发的客户，例如________.

范例五：

Responsibilities:

(1) Being the head of the current staff team, in charge of day-to-day operation

of the ________;

（2） Responsible for various meetings, events and activities of the organization.

参考译文：

职责：

（1） 担任现任工作团队的领导，负责________的日常运营工作；

（2） 负责公司各种会议、活动的组织安排。

◆ 知识点梳理

常见聘任条款句式如下：

· be appointed as the position of……

· The Employer agrees to employ ________ as……

· engage the Employee as Senior Consultant with such duties, authority and responsibilities as……

· be head of the department

· in charge of ……

· be responsible for ……

四、工作时间和休息休假（Working Hours and Holidays）

范例一：

The standard office hours are from 9：00 a. m. to 6：00 p. m. with one hour off for lunch between 1：00 p. m. and 2：00 p. m. Mondays to Fridays, or such other times as the Company may from time to time stipulate. As with any professional office, overtime or alternative working hours may be required.

参考译文：

常规工作时间为周一至周五的上午9点至下午6点，每天包括1小时的午餐时间，或者公司另行规定的其他工作时间。对于专业的职位，有可能需要加班或者安排轮岗。

范例二：

Notwithstanding the foregoing, the both Parties agree that, when the local government authorities adopts measures to avoid traffic jams during peak hours or special event, or where the Company deems necessary due to production and operation, the Company may temporarily change the working hours at its sole discretion.

参考译文：

在当地政府采取避峰措施或有特殊事件安排或公司因生产经营需要时，公司均可自行决定临时性、阶段性地调整工作时间。

范例三：

Party A shall implement the following (　　) type of working hour system for the position of Party B.

(1) Standard working hour system.

(2) Comprehensive working hour system.

(3) Flexible working hour system.

参考译文：

甲方对乙方的职位实行以下（　　）类工作时间制度。

（1）标准工时制。

（2）综合工时制度。

（3）弹性工时制。

有关休息休假的例子如下：

范例一：

The Employee is entitled to days off on Chinese Public Holidays as stipulated in the *Regulation on Public Holidays for National Annual Festivals and Memorial Days* which takes into effect on 1st Jan. 2008.

参考译文：

员工有权按照2008年1月1日生效的《全国年节及纪念日放假办法》享受法定假日休假权利。

范例二：

The Employee is entitled to paid leave per annum in accordance with the *Regulations of Paid Annual Leave of Employees* which takes into effect on January 1, 2008 and other relevant regulations. Such leave is to be taken at such times as the Company considers most convenient having regard to the requirement of the Company's business. Notwithstanding the foregoing, it's acknowledged and agreed by both Parties that the paid leave of the Employee under this Agreement is 5 days per year.

参考译文：

员工有权按照2008年1月1日生效的《职工带薪年休假条例》及相关法规的规定享受带薪年假。年假应由公司根据其业务需求，在方便、可行的时间安排进行。尽管有前述约定，双方一致知悉并同意，就员工在本合同有效期内的带薪年假可按照与公司另行达成的书面协议加以确定（该等带薪年假天数不应低于法律规定的最低天数）。

范例三：

The Employee is entitled to paid maternity leaves for a maximum period of 178 days commencing at any time from 4 weeks before the expected date of birth unless otherwise agreed upon.

参考译文：

除非另有约定，员工有权从预产期前4周开始享受最长期限为178天的带薪产假。

◆ 知识点梳理

与工作及工作时间有关的表达方式汇总如下：

Teleworking	远程办公
Flexitime	弹性上班制
Standard working hour system	标准工时制
Comprehensive working hour system	综合工时制
Flexible working hour system	弹性工时制
Working from home	在家办公
Shift work	轮班制
Day shift	白班
Night shift	晚班
Work extra hours	加班

续表

Hot desking	办公桌轮用制
Part-time job	全职工作
Full-time job	兼职工作
Temping	做临时工
Job sharing	工作分担
Freelancing	自由职业

与休息休假有关的表达方式汇总如下：

Be entitled to days off	有权获得休假
Be entitled to paid leave	有权获得带薪休假
Sick leave	病假
Material leave	产假
Annual leave	年假

五、工作报酬（Remuneration）

提到工资，通常我们想到的词有 salary，wage，compensation 等，但是这些词都是不恰当的，都不如 remuneration 规范。

Salary 一般指劳动者完成既定工作后应得的收入，一般指按月发放的工资。Wage 常常用来表示较短时间内的收入，比如小时工资、周工资等。而 remuneration 一词，是劳动合同中规定的员工获得的所有工资、奖金、补贴、福利等。

范例一：

The salary of the Employee is RMB ________ per month in the probationary period. This salary should not lower than the lowest salary standard on the same position in our company or 80% of its official salary, and it shouldn't be lower than local minimum wage standard.

After the probationary period, the salary of the Employee shall be RMB ________, and the salary will be based on（　　）

a. Hourly wages　　　　b. piece wages

参考译文：

雇员的试用期工资为每月________元。该工资不得低于我们公司同一职位的最低工资标准或其正式工资的80%，并且不得低于当地最低工资标准。

试用期结束后，职工的工资为________元，工资由（ ）决定。

a. 计时　　　　b. 计件

范例二：

The job remuneration is commission based, without base salary.

The Employer pays the employee 5% commission semiannually, based on the total sales volume of the new customers developed by the Employee, including the new customer which the employee developed in 2018 and future new customers developed by the Employee.

参考译文：

此工作工资基于提成，无基本工资。

甲方支付乙方5%的销售提成，以乙方开发的新客户（包括2018年开发的客户和未来开发的新客户）销售总额计提销售提成。提成每半年支付一次。

范例三：

The company agrees that all remuneration payable under this contract of employment shall be paid into the Employee's bank account on the last Friday of each month. In the event of a public holiday falling on a Friday, the payment will be made on the following Monday.

参考译文：

公司同意，根据本雇佣合同应支付的所有报酬应在每个月的最后一个星期五存入员工的银行账户。如果最后一个星期五的是法定假日，则在下星期一支付。

范例四：

In addition to the remuneration specified above in clause 5 the Employee is entitled to be reimbursed by the Employer for all costs incurred in the performance of his/her duties in accordance with the terms of this agreement and with the rules and practices of the Employer's business which are at the time in force.

参考译文：

除上述第 5 条规定的报酬外，雇员有权根据本协议的条款及当时有效的规定和惯例，要求雇主补偿其履行工作职责中所产生的所有费用。

范例五：

Insurance, Welfare and Benefits：

Party A shall pay relevant social insurance to designated authorities on Party B's behalf in a timely manner in accordance with government requirements. And the personal part will be deducted from the salary.

Party B's vocation of pregnancy, childbirth, breast-feeding and the corresponding treatment shall be subject to the relevant regulations, such as maternity insurance, female employee's labor protection, etc.

The treatment for Party B's occupational disease or job-related injuries (death), sickness or Non-job-related injuries, and the medical expenses paid shall be carried out by industrial injury insurance, medical insurance and related provisions.

参考译文：

保险、福利和补贴：

甲方应按照政府要求，及时向指定的有关部门为乙方缴纳有关社会保险。而个人负担部分将从工资中扣除。

乙方的孕期、产期、哺乳期及相关待遇依照有关规定处理，如生育保险、女职工的劳动保护等。

乙方的职业病或工伤（死亡）、疾病或与工作无关的伤害的治疗、以及所支付的医疗费用，应通过工伤保险基金、医疗保险基金和相关规定处理。

六、工作条件和劳动保护（Working Conditions & Working Protection）

Party A and Party B shall strictly comply with the national regulations concerning production safety and abide by regulations of labor protection and occupational hazards and protection of workers.

Party A shall provide Party B protection facilities, equipment and labor protection articles and other labor protection conditions in accordance with the national labor conditions.

Party B shall strictly comply with the safe operation and the relevant rules and regulations prepared by Party A in accordance with law. If Party A illegally command or force risky operation, party B have the right to refuse it.

Party A shall strictly implement relevant Occupational Disease Prevention Laws for the positions exposed to occupational disease hazards, such as exposure to dust, radioactive substances and other toxic and hazardous substances, and Party A shall explain the truth and its consequences on occupational hazards, protective measures adopted and treatment of occupational diseases to Party B, and adopt preventive measures and protection facilities which meet the requirements of the national occupational health.

参考译文：

乙方应严格遵守国家有关安全生产的规定，并遵守有关劳动保护、职业危害防护的规定。

甲方应根据国家劳动条件向乙方提供保护设施、设备和劳动保护用品以及其他劳动保护条件。

乙方应严格遵守甲方依法制定的安全操作规程和有关规定。如果甲方有非法指挥或强迫冒险劳动，乙方有权拒绝。

甲方必须严格执行有关《职业病预防法》，对暴露于粉尘、放射性物质及其他有毒有害物质等职业病危害的岗位，甲方应向乙方说明真相及其对职业危害的后果、采取的防护措施、职业病的治疗和预防，并采取符合国家职业卫生要求的预防措施和保护设施。

◆ 知识点梳理

与劳动保护相关的表达方式归纳如下：

Occupational hazard	职业危害
Production safety	安全生产
Illegally command or force risky operation	非法指挥或强迫冒险劳动

续表

Expose to occupational disease hazards, such as dust, radioactive substances and other toxic and hazardous substances	暴露于粉尘、放射性物质及其他有毒有害物质等职业病危害
Labor protection articles	劳动保护用品
Adopt preventive measures and protection facilities	采取预防措施和保护设施

七、保密义务（Confidentiality）

范例一：

The Employee shall not during or after his/her employment disclose confidential information belonging to the Company. The Employee has a personal responsibility to protect and maintain confidentiality of both the Company's and clients' information. The Employee must not, except as authorized or required by law or the Employee's duties, reveal any confidential information relating to the Company, its subsidiaries, its parent or associates. This obligation will continue after the termination of the Employee's employment unless and until any such information comes into the public domain other than through any breach of this provision by the Employee.

参考译文：

员工不得披露属于公司的保密信息，无论是在受雇期间还是终止雇佣之后。员工对保护和维护公司和客户信息的保密性负有个人义务。员工不得不透露任何与公司、其子公司、母公司或联营公司相关的保密信息，除非得到授权或法律或员工的职责要求。员工雇佣终止之后，仍然负有该义务，直至任何此类信息非由于员工违反本条规定而进入公共领域。

范例二：

To protect the confidentiality of the information the Employee agrees to deliver to the Company, before the end of the Employee's employment, ALL documents and records belonging to the Company which are in the Employee's possession, including all documents and records made by the Employee in the course of the Employee's employment and relating to the affairs of the Company, including computer lists, disks or programs, diaries, client records, cards, telephone lists, pricing lists and technical data and all other tangible items in the Employee's possession or control belonging to or containing any confidential information of the Company.

参考译文：

为了保护保密信息，员工同意：在员工雇佣终止前，向本公司归还员工持有的在雇佣期间产生的及与公司相关的所有属于公司的文档、记录，包括员工所拥有或控制的属于或含有任何本公司的保密信息的计算机列表、磁盘或方案、日记、客户记录、卡片、电话清单、价格表和技术数据及所有其他有形物品。

◆ 知识点梳理

与员工保密义务相关的句式如下：

· The Employee must keep confidential and shall not directly or indirectly disclose, publish or use the following information……

· The Employee shall not during or after his/her employment disclose confidential information belonging to the Company……

· The Employee has a personal responsibility to protect and maintain confidentiality of……

· To protect the confidentiality of the information the Employee agrees to deliver to the Company ALL documents and records……

八、劳动合同的终止（Termination）

范例一：

The employer may terminate this agreement without any period of notice or payment if the Employee at any time:

· is guilty of serious misconduct or neglect or any other conduct in respect of the Employee's employment or personal life which may seriously adversely affect the interests of the Employer;

· is convicted of a criminal offence other than an offence under road traffic legislation in the UK or abroad for which a penalty other than a term of imprisonment is imposed;

· becomes the subject of a bankruptcy order;

· is diagnosed as mentally ill or becomes a patient for the purpose of the Mental Health Act 1983;

· is guilty of any material breach of the provisions of this agreement or any neglect in carrying out his or her duties under the terms of this agreement;

Such termination shall be without prejudice to any other rights of the Employer against the Employee.

参考译文：

如果雇员在任何时候有以下行为，雇主可以终止本协议，且无需任何通知或支付经济补偿：

· 雇员的工作或个人生活中有严重不端、重大过失或任何其他行为，可能严重损害雇主的利益的；

· 雇员被判处刑罚，但因触犯英国或国外道路交通法规而被判处非监禁刑罚的除外；

· 雇员成为破产令的对象；

· 根据《1983 年精神健康法案》雇员被诊断为精神病或成为患者；

· 雇员有任何严重违反本协议规定的行为，或在履行本协议职责中存在重大过失；

该终止不应损害雇主对雇员的任何其他权利。

范例二：

If both Parties cannot agree to renew the agreement, the Contract terminates automatically when it expires. Both Parties shall implement handover procedures timely.

参考译文：

本合同期满如双方未续签，则合同自行终止。双方应及时办理交接手续。

范例三：

The Company may terminate this Agreement without prior notice under any of the following circumstances when the Employee: (i) is found guilty in a criminal lawsuit; (ii) commits a serious malpractice or negligence which results in a significant economic loss of the Company.

参考译文：

公司下列情况下无需提前通知员工即可与员工终止劳动合同：（i）员工被判决承担刑事责任；（ii）员工营私舞弊，有重大过失或失职行为，使公司蒙受重大经济损失。

范例四：

The Company may terminate this Agreement after giving a thirty (30) day prior written notice or by paying one month salary in lieu of notice under any of the following circumstances when:

(i) due to illness or Non-work-related injuries, the Employee is unable to perform his/her original work or is unable to perform alternative duties as arranged by the Company, when the medical treatment period ends;

(ii) the Employee is unable to perform his/her duties to an acceptable standard, even after training has been provided or adjustments have been made to his/her position.

参考译文：

在下列情况下，公司有权经提前30天通知或无需提前30日而支付一个月工资取代提前通知期，通知员工解除本协议：

（i）由于疾病或非因工受伤，医疗期结束后，员工仍无法继续履行本职工作也无法履行公司调岗后的工作；

（ii）员工无法胜任本职工作，在接受培训和岗位调整后仍无法胜任的。

当然，除了用人单位终止劳动合同的情形外，也有劳动者主动提出终止劳动合同的情形，如《劳动合同法》第38条所规定的情形：

Under any of the following circumstances, an employee may rescind the labor contract:

(1) where the employer fails to provide labor protection or labor conditions pursuant to the provisions of the labor contract;

(2) where the employer fails to promptly pay labor remuneration in full amount;

(3) where the employer fails to contribute social security premiums for the em-

ployee pursuant to the law;

(4) where the rules and system of the employer violate the provisions of laws and regulations and are prejudicial to the employee's rights and interests;

(5) where the labor contract is rendered void under any of the circumstances stipulated in the first paragraph of Article 26; or

(6) any other circumstances where the employee may rescind a labor contract as stipulated by the laws and regulations.

Where an employer uses means such as violence, threat or illegal restriction of personal freedom to coerce an employee into provision of labor or where an employer gives illegal orders or forces an employee to engage in risky work which endangers the employee 's personal safety, the employee may forthwith rescind the labor contract and shall not be required to give the employer advance notice thereof.

用人单位有下列情形之一的，劳动者可以解除劳动合同：

（1）未按照劳动合同约定提供劳动保护或者劳动条件的；

（2）未及时足额支付劳动报酬的；

（3）未依法为劳动者缴纳社会保险费的；

（4）用人单位的规章制度违反法律、法规的规定，损害劳动者权益的；

（5）因本法第二十六条第一款规定的情形致使劳动合同无效的；

（6）法律、行政法规规定劳动者可以解除劳动合同的其他情形。

用人单位以暴力、威胁或者非法限制人身自由的手段强迫劳动者劳动的，或者用人单位违章指挥、强令冒险作业危及劳动者人身安全的，劳动者可以立即解除劳动合同，不需事先告知用人单位。

范例五：

The Company shall pay the Employee severance fee in accordance with the relevant national and local laws and regulations.

公司应根据国家和地区相关法律法规的规定向员工支付经济补偿金。

注：在员工无过错的情况下，用人单位终止劳动合同的，用人单位一般需支付劳动者经济补偿金，劳动者有违法犯罪或者严重违反劳动合同的情形除外。但是如果用人单位违法解除劳动合同，则面临支付经济赔偿金的法律责任，经济赔偿金具有惩罚性，是经济赔偿金的两倍。

◆ 知识点梳理

与劳动合同相关的经济补偿金、赔偿金、违约金的表达:

经济补偿金	Severance fee
经济赔偿金	Compensation damages
违约金	Breach of contract damages/ Liquidated damages/penalty

与用人单位和劳动者履行劳动合同情况相关的表达有:

be guilty of serious misconduct or neglect	有严重不端、重大过失行为
commit a serious malpractice or negligence which results in a significant economic loss of the Company	营私舞弊，有重大过失或失职行为，使公司蒙受重大经济损失
be convicted of a criminal offence	被判处刑罚
be found guilty in a criminal lawsuit	被判决承担刑事责任
be diagnosed as mentally ill	被诊断为患有精神疾病
be guilty of any material breach of the provisions of this agreement or any neglect in carrying out his or her duties	有任何严重违反本协议规定的行为，或在履行职责中存在重大过失
medical treatment period	医疗期
be unable to perform his/her duties to an acceptable standard/ be incompetent for the job	无法胜任本职工作
the rules and system of the employer violate the provisions of laws and regulations, and are prejudicial to the employee 's rights and interests	用人单位的规章制度违反法律、法规的规定，损害劳动者权益
the labor contract is rendered void	劳动合同被认定为无效
use means such as violence, threat or illegal restriction of personal freedom to coerce an employee into provision of labor	以暴力、威胁或者非法限制人身自由的手段强迫劳动者劳动的
give illegal orders or force an employee to engage in risky work which endangers the employee's personal safety	违章指挥、强令冒险作业危及劳动者人身安全

终止劳动合同的句式如下：

·在以下情况下，雇主可以终止本协议，且无需任何通知或支付经济补偿 The employer may terminate this agreement without any period of notice or payment under the following circumstances
·在下列情况下，公司有权经提前 30 天通知或无需提前 30 日而支付一个月工资取代提前通知期，通知员工解除本协议 The Company may terminate this Agreement after giving a thirty (30) day prior written notice or by paying one-month salary in lieu of notice under any of the following circumstances
·用人单位有下列情形之一的，劳动者可以解除劳动合同 Under any of the following circumstances, an employee may rescind the labor contract
·劳动者可以立即解除劳动合同，不需事先告知用人单位 The employee may forthwith rescind the labor contract and shall not be required to give the empoyer advance notice thereof if……

第二节　竞业限制协议（Non-Competition Agreement）

竞业限制是《中华人民共和国劳动合同法》的重要内容，根据本法第二十三条、二十四条的规定，它是用人单位对负有保守用人单位商业秘密的劳动者，在劳动合同、知识产权权利归属协议或技术保密协议中约定的竞业限制条款。

具体来说，竞业限制是指用人单位和知悉本单位商业秘密或者其他对本单位经营有重大影响的劳动者在终止或解除劳动合同后的，一定期限内不得在生产同类产品、经营同类业务或有其他竞争关系的用人单位任职，也不得自己生产与原单位有竞争关系的同类产品或经营同类业务。

竞业限制协议，也称非竞争协议，英文表达为 Non-compete agreement 或 Non-competition agreement，更多的是体现在劳动合同中的一个单独的竞业限制条款。

竞业限制协议和保密协议，到底有什么不同呢？其实竞业限制和保密协议，都是为了保护原企业的商业秘密，保护其合法利益。但是很多情况下，一些人会把它们弄混了。保密协议，约定的是保密义务，保密义务是一种法定义务，是离职员工一旦离职就会立刻背上的一种义务，并不因保密协议的存在而存在。而竞业限制协议，背后是竞业限制义务，是为了企业利益而限制、牺牲一部分劳动者利益，但是劳动者此时又处于一个弱势的地位，因此不能用法定的方式直接给他扣上义务，所以要求企业如果有类似要求，就要和劳动者签订竞业限制协议，并约定员工恪守义务的对价，也就是竞业限制补偿金，以平衡双方利益。所以，如果竞业限制协议不存在，或者用人单位不给付补偿金，员工就不必负有竞业限制义务，可以自由择业、就业。

竞业限制协议在雇佣期间和结束后的一段时间内生效，具体时间通常由雇主拟定，一般情况下竞业期最长为两年。

在一个竞业限制协议或条款中，一般包括以下要素：竞业限制的期限、竞争对手的范围、竞业限制补偿金、违反竞业限制违约金等。我们首先了解一下竞业限制协议的序言条款：

Whereas, the information resources and technology of ____________ (hereinafter referred to as the "Company") are confidential and can bring about market benefits;

Whereas, ____________ (hereinafter referred to as "You") will, during your service with the Company, directly or indirectly touch with, know, understand and grasp the business information and technical information of the Company, and such business information and technical information are not known to the public, can bring economic benefits to the Company, have been treated by the Company as confidential, and belong to the Company's trade secrets;

Whereas, You understand and acknowledge that, if you disclose to any existing or potential competitors any above-mentioned business information and technical information, such disclosure will cause the Company to be in a very disadvantageous competitive position and damage the Company's interests; if you are employed by or serve any enterprise in the same trade with the Company, the employment or service will necessarily cause irremediable damage to the Company;

Therefore, according to the Company's Non-disclosure system, both the Company and you (hereinafter collectively referred to as "both parties") agree upon as follows through consultation:

参考译文：

鉴于，____________（下称“公司”）的信息资源及技术具有保密性及市场效益；

鉴于，________________（下称“你”）在公司工作期间，将直接或间接地接触、知悉、了解和掌握公司的经营信息和技术信息，而该经营信息和技术信息均属于不为公众所知悉、能为公司带来经济利益，并已由公司采取保密措施，系属公司的商业秘密；

鉴于，你了解并承认，若你向公司现有或潜在的竞争对手披露任何前述经营信息和技术信息，将会导致公司处于非常不利的竞争地位并损害公司的利益；若你就职或服务于与公司相竞争的企业，则必定会对公司造成无可补救的损害；

因此，根据公司的保密制度，你与公司双方（以下合称“双方”）经协商，达成如下协议条款。

竞业限制义务包括在职竞业限制义务和离职后的竞业限制义务。

在职期间的竞业限制义务条款如下：

范例一：

In-service Non-Competition Obligation: The Employee agrees to refrain from engaging in any competition during the term of employment. The Employee shall refrain from establishing or taking over or participating in, directly or indirectly, a competing enterprise. Furthermore, the Employee shall refrain from any contract or support for a competing enterprise. Within the scope of the business of the Company, the Employee shall refrain from engaging in any business for his/her own or other person's account.

参考译文：

在职竞业限制义务：员工同意在其任职期间不与公司进行任何形式的竞争。员工承诺不直接或间接地参与竞争对手公司的设立、接管、不直接或间接参与竞争对手企业。员工进一步承诺：不接触、不支持竞争对手企业。在公司等业务范围内，员工不得为自营或为他人经营与公司有竞争的业务。

离职后的竞业限制义务条款如下：

范例二：

Post-employment Non-Competition Obligation: The business of Party A is highly competitive and depends on information and actions that require the full involvement of Parties and Party A's clients and contacts in current and future business actions. Even some of the information and actions will not develop into a business relationship for a period of time after disclosure to the Party B, Party B agrees to NOT COMPETE with Party A in any form, individually or as an employee of another business enterprise, for a period of two years from the Party B's relationship termination with Party A.

参考译文：

离职后竞业限制义务：甲方从事的业务处于高度竞争状态，且充分依赖于甲乙双方间及与甲方客户间现在及未来的所有信息及动态之沟通与联络。对于乙方获知的甲方一些信息和动态即使在一时间段内尚未与甲方形成业务关系，乙方亦承诺在与甲方终止关系之后的两年内，不得以任何形式、单独或以其他公司雇员的名义与甲方进行竞争。

范例三：

Both parties acknowledge that the Company has the sole discretion to decide whether or not it will request your compliance with Post Employment Non-Competition. If the Company does not request you to comply with the Non-competition restrictions in post-employment, the Company may provide you with a prior notice to terminate this Agreement. If the Company requests you to comply with the Non-competition restrictions, it will pay you reasonable compensation.

参考译文：

双方同意，公司有权决定是否要求你遵守离职后竞业禁止的条款。若公司不要求你遵守离职后竞业禁止义务，公司可提前通知你解除本协议；若公司决定要求你履行竞业禁止义务，公司将给予合理的竞业禁止补偿。

劳动法仅规定了离职后竞业限制经济补偿金，未规定在职期间竞业限制经济补偿金，如下条款所示：

范例四：

Compensation for Post-Employment Non-Competition: In consideration of you agreeing to perform the Non-competition obligations as outlined above during the Post-employment Non-competition Period, the Company agrees to pay you monetary compensation on a monthly basis during the Post-employment Non-competition Period. The aforesaid monetary compensation shall be paid in the amount of 30% of your average monthly salary for the last twelve (12) months preceding to your departure if you are employed by a Non-competitor of the Company, or the Company will pay you the average of your monthly salary for the last twelve (12) months preceding to your departure if you are unemployed due to the Non-competition restrictions and you do not engage in any actions which violate your Non-competition obligations with the Company ("Non-competition Compensation"). For the purpose above, you shall provide proof of your employment with a new employer or proof that you are unemployed on a monthly basis during the Post-employment Non-competition Period, and the proof you provide shall be used as the basis of Non-competition compensation to be paid by the Company.

参考译文：

离职后竞业禁止之补偿：在你同意于离职后竞业限制期内履行上述所言之竞业限制义务的条件下，公司同意在离职后竞业限制期内按月给予你相应的经济补偿，若你离职后在非与本公司竞争的单位就业的，该等经济补偿的金额应为你离职前十二个月的月平均工资的30%，若你离职后因竞业限制而失业，并且你也未从事任何与公司竞争的业务的，则该等经济补偿金应为你离职前十二个月的月平均工资（“竞业限制经济补偿金”）。为此目的，你应按月向公司提交竞业限制期间在新雇主就业的证明，或你离开本公司后的失业证明，作为公司向你支付经济补偿金的依据。

违反竞业限制义务的违约责任条款如下：

范例五：

Breach of Non-Competition Obligation: If you breach the Non-Competition clause contained herein, the Company shall not be required to pay any compensation described in the preceding paragraph, and you agree to pay to the Company the following:

(a) The equivalent of the amount already paid by the Company to you for Post-Employment Non-Competition; and

(b) Penalty equal to six (6) times the average monthly salary of the twelve (12) months preceding to your departure; and

(c) Any other damages caused by you due to your breach of the covenants herein, including but without limitation legal fees, witness fees, etc.

参考译文：

违反竞业禁止：若你违反本竞业禁止协议的规定，公司不会给予任何上述补偿金，同时你同意支付公司下列款项：

(a) 公司已经给付你的离职后竞业禁止补偿金全额，以及

(b) 相当于你离职前十二个月的月平均工资的六倍的违约金；以及

(c) 其他任何因你违反此竞业禁止条款所造成的公司损失，包括律师费、举证费等。

◆ 知识点梳理

竞业限制相关的表达归纳如下：

Non-compete/Non-competition (restrictions)	竞业限制
In-service Non-Competition Obligation	在职竞业限制义务
Post-Employment Non-Competition Obligation	离职后竞业限制义务
Non-competition Compensation	竞业限制经济补偿金
Penalty	违约金
Engage in the same trade as the company for his own account or for any other person's account	自营或者为他人经营与公司营业范围相同的业务

与竞业限制相关的句式表达归纳如下：

· The Employee agrees to refrain from engaging in any competition during the term of employment.

· Party B agrees to NOT COMPETE with Party A in any form, individually or as an employee of another business enterprise, for a period of two years.

· In consideration of you agreeing to perform the Non-competition obligations as outlined above during the Post-employment Non-competition Period, the Company agrees to pay you monetary compensation on a monthly basis during the Post-employment Non-competition Period.

第六章 公司经营管理类常见涉外法律文书

在公司管理中，经常会出现一些经营管理类法律文书，如被称为公司“小宪法”的公司章程、董事会决议、隐名股东与显名股东之间的委托持股协议、股权凭证和银行资信证明等。另外，对于中外合资经营企业和中外合作经营企业而言，合资经营协议为必备的法律文书。本章节我们将主要围绕以上几种常见法律文书展开。

第一节 中外合资经营协议（Sino-Foreign Equity Joint Venture Agreement）

在研究合资经营协议之前，我们首先应该区分中外合资经营企业与中外合作经营企业。中外合资经营企业，是指中国经营者与外国经营者按照中国法律的规定，在中国境内共同投资、共同经营，并按投资比例分享利润、分担风险及亏损的企业。而中外合作经营企业，是指中国合作者与外国合作者依照中国法律的规定，在中国境内共同举办的，按合作企业合同的约定分配收益或者产品、分担风险和亏损的企业。从定义可见，两者的主要区别在于合资经营企业是按照投资比例享受分红和分担亏损，而合作经营企业是按照双方约定分配收益和承担亏损，因此中外合作经营企业是一种契约式的合营企业。因此，以示区分，中外合资经营协议一般用英文 Sino-Foreign Equity Joint Venture Agreement 表达，而中外合作经营协议一般用 Sino-Foreign Cooperative Joint Venture Agreement 表达。我们在本节则主要研究中外合资经营协议的写作。

一、序言（Preamble）

有些合资经营协议会先在序言中写明合作所依据的法律法规、合资企业适用的法律以及合资对于中国经济的促进作用等，如：

范例一：

The Joint Venture established within Chinese territory shall be beneficial for promoting the development of the economy, the enhancement of the science and technology of China and facilitating China's socialist modernization.

参考译文：

在中国境内设立的合营企业，应当能够促进中国经济的发展和科学技术水平的提高，有利于社会主义现代化建设。

范例二：

Chinese-foreign equity joint ventures (hereinafter referred to as joint ventures) established within Chinese territory upon the approval in accordance with the *Law on Chinese-Foreign Equity Joint Ventures* are Chinese legal persons, who shall be governed and protected by Chinese law.

参考译文：

依照《中外合资经营企业法》批准在中国境内设立的中外合资经营企业（以下简称合营企业）是中国的法人，受中国法律的管辖和保护。

目前，大多数的合资经营协议总则中已经省略了以上内容，直接介绍双方合作的背景或者合作基础，如下：

范例三：

WHEREAS Party A is engaged in manufacturing and selling ________ in China; and

WHEREAS Party B is engaged in manufacturing and selling ________ (hereinafter called "Licensed Product") and has Japanese patent rights to Licensed Product (hereinafter called "Patents") and registered Trademark No. ________ (hereinafter called "Trademark"); and

WHEREAS the Parties consider it mutually advantageous to organize a jointly owned corporation (hereinafter called "Joint Venture") under the laws of the People's Republic of China to engage in the manufacture, sale and development of Licensed Product in ________.

NOW IN WITNESS WHEREOF, in consideration of the premises and mutual agreement described hereinafter Party A and Party B agree as follows:

参考译文：

甲方在中国生产和销售________产品；

乙方生产和销售________产品（以下称“许可产品”），拥有许可产品的日本专利（以下称“专利”）和________号注册商标；

甲乙双方认为按照中华人民共和国的法律成立共同所有的公司（以下称“合资公司”），在________从事生产、销售和开发许可产品，对双方都是有利的；

为此，鉴于本协议所述的前提与约定，特此立约如下：

范例四：

This Joint Venture Contract (hereinafter referred to as "this Contract") is signed in Zhuhai, Guangdong China on March 20, 2019 by and between:

Party A: ________ (America) Holdings Limited, a limited liability company registered in America with its legal address at ________________ (hereinafter referred to as "Party A" or "foreign shareholder");

Party B: Zhuhai ________________ Co., Ltd., a limited liability company registered within the territory of China with its legal address at Zhuhai City (hereinafter referred to as "Party B" or "Chinese shareholder").

In accordance with the *Law of the People's Republic of China on Chinese-Foreign Equity Joint Ventures*, *Regulation on the Implementation of the Law of the People's Republic of China on Chinese-Foreign Equity Joint Ventures*, *Company Law of the People's Republic of China* and other applicable laws and regulations of the People's Republic of China, based on the principles of equality and mutual benefit and through friendly negotiation, both parties reach a consensus on the establishment of the Company in Zhuhai City, China, which will be a Chinese-Foreign equity joint venture limited liability company and this Contract is hereby concluded.

参考译文：

本合资经营合同（下称“本合同”）由以下双方于2019年3月20日在中

国珠海签署：

甲方：________（美国）控股有限公司，一家于美国注册的有限责任公司，其法定地址为________________（下称“甲方”或“外方股东”）；

乙方：珠海________有限公司，一家于中国境内注册的有限责任公司，其法定地址为珠海市（下称“乙方”或“中方股东”）。

根据《中华人民共和国中外合资经营企业法》、《中华人民共和国中外合资经营企业法实施条例》、《中华人民共和国公司法》及中华人民共和国适用的法律和法规，双方本着平等互利的原则，经友好协商后，就在中国珠海市设立公司并使之成为一家中外合资的有限责任公司达成了一致，并特此签订本合同。

范例五：

In accordance with the *Law of the People's Republic of China on Chinese-Foreign Equity Joint Ventures* and other relevant Chinese laws and regulations, Shanghai ________ Co., Ltd. (hereinafter referred to as "Party A") and Hongkong ________ Inc. (hereinafter referred to as "Party B"), adhering to the principles of equality and mutual benefit, and through friendly consultations, agree to jointly establish an equity joint venture company (the "JV company") in Shanghai, the People's Republic of China ("China"), and hereby enter into this Equity Joint Venture Contract ("Contract").

参考译文：

根据《中华人民共和国中外合资经营企业法》和中国其他有关法律法规，上海________有限公司（以下简称“甲方”）与香港________有限公司（以下简称“乙方”）本着平等互利的原则，通过友好协商，同意在中华人民共和国（“中国”）上海共同成立一家合资经营公司（“合营公司”），特签订本合资经营合同（“合同”）。

二、公司的成立（Formation of Joint Venture）

范例一：

Party A and Party B shall spare no efforts for the organization of Joint Venture under the laws of the People's Republic of China.

The name of Joint Venture is ________ with its legal address: ________.

All activities of Joint Venture shall comply with the provisions of the laws, decrees and pertinent regulations of the People's Republic of China.

Joint Venture shall take the form of a limited liability company. The profits, risks and losses of Joint Venture shall be shared by both Party A and Party B in proportion to the contributions to the registered capital.

The expenses of organizing Joint Venture shall be equally borne by Party A and Party B.

参考译文：

甲方和乙方按照中华人民共和国的法律建立合资企业。

合资企业称为________，地址为________________。

合资企业的一切活动，必须遵守中华人民共和国的法律、法令和有关条例规定。

合资企业的组织形式为有限责任公司。甲乙双方以各自认缴的出资额对合资公司的债务承担责任。各方按其出资额在注册资本中的比例分享利润和分担风险及亏损。

合资企业的组建费用由甲乙双方平均分担。

范例二：

Both parties agree that the Company which is a Chinese-Foreign equity joint venture shall be established according to the articles of this Contract on the date when it obtains the Business License of Sino-Foreign Equity Joint Venture issued by Administration for Industry and Commerce.

参考译文：

双方同意，该中外合资企业应从工商局获发中外合资经营企业营业执照之日起成立。

范例三：

The name of the Company is ________ (tentatively, subject to the industrial and commercial registration).

The legal address of the Company is ________ (tentatively, subject to the industrial and commercial registration).

参考译文：

公司的名称为________（暂定名，以工商登记为准）。

公司的法定地址为________（暂定地址，以工商登记为准）。

范例四：

The parties hereby form and establish an equity Joint Venture under the name of ________ in accordance with the laws of the People's Republic of China. The principal place of business of the joint venture shall be located at ________. The term of the JV shall commence on the execution date hereof and shall continue in perpetuity until mutual agreement to end the JV by both parties of the JV.

参考译文：

双方根据中华人民共和国法律成立合资经营企业，企业名称为________。合资企业的主要营业地点在________。合资企业的经营期限自签署本协议之日起开始，并永久存续，直至合资双方同意终止合资企业为止。

范例五：

The Company is a limited liability company established according to the laws of China. Each party shall assume limited liability to the Company to the limit of its respective contribution amount and the Company shall assume liability for the debts of the Company based on all its assets. The profits, risks and losses of the Joint Venture shall be shared by the parties in proportion to their contributions to the registered capital.

参考译文：

公司是按中国法律成立的有限责任公司。各方以其所认缴的出资额为限对公司承担有限责任，公司以其全部财产对公司的债务承担责任。各方按其出资额在注册资本中的比例分享利润、承担风险及亏损。

◆ 知识点梳理

合营企业建立条款常用表达如下：

合资经营企业	Equity joint venture
合作经营企业	Cooperative joint venture
经营地址	Legal address/ place of business/premises
注册资本	Registered capital
出资额	Capital contribution
以出资额为限承担有限责任	Assume limited liability in proportion to the contribution to the registered capital
承担合资企业债务的责任	Be liable to joint venture/assume liability to joint venture
按其出资额在注册资本中的比例分享利润、承担风险及亏损	Share the profits, risks and losses in proportion to their contributions to the registered capital

三、注册资本和出资比例（Registered Capital and Contribution Proportion）

范例一：

The registered capital of the joint venture refers to the total capital registered with the registration authority for the establishment of the joint venture. It shall be the sum of the capital contributions subscribed by all parties to the joint venture. The registered capital is denominated in Renminbi.

参考译文：

合资企业的注册资本，是指为设立合资企业在登记管理机构登记的资本总额，应为合资本各方认缴的出资额之和。合资企业的注册资本以人民币表示。

范例二：

The registered capital of Joint Venture shall be (amount of capital) ________, of which half (50%) will be contributed by each Party.

参考译文：

合资企业的注册资本为（资本金）________，其中一半（50%）由双方共同出资。

范例三：

Party A and Party B shall contribute according to the operating and development demand of the Company and they shall complete contribution before Dec. 31, 2020 in any case.

参考译文：

甲方和乙方应根据公司经营发展的需要进行出资，在任何情况下，甲方和乙方应在 2020 年 12 月 31 日前完成出资。

范例四：

Where the shareholder of the Company contributes in USD, the actual contribution amount shall be converted according to the central parity rate of bank between RMB and USD published by the People's Bank of China at the current date of payment.

参考译文：

公司股东以美元出资的，实际出资金额按付款当日中国人民银行公布的人民币与美元汇率的银行中间价折换。

范例五：

Each Party to Joint Venture shall pay in its contributions prior to ________ (date). Any delay in payment shall be subject to a payment of interest accrued and a penalty to the other party.

参考译文：

合营企业各方应在________（日期）前缴付其出资。如延迟缴付出资，应交纳利息，并向另一方支付违约金。

范例六：

The total investment of the Joint Venture shall be ________. The investment shall be paid up in two installments as follows: the first installment of ________ shall be paid up before ________ and the second installment of ________ shall be paid up before ________.

参考译文：

合资企业的总投资额为________。出资分两个阶段缴清：第一笔________于________之前缴清；第二笔________于________之前缴清。

范例七：

Both parties shall pay up their contributions in a lump sum within one (1) month from the effective date of the contract.

参考译文：

双方应在合同生效之日起一（1）个月内一次性缴清出资额。

范例八：

After the parties have made their capital contributions to the joint venture, such contributions shall be verified by a certified public accountant registered in China. Upon the issuance of the capital verification report by the said accountant, the joint venture shall issue a capital contribution certificate to each party, which shall contain the following particulars: the name of the joint venture, the date of establishment of the joint venture, the names of the parties and their capital contribution, the date on which their capital contribution is made, and the date of the issuance of the capital contribution certificate.

参考译文：

合营各方缴付出资额后，应当由中国的注册会计师验证，出具验资报告后，由合营企业据以发给出资证明书。出资证明书载明下列事项：合营企业名称、合营企业成立的日期、合营者名称（或者姓名）及其出资额、出资的日期、签发出资证明书的日期。

◆ 知识点梳理

与出资相关的条款常用表达如下：

认缴出资额	Subscribed capital
实缴出资额	Paid-up capital/paid-in capital
货币以人民币表示	Denominated in Renminbi
出资证明书	Capital contribution certificate

续表

持股比例	Shareholding proportion
一次性缴清出资	Pay up their contributions in a lump sum
分期缴清出资	Pay up capital in installments
验资报告	Capital verification report

注：之前注册公司实行实缴制，需要股东在设立公司的时候就将投资款缴纳到公司账户，无疑增加了设立公司的成本，也抬高了创业的门槛。目前新《公司法》实行注册资本认缴制，认缴制并不需要股东在设立公司的时候就将投资款缴纳到位，股东可以约定在一定期限内完成出资，大大降低了设立公司的门槛。同样，对于合资公司而言，也存在实缴和认缴之分。在上面的例子中我们可以看到多处出现 paid up capital（实缴出资），subscribed capital（认缴出资）。

四、股权转让（Stock Equity Transfer）

合资经营企业在注册的时候需要经过商务部的审批，同样，合资经营企业的股东在转让股权的时候，除了遵循普通类型的公司的股权转让规则外，还需要相关部门的批准。

范例一：

If a party to the joint venture intends to assign all or part of its investment subscribed to a third party, written consent shall be obtained from the other party, and approval from the relevant competent authorities shall be required.

参考译文：

如果合资企业任何一方有意将其全部或部分认缴出资转让给第三方，则应获得合资企业另一方的书面同意以及有关部门的批准。

范例二：

Ifa party proposes to transfer all or any part of its interest of the Joint Venture, the party shall notify the other party in writing of the terms and conditions of the proposed transfer at least thirty (30) days in advance.

参考译文：

如果一方提出转让其在合营企业的全部或部分利益，则该方应至少提前三十（30）天以书面形式通知另一方拟转让的条款与条件。

范例三：

If a party proposes to transfer all or any part of its interest of the Joint Venture to a third party, the other Party shall have a pre-emptive right to purchase such interest. If the other Party does not exercise its pre-emptive right of purchase within ninety (90) days after delivery of such notice, such other Party shall be deemed to have consented to such transfer.

参考译文：

如果一方提出转让其在合营企业的全部或部分利益给第三方，则另一方应拥有购买该利益的优先购买权。如果另一方在发出通知后九十（90）天内未行使其优先购买权，则该方被视为已同意转让。

范例四：

If the Board of Directors decides to increase the registered capital of the Joint Venture, either Party shall have to right to subscribe the increase in proportion to their contributions to the registered capital.

参考译文：

如果董事会决定增加合资企业的注册资本，任何一方均有权按其在注册资本的出资比例认购新股。

范例五：

Should one Party transfer all or part of its share of the registered capital of the JV Company, prior consent shall be obtained in writing from the other Party. In addition, the other Party shall have the preemptive right on the same terms and conditions and to the extent permitted by law.

参考译文：

如果一方转让其对合营公司注册资本的全部或部分出资，应事先获得另一方的书面同意。此外，该另一方在相同的条款和条件下，在法律允许范围内有优先购买权。

范例六：

Restricted by other agreements in this Article 5, when Quasi Transferor intends to transfer, sell or otherwise dispose all or part of its stock equity in the Company (hereinafter referred to as "transfer"), it shall notify the other shareholders in writing in advance thereof: (i) its intention to transfer, (ii) the rights and interests which it intends to transfer, (iii) terms and conditions of transfer, and (iv) the identity of the Quasi Transferee (called "Transfer Notice" collectively). The other shareholders have the right to decide at its own option within thirty (30) days after receipt of such Transfer Notice: (i) to purchase such stock equity in priority under the condition equal to that of the Quasi Transferee; or (ii) to sell the held stock equity in priority according to the shareholding proportion with the equal condition raised by the Quasi Transferee for purchase of stock equity.

参考译文：

受制于本第5条的其他约定，当拟转让方意图转让、出售或以其他方式处置其在公司中的全部或部分股权（下称“转让”），其应首先以书面方式通知其他股东：(i) 其转让的意图，(ii) 其意图转让的权益，(iii) 转让的条款，及 (iv) 拟受让方的身份（合称“转让通知”）。其他股东有权在收到该等转让通知后三十（30）日内自行选择决定：(i) 以和拟受让方同等的条件优先购买该等股权；或 (ii) 以和拟受让方为购买股权而提出的同等条件按持股比例优先出售持有的股权。

范例七：

If the other stockholder fails to make the above decision or it clearly notifies the Quasi Transferor that it has no intention to exercise the aforesaid rights within thirty (30) days after receipt of the Transfer Notice, the Quasi Transferor may transfer the relevant stock equity to the Quasi Transferee based on the terms and conditions mentioned in such Transfer Notice and provide one photocopy of such agreement sealed by the Company to other shareholders within fifteen (15) days after the agreement on such transfer has been signed.

参考译文：

如果其他股东未能在收到转让通知后三十（30）日内作出以上决定或其明确通知拟转让方其无意行使上述权利，则拟转让方可基于该等转让通知所述的条款和条件将有关股权转让给拟受让方，并应在签署关于该等转让的协议后的十五（15）日内向其他股东提供该等协议的一份经公司盖章的复印件。

范例八：

Notwithstanding the foregoing, both parties agree that the foreign shareholder may sell or transfer all or part of its rights and interests owned by it in the registered capital of the Company to its affiliated party without restrictions of Article 5 and Article 6.

参考译文：

尽管有前述规定，双方同意，外方股东可将其在公司注册资本中拥有的全部或部分权益出售或转让给其关联方，而不受第5条和第6条的限制。

◆ 知识点梳理

转让股权中的常用表达如下：

拟转让方	Quasi Transferor
拟受让方	Quasi Transferee
优先购买权	Pre-emptive right to purchase
向第三方转让全部或者部分股权	Assign/transfer all or part of stock equity to a third party

五、不竞争（Non-compete）

Except as agreed by the foreign shareholder in writing beforehand, the Chinese shareholder shall not facilitate each of its affiliated parties at any time during the period from the date when this Contract is signed to expiration of two (2) years after the Chinese shareholder ceases to act as the shareholder of the Company, directly or indirectly to induce or try to induce those which are or have been the customers, suppliers, agents, traders, distributors or clients of the Company or any person, partner or company which has got used of transactions with the Company to leave the Company.

参考译文：

除非经外方股东事先书面同意，自本合同签订日起至中方股东不再作为公司股东之日后的二（2）年期限届满之日止的这段期间内的任何时间，中方股东不得且应促使其每一关联方不得，直接或间接地招引或试图诱使任何公司当前的顾客、供应商、代理商、贸易商、分销商或客户或已习惯同公司交易的任何人士、合伙商或公司离开公司。

注：本句结构比较复杂，我们可以提取句子主干为：the Chinese shareholder shall not facilitate each of its affiliated parties to induce or try to induce those or any person, partner or company，句子结构为：主语 + 谓语 + 宾语 + 宾补，其中主语为 the Chinese shareholder，谓语为 shall not facilitate，宾语为 each of its affiliated parties，补语为 to induce or try to induce those or any person, partner or company. 下划线部分是时间状语，该时间状语导致句子宾语和宾语补足语被隔离，从而导致阅读困难。

六、陈述和保证（Representation and Warranties）

范例一：

The foreign shareholder makes the following representations and warranties respectively:

It is a validly existing company or for-profit organization incorporated duly according to its local laws;

It owns full legal right, power and authority to sign this Contract and all the contracts and documents to which it acts as one party mentioned in this Contract, and to observe and fulfil its obligations under this Contract and other such contracts and documents;

It has obtained all consents, approvals and authorizations and has adopted other required measures to sign this Contract and all contracts and documents to which it acts as one party mentioned in this Contract effectively and to observe and fulfil its obligations under this Contract and such contracts and documents;

There are not any civil, criminal or administrative judgment, action, lawsuit, request, claims, hearing, notice of violation, investigation or procedure filed to it in

China and its registered location, which are pending or potentially threatening, will cause major debts, fine, punishment or other obligations and will create negative impact on its capacity to fulfil this Contract through reasonable estimate.

参考译文：

外方股东在此分别陈述和保证如下：

其是一家根据其注册地法律正式组建并有效存续的公司或营利性组织；

其拥有全面的法律权利、权力和权限签署本合同以及本合同中所述的其作为签约一方的所有合同和文件，并遵守和履行其在本合同及该等其他合同和文件项下的义务；

其已获得一切同意、批准、授权且已采取其他所需措施，用以有效签署本合同及本合同所提及的、其作为签约一方的所有合同和文件，以及用以遵守和履行其在本合同及该等合同和文件项下的义务；及

在中国及其注册地无针对其而提起的悬而未决或具有潜在威胁的、经合理预计将会造成重大债务、罚款、惩罚或其他义务且会对其履行本合同的能力产生负面影响的任何民事、刑事或行政判决、行为、诉讼、要求、权利主张、听证会、违法通知、调查或程序。

范例二：

The Chinese shareholder makes the following representations and warranties respectively:

It is a validly existing company incorporated duly according to the laws of China;

It owns full legal capacity, right, power and authority to sign this Contract and all the contracts and documents to which it acts as one party mentioned in this Contract and to observe and fulfil its obligations under this Contract and such other contracts and documents;

It has obtained all consents and has adopted other required measures to sign this Contract and all contracts and documents to which it acts as one party mentioned in this Contract effectively and to observe and fulfil its obligations under this Contract and such contracts and documents; and

There are not any civil, criminal or administrative judgment, action, lawsuit, request, claims, hearing, notice of violation, investigation or procedure filed to it in China, which are pending or potentially threatening, will cause major debts, fine, punishment or other obligations and will create negative impact on its capacity to fulfil this Contract through reasonable estimate.

参考译文：

中方股东在此分别陈述和保证如下：

其是一家根据中国法律正式组建并有效存续的公司；

其拥有全面的法律能力、权利、权力和权限，用以签署本合同和本合同中所提及的、其作为签约一方的所有合同与文件，以及用以遵守和履行其在本合同及该等其他合同和文件项下的义务；

其已获得一切同意且已采取其他所需措施，用以有效签署本合同及本合同中所提及的、其作为签约一方的所有合同和文件，以及用以遵守和履行其在本合同以及该等合同和文件项下的义务；及

在中国无针对其而提起的悬而未决或具有潜在威胁的、经合理预计将会造成重大债务、罚款、惩罚或其他义务且会对其履行本合同的能力产生负面影响的任何民事、刑事或行政判决、行为、诉讼、要求、权利主张、听证会、违法通知、调查或程序。

七、税务、外汇管理（Taxation, Foreign Exchange Administration）

有关合资企业的税务条款如下：

范例一：

Joint venture shall pay taxes in accordance with the provisions of the relevant laws of the People's Republic of China.

参考译文：

合营企业应当按照中华人民共和国有关法律的规定，缴纳各种税款。

范例二：

Staff and workers of joint ventures shall pay individual income tax in accordance with the Individual Income Tax Law of the People's Republic of China.

参考译文:

合营企业的职工应当按照《中华人民共和国个人所得税法》缴纳个人所得税。

范例三:

Taxes on export products manufactured by a joint venture other than those restricted by China shall be reduced, exempted or refunded in accordance with the relevant provisions of the Chinese tax law.

参考译文:

合营企业生产的出口产品，除中国限制出口的以外，依照中国税法的有关规定减税、免税或者退税。

范例四:

The company shall pay taxes and enjoy preferential tax treatment in respect of its economic activities in accordance with the relevant laws and regulations of PRC and the relevant policies of (or applicable in) the Industrial Park.

参考译文:

公司应根据中国的有关法律法规和工业园区的有关政策（或适用政策），就其经济活动缴纳税收并享受税收优惠待遇。

有关合资企业的外汇管理条款如下:

范例五:

All matters relating to foreign exchange of joint ventures shall be handled in accordance with the *Regulations of the People's Republic of China on Foreign Exchange Control* and the provisions of relevant administrative measure.

参考译文:

合营企业的一切外汇事宜，按照《中华人民共和国外汇管理条例》和有关管理办法的规定办理。

范例六:

A joint venture shall, on the strength of its business license, establish accounts in foreign exchange and in Renminbi with banks in China, which shall supervise its receipts and payments.

参考译文：

合营企业凭营业执照，在境内银行开立外汇账户和人民币账户，由开户银行监督收付。

范例七：

Branches set up by a joint venture in foreign countries or in Hong Kong SAR or Macao SAR shall submit their annual balance sheet and annual profit statement to the State Administration of Exchange Control or its branches through the joint venture.

参考译文：

合营企业在国外或者港澳地区设立分支机构，其年度资产负债表和年度利润表，应当通过合营企业报送国家外汇管理局或者其分局。

范例八：

A joint venture may, in light of its operation needs, apply to financial institutions in China for loans in foreign exchange and in Renminbi. It may also borrow funds in foreign exchange from banks abroad or in Hong Kong SAR or Macao SAR in accordance with the relevant stipulations of the State and carry out the procedures for registration or filing for the record with the State Administration of Exchange Control or one of its branches.

参考译文：

合营企业根据经营业务的需要，可以向境内的金融机构申请外汇贷款和人民币贷款，也可以按照国家有关规定从国外或者港澳地区的银行借入外汇资金，并向国家外汇管理局或者其分局办理登记或者备案手续。

范例九：

After paying taxes on their salaries and other legitimate incomes according to law and deducting their expenses in China, foreign employees and employees from Hong Kong SAR and Macao SAR may remit the remainder of their foreign exchange out of China in accordance with the relevant stipulations of the State.

合营企业的外籍职工和港澳职工的工资和其他正当收益，依法纳税后，减去在中国境内的花费，其剩余部分可以按照国家有关规定购汇汇出。

范例十：

The staff and workers of the company shall pay individual income tax in accordance with the relevant PRC laws and regulations. All profits and salaries of the expatriate staff of the company may be freely remitted out of the PRC, provided that matters relating to taxation and foreign exchange control shall be handled in accordance with the relevant laws and regulations of PRC.

参考译文：

公司职工应按中国有关法律法规缴纳个人所得税。公司外籍员工的所有利润和工资可以自由的汇出中国，但条件是与税收、外汇管理有关的事宜须按中国的有关法律法规办理。

范例十一：

All transactions of the Company's foreign exchange shall be handled through the Bank of China or other banks authorized by the State Administration of Exchange Control.

参考译文：

公司的所有外汇交易，应通过中国银行或国家外汇管理局授权的其他银行办理。

◆ 知识点梳理

有关合营企业的税务、外汇管理常用表达如下：

个人所得税	Individual income tax
企业所得税	Corporate income tax
…产品享受减税、免税或者退税	Taxes on…are reduced, exempted or refunded
享受税收优惠待遇	Enjoy preferential tax treatment
凭营业执照	On the strength of its business license
资产负债表	Balance sheet
损益表/利润表	Income statement/profit statement
其外汇的剩余部分汇出中国	Remit the remainder of their foreign exchange out of China

续表

合营企业的一切外汇事宜，按照……办理	All matters relating to foreign exchange of joint ventures shall be handled in accordance with ……
在境内银行开立外汇账户和人民币账户	Establish/open accounts in foreign exchange and in Renminbi with banks in China
向境内的金融机构申请外汇贷款和人民币贷款	Apply to financial institutions in China for loans in foreign exchange and in Renminbi
公司的所有外汇交易，应通过中国银行或国家外汇管理局授权的其他银行办理	All transactions of the Company's foreign exchange shall be handled through the Bank of China or other banks

第二节　公司章程（Articles of Association）

公司章程是公司设立最重要的书面文件，主要规定与公司相关的基本事项和重大事项，如公司名称与住所、经营范围、经营管理、法定代表人、公司股东会和董事会的表决程序等，对公司经营具有重要意义，是公司组织与行为的基本准则，被称为是一个公司的“小宪法”（constitution）。公司章程英文可写作 Articles of Association，Articles of Incorporation，Constitution。

另外，中国有两种基本的公司形式，即有限责任公司（limited company）和股份有限公司（company limited by shares/joint stock limited company）。这两类公司本质上都是股东以其出资额为限对公司的债务承担有限责任。两者不同的是，股份有限公司将公司全部资产分为等额股份，且可以从特定或者不特定的公众公开募集股份，因此，在英美法中，股份有限公司被称为 public company（股份公开公司或公众公司）。而有限责任公司只能从有限人数的股东募集资金（中国公司法规定有限责任公司股东人数为 1－50 人），因此在英美法中被称为 closed company/private company（封闭型公司/股份不公开公司）。根据以上不同点，有限责任公司更多的体现的是人合性，而股份有限公司则更多表现为资合性。

另外，股份有限公司的设立方式，又分为两种形式，即发起设立（established by promotership）和募集设立（established by public share offer）。发起设立指发起人（promoter/initial incorporator）认购公司发行的所有股份，而募集设立则指发起人认购部分股份（不低于总计股份的35%），剩余的股份从社会公众募集。因此，股份有限公司只对发起人的人数有要求（2－200人），对股东人数只有最低要求（不低于2人），没有最高要求，由于股东人数多而且分散，也造成公司管理方面比较复杂。而有限责任公司的成立以及管理等方面，则相对简单。

基于以上差异，造成有限责任公司和股份有限公司之间的公司章程有很多的不同，特列表对比如下：

有限责任公司	股份有限责任公司
（1）公司名称和住所	（1）公司名称和住所
（2）公司经营范围	（2）公司经营范围
	（3）公司设立方式
（3）公司注册资本	（4）公司股份总数、每股金额和注册资本
（4）股东的姓名或者名称	（5）发起人的姓名或者名称、认购的股份数、出资方式和出资时间
（5）股东的出资方式、出资额和出资时间	（6）董事会的组成、职权和议事规则
（6）公司的机构及其产生办法、职权、议事规则	（7）监事会的组成、职权和议事规则
（7）公司法定代表人	（8）公司法定代表人
（8）股东会会议认为需要规定的其他事项	（9）公司利润分配办法
	（10）公司的解散事由与清算办法
	（11）公司的通知和公告办法
	（12）股东大会会议认为需要规定的其他事项

本章将主要围绕以上公司章程的内容展开对比研究：

一、公司名称和住所（Name and Residence of Company）

范例一：

The Company, domiciled at ________________, is registered with Zhuhai Industrial and Commercial Administration Bureau under the name of

________________ Electronics Co. , Ltd.

参考译文：

公司在珠海市工商行政管理局登记注册，公司名称为________________电子有限公司，住址为________________.

范例二：

The Corporation is incorporated in accordance with the *Company Law of the People's Republic of China* as a company limited by shares. The name of the Corporation is __________ and its residence is: __________.

参考译文：

本公司依照《中华人民共和国公司法》规定组建为股份有限公司，公司名称为______________，地址为______________。

范例三：

The Company is headquartered in ________ and may, according to actual development, make investment and establish branches and offices in foreign countries as resolved by the Board of Directors and approved by the competent authority.

参考译文：

本公司总公司设于________，可根据实际发展需要，经董事会决议及主管机关核准，在海外投资并成立分支机构或者办事处。

范例四：

The Company shall be an independent legal person under the Company Law. The Company shall be subject to the jurisdiction of and shall be protected by the Applicable Laws. The activities of the Company shall comply with the Applicable Laws.

参考译文：

按照《公司法》的规定，公司应为独立法人。公司受相关法律的管辖和保护。公司的活动应该遵守相关法律。

范例五：

The form of organization of the Company is limited liability company. The liability of a shareholder of the Company shall be limited to the registered capital paid-in or subscribed by such shareholder. Unless otherwise specifically agreed in writing by the shareholders, creditors of the Company shall only have recourse to the assets of the Company and shall not seek repayment from the shareholders of any debt, liability or obligation of the Company.

参考译文:

公司的组织形式为有限责任公司。公司股东以其实缴出资额或者认缴出资额为限对公司承担有限责任。除非经股东明确书面同意,公司的债权人仅对公司的资产享有追索权,无权要求股东对公司的债务、责任以及义务承担偿还责任。

◆ 法律知识补充

◇公司为拟制法人,具有独立人格,股东仅以其出资额为限对公司承担有限责任。在股东已经实缴出资的情况下,债权人不得要求股东承担公司债务,即使在认缴出资的情况下,股东也仅在未出资的本息范围内对公司债务不能清偿部分承担补充赔偿责任。

◇但是,在某些的情况下,可能会出现股东滥用股东有限责任和公司独立法人人格地位,损害公司利益的情形,公司法赋予了债权人一项保护自己的制度:公司独立法人人格否认制度,在英美法中叫揭开公司的面纱,即,债权人突破股东的有限责任和公司的独立法人地位,要求股东对公司的债务承担连带责任。

◆ 本节知识点梳理

Limited liability company	有限责任公司
Company limited by shares/joint stock company	股份有限公司
Be incorporated as a company limited by shares	组建为股份有限公司
Domicile/residence/place of business	公司住所地,营业地
Head office/headquarters	总部
Be headquartered in	总部位于
Paid-in capital, contributed capital	实缴资本
Subscribed capital	认缴资本
Disregarding the corporate entity	公司独立法人人格否认

续表

Piercing/lifting the corporate veil	揭开公司的面纱
Have recourse to the assets of the Company	对公司资产享有追索权

二、公司经营范围（Scope of Business of Company）

范例一：

The scope of business of the Company: production, sale and operation of ________.

The scope of business as approved by the registration authority shall be final and valid. The Company shall conduct business within the approved business scope.

参考译文：

公司经营范围为：________的生产、销售、经营。

经营范围以登记机关核准登记的为准。公司应当在登记的经营范围内从事活动。

范例二：

The scope of business of the Company is subject to approved items in business license.

参考译文：

公司的经营范围以执照核准为准。

范例三：

The scope of business of the Company shall be as follows: electronic parts and components manufacturing, product designing, international trade, integrated circuits; various semiconductor parts and components.

参考译文：

公司的经营范围为：电子零部件制造、产品设计、国际贸易、集成电路、各种半导体零件和组件。

三、公司注册资本（Registered Capital of Company）

适用于有限责任公司的条款如下：

范例一：

The Company has a registered capital of 1 million yuan, of which each shareholder contributes:

Name of shareholder:

Contribution:

Percentage:

……

参考译文：

公司注册资本总额为 100 万元人民币。各股东出资额及所占比例如下：

股东名称：

出资额：

出资比例：

……

范例二：

Shareholders shall contribute capital in currency.

参考译文：

股东以货币出资。

范例三：

The registered capital of the Company shall be: ________________.

The personal (or corporate) names of the shareholders, subscribed and paid-in capital contribution, schedule for making the contribution, and the type of contribution are as follows:

参考译文：

公司注册资本：________________。

股东的姓名（名称）、认缴及实缴的出资额、出资时间、出资方式如下：

范例四：

Each shareholder shall make its capital contribution in full amount within three years after the registration of the Company.

In case a shareholder refuses to make its respective capital contribution, it shall be liable to other shareholders who have already made capital contribution for breach of obligation.

参考译文：

各股东应当于公司注册成立后三年内足额缴纳其所认缴的出资额。

股东不缴纳所认缴的出资的，应当向已足额缴纳出资的股东承担违约责任。

范例五：

Capital contribution may be made in Non-monetary form, provided that relevant procedures must be gone through according to laws and regulations.

股东可以以非货币形式出资，但必须按照法律法规的规定办理有关手续。

范例六：

Once the Company is established, a capital-contribution certificate shall be issued to the shareholders, on which the following items are indicated:

(1) Company name;

(2) Date of registration;

(3) Registered capital;

(4) Name and contributed capital of shareholder;

(5) Number and issuance date of such certificate.

The certificate shall bear the legal representative's signature and the company seal.

参考译文：

公司成立后，应当向股东签发出资证明书，出资证明书载明下列事项：

(1) 公司名称；

(2) 公司登记日期；

(3) 公司注册资本；

(4) 股东的姓名或名称，缴纳的出资；

(5) 出资证明书的编号和核发日期。

出资证明书应当由公司法定代表人签名并由公司盖章。

◆ 法律知识补充

◇股东可以用货币出资，也可以用实物出资，如动产、不动产、知识产权、土地使用权等。

◇用实物出资的，应该办理评估作价手续；如果用以出资的实物上有权利负担的，应该办理解除权利负担的手续；用划拨土地使用权出资的，应该办理变更手续，将土地性质从划拨变更为出让。

有关出资的表述总结如下：

货币出资	Contribution in currency
实物出资	Contribution in real object, contribution in kind, Non-monetary contribution
向其他股东承担违约责任	Be liable to other shareholders for breach of obligation

以上的例子适用于有限责任公司。适用于股份有限公司的条款如下：

范例一：

The total capital amount of the Company shall be RMB Ten Billion Yuan accounting for ten billion shares, at a par value of RMB One Yuan per share. The Board of Directors is authorized to issue the unissued shares in installments. The issue price per share will be determined by the Board of Directors pursuant to the Company Law or relevant securities-related laws and regulations.

参考译文：

公司总股本为100亿人民币，占100亿股，每股面值一元，并授权董事会分批发行。每股发行价将由董事会根据《公司法》或相关的证券法律法规确定。

范例二：

The authorized capital of the Company is RMB 5 billion Yuan consisting of 500 million shares. The par value of each share is RMB 10 Yuan, and such shares can be issued in separate installments.

Among these shares, 5 million shares are reserved for the holders of employee stock warrants, and the Board of Directors is authorized to issue the shares in separate installments.

参考译文：

公司的法定股本为人民币50亿元，共计5亿股，每股面值为10元，可以分批发行。

在这些股份中，有500万股保留给员工认股权证的持有人，并授权董事会分批发行。

范例三：

The company's registered capital is RMB ________ Yuan. The company's registered capital is contributed in a lump sum (or in installments).

The total number of shares of the company is ________ shares, and the par value of each share is ________ Yuan.

Name of initial incorporator:

Number of shares subscribed:

Type of contribution:

Time of contribution:

……

参考译文：

本公司注册资本人民币________元。本公司注册资本实行一次性（或分期）出资。

公司的股份总数为________股，每股面值________元。

公司的发起人姓名：

认购的股份数：

出资方式：

出资时间：

……

范例四：

The share certificate of the Company can be all name-bearing share certificates and shall be signed by, and stamped with the seals or by signature of, at least three directors of the Company, and issued after duly authentication pursuant to the law.

参考译文：

公司股票可以是记名股票，由至少三名董事签名和公司盖章，并依法经适当认证后发行。

范例五：

The share certificates of the Company shall be in unregistered form, signed by, or affixed with seals of, at least three directors, and authenticated by the competent authority before issuance.

参考译文：

本公司股票为无记名式，由董事三人以上签名或盖章，经主管机关认证后发行。

◇与股份有限公司资本相关的表达方式如下：

Capital/capital amount	股本
Par value	面值
Name-bearing share, registered share	记名股票
Bearer share, unregistered share	无记名股票
Issue shares in installments	分期发行股份
Issue shares in a lump sum	一次性发行股份
Employee stock warrants	员工认股权证
Initial incorporator/promoter	发起人

四、公司治理机构（Corporate Governance Institutions）

公司的三大治理机构分别为：股东（大）会、董事会、监事会。股东（大）会是公司的最高权力机关，董事会是公司的执行机关，监事会是公司的监督机关。另外，董事会下管理层，负责公司具体的经营管理事务，并对董事会负责。一个公司的治理架构可以用下面的图示进行表示：

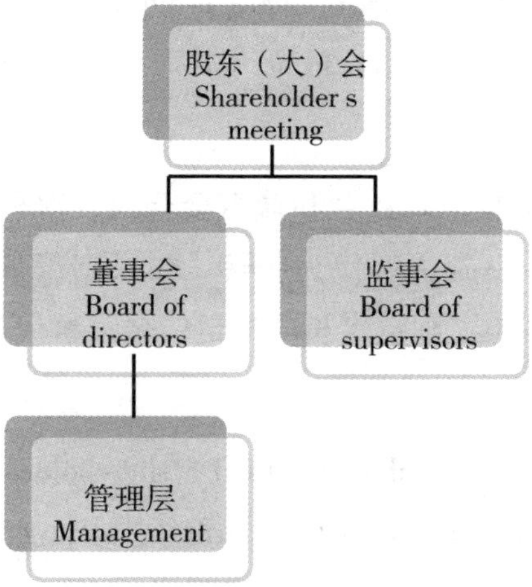

接下来将分别介绍三大治理机构及管理层的组成、职权和议事规则条款。

（一）股东（大）会（Shareholders' Meeting）

为了区分，公司的权力机关在有限责任公司被称为股东会，在股份有限公司被称为股东大会，股东（大）会分为定期会议和临时会议。一般而言，有限责任公司的定期会议一年召开两次，而股份有限公司由于股东人数多且分散，一般一年召开一次，因此也被称为年度股东大会。

1. 适用于两种类型的公司的条款如下：

范例一：

The Company shall set up shareholders' meeting, composed of all shareholders. The shareholders' meeting has the highest authority within the Company.

参考译文：

公司设股东（大）会，股东（大）会由全体股东组成，是公司的最高权力机构。

范例二：

The chairperson shall chair the shareholders' meeting and the meeting of the Board of Directors internally and represent the Company in external matters. Where the chairperson of the Board is on leave or unable to perform his/her duties, the vice chairperson shall act on the chairperson's behalf. If vice chairperson is also on leave or unable to perform his/her duties or there is no vice chairperson appointed, the chairperson shall designate a director to act on his/her behalf.

参考译文：

董事长对内主持股东（大）会和董事会会议，对外代表公司。董事长休假或无法履行职责时，由副主席代为履行。如果副董事长也休假或无法履行职责，或者没有副董事长，则董事长应指定一名董事代为履行。

范例三：

In case a shareholder is unable to attend a shareholders' meeting, he/she may issue proxy printed by the Company setting forth the scope of authorization by signing or affixing his/her seal on the proxy form for the representative to be present on his/her behalf.

参考译文：

如果股东无法出席股东大会，他/她可以签发由公司印制的授权委托书，载明授权范围，在委托书上签字或盖章，以使委托人凭委托书代表该股东出席会议。

范例四：

Any resolution of any type of shareholders' meeting relating to the amendment of the Articles of Association, an increase or reduction of the registered capital of the Company, or any merger, division, dissolution or change of corporate form in relation to the Company requires the affirmative votes by shareholders representing over two-thirds of the voting rights.

参考译文：

股东（大）会会议作出修改公司章程、增加或者减少注册资本的决议，公司合并、分立、解散或者变更公司形式的决议，以及选举或更换执行董事的决议必须经代表三分之二以上表决权的股东通过。

2. 适用于股份有限责任公司的条款如下：

范例一：

Shareholders' meeting shall be of two types, namely regular and ad hoc shareholders' meeting; the former shall be convened once a year by the Board of Directors in accordance with laws within six months after the close of each accounting fiscal year and the latter shall be convened in accordance with laws whenever necessary.

参考译文：

股东大会分为定期股东大会和临时股东大会两种。前者应在每个会计年度结束后的六个月内，由董事会每年依法召集一次，后者应在必要时依法召集。

◆ 法律知识补充：究竟在什么情形下会召开临时股东（大）会呢？有限责任公司与股份有限责任公司的规定是不一样的，对比如下：

有限责任公司	股份有限公司
Regular meetings shall be convened regularly in accordance with the provisions of the articles of association of the company. Shareholders holding more than one-tenth of the voting rights, or over one-third board directors, or board of supervisors or the supervisors (in the case of a company which does not set a board of supervisors) may propose to convene an ad hoc meeting. ——Article 40 of the Company Law of the PRC	SA shareholders' general meeting shall be convened once every year. A shareholders' general meeting shall be convened within two months of any of the following events: (1) the number of directors falls below two-thirds of the quorum stipulated in this Law or articles of association of the company; (2) the losses of the company which have not been made good equal over one-third of the paid-up capital of the company; (3) requisition of a shareholders' general meeting by a shareholder who holds over 10% of the company's shares or several shareholders who hold over 10% of the company's shares jointly; (4) the board of directors deems it necessary to convene a shareholders' general meeting; (5) the board of supervisors proposes to convene a shareholders' general meeting; or (6) other events stipulated by the articles of association of the company. —— Article 101 of the Company Law of the PRC

续表

有限责任公司	股份有限公司
定期会议应当依照公司章程的规定按时召开。代表十分之一以上表决权的股东，三分之一以上的董事，监事会或者不设监事会的公司的监事提议召开临时会议的，应当召开临时会议。 ——《中华人民共和国公司法》第40条	股东大会应当每年召开一次年会。有下列情形之一的，应当在两个月内召开临时股东大会： （1）董事人数不足本法规定人数或者公司章程所定人数的三分之二时； （2）公司未弥补的亏损达实收股本总额三分之一时； （3）单独或者合计持有公司百分之十以上股份的股东请求时； （4）董事会认为必要时； （5）监事会提议召开时； （6）公司章程规定的其他情形。 ——《中华人民共和国公司法》第101条

范例二：

Unless otherwise provided in the Company Law, a shareholder of the Company shall have one vote for each share held by him or her.

Unless otherwise provided in the *Company Law* or other Laws, resolution (s) shall be made at the meeting attended by shareholders holding and representing a majority of the total number of issued and outstanding shares and at which meeting a majority of the shareholders shall vote in favor of the resolution.

参考译文：

除法律另有规定外，股东对其所持每股股份享有一票表决权。

除非《公司法》或其他法律另有规定，股东大会应由代表已发行股份总数过半数股东出席，股东会决议由出席股东所占表决权的过半数同意方可通过。

范例三：

For regular shareholders' meetings, the notice of meeting shall be served to each shareholder at least thirty days prior to the meeting; for ad hoc shareholders' meetings, a notice of meeting shall be served to each shareholder at least fifteen days prior to the meeting. The notice of meeting shall specify the date, location and reasons for convening the meeting.

参考译文：

对于定期股东大会，会议通知应至少在会议召开前三十天送达每位股东；对于临时股东大会，应在会议召开至少十五天之前将会议通知送达每位股东。会议通知应注明召开会议的日期、地点和事由。

3. 适用于有限责任公司的条款如下：

范例一：

The first shareholders' meeting shall be convened and presided over by: (1) the shareholder who made the largest capital contribution; or (2) if all shareholders have made an equal capital contribution, then by ________________.

Shareholders shall exercise their voting rights at shareholders' meetings in proportion to their respective shares of capital contributions.

参考译文：

股东会的首次会议由：（1）出资最多的股东；或（2）如果各股东的出资相同，由________________召集和主持。

股东会会议由股东按照出资比例行使表决权。

范例二：

The board of shareholders shall exercise the following duties and powers:

(1) decide on the business direction and investment plans of the company;

(2) elect and remove directors and supervisors who are not representatives of the employees and decide on the remuneration of directors and supervisors;

(3) review and approve reports of the board of directors;

(4) review and approve reports of the supervisors or the board of supervisors;

(5) review and approve the annual financial budget and financial accounting plan of the company;

(6) review and approve the profit distribution plan and loss recovery plan of the company;

(7) resolve on increase or reduction of registered capital of the company;

(8) resolve on issue of corporate bonds;

(9) resolve on merger, division, dissolution, liquidation or change of company

structure;

(10) amend the articles of association of the company; and

(11) other duties and powers stipulated in the articles of association of the company.

The shareholders may pass a resolution in writing unanimously for a decision on the aforesaid matters without convening a shareholders' meeting and all the shareholders shall sign and affix their seal on the decision document.

参考译文：

股东会行使下列职权：

(1) 决定公司的经营方针和投资计划；

(2) 选举和更换非由职工代表担任的董事、监事，决定有关董事、监事的报酬事项；

(3) 审议批准董事会的报告；

(4) 审议批准监事会或者监事的报告；

(5) 审议批准公司的年度财务预算方案、决算方案；

(6) 审议批准公司的利润分配方案和弥补亏损方案；

(7) 对公司增加或者减少注册资本作出决议；

(8) 对发行公司债券作出决议；

(9) 对公司合并、分立、解散、清算或者变更公司形式作出决议；

(10) 修改公司章程；

(11) 公司章程规定的其他职权。

对前款所列事项股东以书面形式一致表示同意的，可以不召开股东会会议，直接作出决定，并由全体股东在决定文件上签名、盖章。

◆ 知识点汇总

有关股东（大）会的相关术语表达方式如下：

Regular shareholders' meeting	定期股东大会
Ad hoc/interim shareholders' meeting	临时股东大会
Convene the shareholders' meeting	召集股东大会
Chair/preside over the shareholders' meeting	主持股东大会

续表

Proxy	委托书
Shareholders representing over two-thirds of the voting rights	代表 2/3 以上表决权的股东
Issued and outstanding shares	已发行股票
Exercise voting rights in proportion to their respective shares of capital contributions	按照出资比例行使表决权

（二）董事会（Board of Directors）

董事会是一个公司的执行机关，对股东大会负责。有限责任公司的董事会人数是 3 - 13 人，股份有限公司的董事会人数是 5 - 19 人，其中上市的股份有限公司还设置了独立董事制度，要求董事会成员中必须设置独立董事，独立董事既不是公司股东，也不在公司担任除董事外的其他职务，主要职责在于对控股股东及其选任的上市公司的董事、高级管理人员，以及其与公司进行的关联交易等进行监督，并对公司重大事项发表独立意见。

1. 两种类型的公司均适用的条款如下：

范例一：

The company shall establish a board of directors. The board of directors shall be accountable to the board of shareholders and shall exercise the following duties and powers:

(1) convene shareholders' meetings and report to the board of shareholders;

(2) implement the resolutions passed by the board of shareholders;

(3) decide on the business plans and investment programs of the company;

(4) prepare the annual financial budget and financial accounting plan of the company;

(5) prepare the profit distribution plan and loss recovery plan of the company;

(6) prepare the plan for increase or reduction of registered capital and issue of corporate bonds;

(7) draft the plan for merger, division, dissolution or change of company form;

(8) decide on the structure of the company's internal management;

(9) appoint or remove the officers of the company, appoint or remove, upon

the general manager's recommendation, deputy manager of the company and the officer in charge of finance, and determine the remuneration of those officers;

(10) formulate the basic management scheme of the company; and

(11) other duties and powers stipulated by the articles of association of the company.

参考译文:

公司设置董事会，董事会对股东会负责，并行使下列职权:

(1) 召集股东会会议，并向股东会报告工作;

(2) 执行股东会的决议;

(3) 决定公司的经营计划和投资方案;

(4) 制订公司的年度财务预算方案、决算方案;

(5) 制订公司的利润分配方案和弥补亏损方案;

(6) 制订公司增加或者减少注册资本以及发行公司债券的方案;

(7) 制订公司合并、分立、解散或者变更公司形式的方案;

(8) 决定公司内部管理机构的设置;

(9) 决定聘任或者解聘公司经理及其报酬事项，并根据经理的提名决定聘任或者解聘公司副经理、财务负责人及其报酬事项;

(10) 制定公司的基本管理制度;

(11) 公司章程规定的其他职权。

范例二:

The tenure of the director is three years and is subject to reelection and reappointment. A director shall not be removed by the shareholders' meeting before the expiration of the tenure. In order to maintain the continuity of the company's business activities, the number of directors changed shall not be higher than one-third of the total number of directors each time they change office.

参考译文:

董事每届任期年限为三年，可连选连任。任期届满前股东会不得无故解除其职务。为保持公司经营活动具有连续性，每次换届，董事变动人数不应高于董事总数的三分之一。

范例三：

If the director's tenure expires without being re-elected, or if the director resigns during the term of office and the number of board members is less than the quorum, the former director shall still perform the duties in accordance with laws, administrative regulations and the articles of association before the newly elected director takes office.

参考译文：

董事任期届满未及时改选，或者董事在任期内辞职导致董事会成员低于法定人数的，在改选出的董事就任前，原董事仍应当依照法律、行政法规和公司章程的规定，履行董事职务。

范例四：

The Board of Directors shall be organized by directors. The Chairman of the Board shall be elected by the majority of directors present at a meeting attended by more than two thirds of directors. The directors may also elect a vice Chairman of the Board whenever they may deem necessary to carry out the Company's activities.

参考译文：

董事会由董事组成。董事会主席应由半数以上董事选举产生，且会议应由三分之二以上董事出席。董事还可以在公司营业活动必要时选举产生董事会副主席。

范例五：

In case the Chairman of the Board of Directors is on leave or unable to perform his duties for cause, the vice Chairman of the Board of Directors, if any, shall act as the Chairman. If there is no vice Chairman of the Board or the vice Chairman of the Board is also on leave or unable to perform his duties for cause, the Chairman of the Board shall designate a director to act as the chairman. If there is no such designation, the directors shall elect one from amongst themselves.

参考译文：

董事长休假或者因故无法履行职责的，由副董事长（如有）代理。没有副董事长或者副董事长休假或者因故不能履行职务的，董事长应当指定一名董事代理。如果没有这样的指定，则应由全体董事推选一人代理。

范例六：

In case a board member is unable to attend the Board of Directors' meeting, he/she may issue proxy setting forth the scope of authorization by signing or affixing his/her seal on the proxy form for another board member to present on his/her behalf. The representative shall serve as the proxy for one director only.

参考译文：

董事不能出席董事会会议的，他/她可书面委托其他董事代为出席，委托书应载明授权范围，并签字或者盖章。前述代理人，以受一人委托为限。

范例七：

The directors' meeting shall be held at least once every quarter, and the notice for the meeting shall specify the reasons for the meeting and shall be served to each director and supervisor at least seven days prior to the meeting. A directors' meeting may be held at any time in case of an emergency.

参考译文：

董事会会议应至少每季召开一次，召集时应将载明事由的通知至少于会议召开七日前送达各董事及监事；但有紧急情况时，可随时召集董事会会议。

范例八：

The board of directors shall make a minute about the resolutions made on the meeting, and the directors attending the meeting shall sign their names on it.

参考译文：

董事会应当对所议事项的决定作成会议记录，出席会议的董事应当在会议记录上签名。

2. 适用于股份有限公司的条款如下：

范例一：

The Company shall have eleven (11) to fifteen (15) directors to be elected at a shareholders' meeting through a nominating system from persons of full legal capacity to serve a term of three years. A director may be re-elected.

At least three (3) directors or one-fifth of all directors, whichever is higher, shall be the independent directors. The qualification, the limitations of shareholding and concurrently serving other positions, the methods of nomination and election and other related matters shall be subject to the applicable laws.

参考译文：

公司应通过候选人提名制度从具有完全的民事行为能力的人中选出十一（11）到十五（15）名董事，任期三年。董事可以连选连任。

全体董事中，独立董事至少应为三（3）名，或全部董事的五分之一，以较高者为准。独立董事的任职资格、持股限制和任职限制、提名和选任方法以及其他相关事项，依相关可适用法律法规办理。

范例二：

Other than what is required by Company Law, the resolution of the board of directors shall be adopted by a majority of all the directors at the meeting attended by more than half of the directors.

参考译文：

除《公司法》另有规定外，董事会会议应有过半数的董事出席方可举行，董事会作出决议，必须经全体董事的过半数同意方可通过。

范例三：

For the election of Directors, each share has the same voting rights equal to the number of Directors to be elected, and a shareholder may cast all his/her voting rights to one candidate or among several candidates; those candidates receiving more voting rights shall be elected as Directors.

参考译文：

选举董事时，每一股份有与应选出董事人数相同的表决权，股东可集中选举一人，或选举数人；获得更高选票的候选人当选为董事。

◆ 法律知识补充

本条款所表达的股份有限公司召开股东大会的一种表决方式，即，累积投票制（cumulative voting），其主要目的是为了保护中小股东的利益。累积投票制，是指股东大会选举董事或者监事时，每一股份拥有与应选董事或者监事人数相同的表决权，股东拥有的表决权可以集中使用。例如，某股东拥有100股，每股代表一票，如公司要选出5位董事，则该股东共有500票。通过累积投票，股东就可以将这500票投给1位董事候选人，或根据自己的意愿分投给选中的各候选人，这样就使小股东集中有限的票数投给自己意向的候选人，被选举出的董事就可以进入董事会从而增加小股东在公司的参与度。可以看出，采取累积投票制度确实可以缓冲大股东利用表决权优势产生的对公司的控制，增强小股东在公司治理中的话语权，有利于公司治理结构的完善。

范例四：

In the case that vacancies on the Board of Directors exceed, for any reason, one third of the total number of the Directors stipulated in the Articles of Association, or the number of directors is lower than the quorum required in the *Company Law*, then the Board of Directors shall convene a shareholders' meeting to elect new Directors to fill such vacancies in accordance with relevant laws, rules and regulations.

参考译文：

如因任何理由导致董事缺额超过公司章程规定董事人数的1/3或者公司法所要求的法定人数，董事会应依法召开股东大会补选新董事。

3. 对于规模较小的有限责任公司而言，可能不设董事会而只设一名执行董事，如下面条款所示：

范例一：

The Company shall not have a board of directors but shall have an executive director to be appointed by the shareholders' meeting. The term of the executive director shall be three years. An executive director may serve consecutive terms upon expiration of his term if re-appointed.

参考译文：

公司将不设董事会，而设执行董事一名，由股东会选举产生。执行董事任期三年，任期届满，可连选连任。

范例二：

The executive director shall be the legal representative of the Company, elected by the shareholders' meeting with a term of three years.

参考译文：

执行董事为公司法定代表人，由股东会选举产生。任期为三年。

◆ 知识点梳理

有关董事会的表达方式如下：

The board of directors	董事会
Be accountable to	对……负责
Legal capacity	行为能力
Tenure	任期
Subject to reelection and reappointment	可连选连任
Quorum	法定人数
Serve notice of the meeting	送达会议通知
Voting right	表决权、投票权
Cumulative voting	累积投票制

（三）监事会（Board of Supervisors）

监事会是一个公司的监督机关，主要监督董事、高级管理人员在经营管理公司中的行为，防止其滥用职权、损害公司利益情形的发生。股份有限公司要求必须设立监事会，而对于有限责任公司而言，则不强制要求设立监事会，但是要设置 1 – 2 名监事代为行使监事会的职权。

另外，对于股份有限公司而言，监事会中应当包括股东代表和适当比例的公司职工代表，且要求职工代表的比例不得低于 1/3，具体比例由公司章程规定。而监事会中的职工代表则由公司职工通过职工代表大会、职工大会或者其他形式民主选举产生。同时，董事、高级管理人员不得兼任监事，正如不能既当球员又当裁判员。

范例一：

The Company does not set up a board of supervisors. It shall have one supervisor (with a tenure of 3 years) appointed by the shareholders' meeting. The shareholders' meeting shall not remove the supervisor unreasonably prior to the expiration of his tenure. The executive director, manager or financial director shall not hold the post of supervisor concurrently. The supervisor shall carry out the following functions:

(1) Supervisor the Company's financial situation;

(2) Supervisor any behavior of the executive director or the manager that violates laws, regulations, or the Articles of Association of the Company;

(3) Demand the executive director or the manager to correct any of their behaviors that damage the Company's interests;

(4) Propose to hold an ad hoc shareholders'meeting.

参考译文:

公司不设监事会，设监事一名，监事由股东会委任，任期三年。监事在任期届满前，股东会不得无故解除其职务。执行董事、经理及财务负责人不得兼任监事。监事行使下列职权:

(1) 检查公司财务;

(2) 对执行董事、经理执行公司职务时违反法律法规或者公司章程的行为进行监督;

(3) 当执行董事和经理的行为损害公司的利益时，要求执行董事和经理予以纠正;

(4) 提议召开临时股东会会议。

范例二:

The board of supervisors shall consist of five supervisors. The five supervisors including: one candidate recommended by ____________, one candidate recommended by ____________, one candidate and two employee supervisors recommended by ____________.

Directors or senior officers shall not concurrently work as a supervisor.

参考译文:

监事会由5名监事组成，其中，_______推荐监事候选人1人，_______推荐监事候选人1人，_______推荐监事候选人1人，职工监事2人。

董事、高级管理人员不得兼任监事。

范例三：

The board of supervisors shall set one chairman, who are recommended by ________________ and elected by more than half supervisors. If the chairman of the board of supervisors is unable to perform duties or fail to perform the duties, one supervisor would be elected by more than half supervisors to convene and preside over the meetings of the board of supervisors.

参考译文：

监事会设监事会主席一名，由____________推荐的监事候选人担任，由监事会经全体监事过半数同意选举产生。监事会主席不能履行职务或者不履行职务的，由半数以上监事共同推举一名监事召集和主持监事会会议。

范例四：

The supervisor may attend the board of directors' conference as an observer without voting right and raise questions or make suggestions to the decision of the board of directors.

参考译文：

监事可以列席董事会会议，并对董事会决议事项提出质询或者建议。

范例五：

The board of supervisors shall make a minute about the resolutions made on the meeting, and the supervisors attending the meeting shall sign their names on it.

参考译文：

监事会应当对所议事项的决定做成会议记录，出席会议的监事应在会议记录上签名。

（四）管理层（Management）

公司的管理层由高级管理人员组成，高级管理人员简称高管，是董事会下设置的一个具体负责公司经营管理的机构，对董事会负责。

高级管理人员的英文表述，有多种表达方式：senior management personnel, senior managers, officers 等。个人认为 officer 最为规范，有些法律英语资料中将 officer 翻译为官员，实为望文生义。

究竟哪些人属于一个公司的高级管理人员呢?《中华人民共和国公司法》第217条规定:“高级管理人员,是指公司的经理、副经理、财务负责人、上市公司董事会秘书和公司章程规定的其他人员。”因此,法律中明确列为高管的人员有:经理(manager)、副经理(deputy manager)、财务负责人(chief financial officer)、上市公司的董事会秘书(secretary of the board of directors of a listed company)。上市公司董事会秘书的职位,仅出现于上市公司才有。各个公司根据其管理架构的不同,还可以设置其他的高级管理人员职位,如总经理助理、首席技术官、法务总监等。

范例一:

The Company may have one president and several vice presidents. The appointment, dismissal and remuneration of the president shall be resolved by two-third of the votes of the directors present at a meeting attended by the majority of all directors. The appointment, dismissal and remuneration of the vice president shall, under the recommendation of the president, be resolved by majority votes of the directors present at a meeting attended by a majority of all directors.

参考译文:

本公司设总经理一人,副总经理数人。总经理的委任、解任及薪酬应由出席会议的董事的三分之二表决通过,且会议应由过半数董事出席方可举行。副总经理的委任、解任及薪酬,由总经理提请后,应由出席会议的董事的过半数表决通过,且会议应由过半数董事出席方可举行。

范例二:

The president shall adhere to the resolutions of the Board to manage Company's affairs.

参考译文:

总经理依照董事会决议主持公司业务。

范例三:

Without written consent from the shareholder's meeting, the President and the Vice Presidents shall not concurrently assume posts in any other organizations in the same trade with the Company.

参考译文：

未经股东会书面同意，总经理和副总经理不得同时在与公司处于相同行业的其他任何组织任职。

范例四：

The Company may purchase liability insurance for its directors, supervisors and officers.

参考译文：

本公司可以为其董事、监事及高级管理人员购买责任保险。

◆ 法律知识补充

公司的董事、高管，对公司负有一种忠实义务（fiduciary duties），要求其勤勉尽责地为公司服务，该忠实义务，根据《中华人民共和国公司法》第148条，具体表现在以下八个方面：

A director or officer shall not:

（1） Misappropriating company's funds;

（2） Depositing company's assets into an account in his own name or in any other individual's name;

（3） Loaning company's funds to others or secure company's assets for the debt of any other individual without the approval of the shareholder's meeting, or the board of directors in violation of the articles of association;

（4） Entering into any contract or engage in any transaction with the company in violation of the articles of association or without the approval of the shareholder's meeting;

（5） Taking advantage of the conveniences to seek the company's business opportunities; engaging in the same trade as the company for his own account or for any other person's account without the approval of the shareholder's meeting;

（6） Accepting and possessing the commissions paid by others for transactions conducted with the company;

（7） Disclosing company's confidential information without authorization;

（8） Engaging in other activities in violation of his duty of royalty.

Income received by directors and officers in violation of the aforesaid provisions shall belong to the company.

参考译文：

董事、高级管理人员不得有下列行为：

（1）挪用公司资金；

（2）将公司资金以其个人名义或者以其他个人名义开立账户存储；

（3）违反公司章程的规定，未经股东会、股东大会或者董事会同意，将公司资金借贷给他人或者以公司财产为他人提供担保；

（4）违反公司章程的规定或者未经股东会、股东大会同意，与本公司订立合同或者进行交易；

（5）未经股东会或者股东大会同意，利用职务便利为自己或者他人谋取属于公司的商业机会，自营或者为他人经营与所任职公司同类的业务；

（6）接受他人与公司交易的佣金归为己有；

（7）擅自披露公司秘密；

（8）违反对公司忠实义务的其他行为。

董事、高级管理人员违反前款规定所得的收入应当归公司所有。

注：有些公司章程直接将《公司法》第148条的内容作为董、高的任职义务写入章程中，或者根据公司或者行业情况进行局部修改，一般都大同小异，此处不再举例。

◆ 知识点汇总

有关管理层的相关术语表达方式如下：

Officer	高级管理人员
Appointment, dismissal/discharge and remuneration of……	……的聘任、解聘和薪酬
Fiduciary duty	忠实义务
Liability insurance	责任保险
Legal capacity	行为能力
Secure the company's assets for the debt of any other individual	以公司财产为他人提供担保

续表

Concurrently assume posts in other organizations in the same trade with the Company	同时在与公司处于相同行业的其他组织任职
Engaging in the same trade as the company for his own account or for any other person's account	自营或者为他人经营与所任职公司同类的业务
Commissions	佣金
Disclose company's confidential information without authorization	擅自披露公司秘密

五、公司财务、会计（Corporate Finance and Accounting）

范例一：

The Company shall set up a financial and accounting system according to laws, regulations, and the rules of relevant authorities, and pay taxes in accordance with laws.

The Company shall, upon the end of each accounting year, prepare a financial and accounting report, which shall be audited by a Chinese certified public accountant.

参考译文：

公司应当依照法律法规和有关主管部门的规定建立财务会计制度，依法纳税。

公司应当在每一会计年度终了时制作财务会计报告，并依法经中国注册会计师审计。

范例二：

The Company shall adopt the calendar year as its fiscal year, which shall begin on January 1 and end on December 31 of the same year, except that the first fiscal year of the Company shall be deemed to have commenced on the business license issuance date and shall be deemed to have ended on the immediately succeeding December 31.

参考译文：

公司会计年度采用日历年制，日历年制从每年一月一日开始，到当年十二月三十一日结束；但是，公司的第一个会计年度应被视为从营业执照颁发日开始，到当年的十二月三十一日结束。

范例三：

The Board of Directors shall prepare at the close of each accounting fiscal year for the Company (1) Business Report, (2) Financial Statements, (3) Proposal of Distribution of Earnings or Making Up of Loss, etc. and submit the same to the general shareholders meeting for acceptance.

参考译文：

本公司应于每会计年度终了，由董事会制备：（1）营业报告书，（2）财务报表，（3）盈余分配或亏损弥补方案等，并提交股东（大）会审议通过。

范例四：

The Company's independent auditor shall be engaged by the Company as its auditor to examine and verify the annual financial report. The Company's independent auditor shall be appointed and removed by the executive director.

Quarterly and annual financial statements, and such other reports as the executive director may require to be prepared shall be prepared and submitted by the chief financial officer (or if none appointed, by the general manager) to the executive director. Such statements shall be in Chinese and English and shall refer to both RMB and any other supplementary bookkeeping currency adopted by the Company. Except as otherwise determined by the executive director, the annual financial statements will include the following statements (including footnotes):

1. balance sheet;
2. statement of profit and loss;
3. statement of changes in financial position; and
4. profit distribution recommendations.

参考译文：

公司应聘请独立审计师对公司年度财务报告进行审核。公司的独立审计师由执行董事聘请和解雇。

财务总监（如未指定，应为总经理）应该编制并向执行董事提交季度和年度财务报表和执行董事要求的其他报告。前述报表应以中文及英文编制，相关金额应同时采用人民币和公司采用的其他辅助记账币种表示。除执行董事另有决定外，年度财务报表应包括以下报表（包括说明）：

1. 资产负债表；

2. 损益表；

3. 财务情况变动说明书；

4. 利润分配建议书。

范例五：

After making the final settlement of account, the Company shall allocate the net profit ("earnings"), if any, according to the following sequence:

1. Payment of taxes;

2. Making up for loss in preceding years;

3. Setting aside 10% for statutory reserve except for when accumulated statutory reserve has reached 50% of the Company's registered capital;

4. The remaining, plus the previous year's unappropriated earnings, shall be distributed to the shareholders in accordance with their respective capital contributions.

参考译文：

本公司年度结算如有盈余，依下列顺序分派：

1. 支付税款；

2. 弥补以前年度亏损；

3. 提存百分之十为法定盈余公积金。但法定盈余公积金累计达本公司注册资本的50%时可不再提取；

4. 余额加计以前年度未分派盈余，按照股东出资比例分配盈余。

范例六：

The Company's reserve fund is for the purposes of loss compensation, business expansion, or capital increase.

参考译文：

公司公积金用于弥补公司亏损、扩大公司生产经营或转增公司资本。

◆ 知识点汇总

有关公司财务会计的术语表达方式如下：

Fiscal year	会计年度
Certified public accountant	注册会计师
Balance sheet	资产负债表
Income statement	损益表、利润表
Proposal of Distribution of Earnings or Making Up of Loss	盈余分配或亏损弥补方案
Profit distribution plan	利润分配计划
Statutory reserve	法定公积金
Capital reserve	资本公积金
Cumulative losses	累计亏损

六、公司的解散和清算（Dissolution and Liquidation）

根据《中华人民共和国公司法》的规定，公司解散的原因有如下几种：

（1）公司章程规定的营业期限届满或者公司章程规定的其他解散事由出现；

（2）股东会或者股东大会决议解散；

（3）因公司合并、分立需要解散；

（4）依法被吊销营业执照、责令关闭或者被撤销；

（5）人民法院依法予以解散。

公司解散之后，除了合并、分立的情形外，都需要清算，并编制清算报告，之后向工商局申请注销公司。有关公司解散和清算的情况，有些公司也会在章程中加以规定，如以下示例：

范例一：

The company will be dissolved when the operation period specified in the company's articles of association expires.

参考译文：

公司章程规定的营业期限届满时公司解散。

范例二：

The shareholders' meeting shall have the right to pass a resolution to terminate and liquidate the Company. Shareholders holding at least one-third of all voting rights may submit for consideration at the shareholders' meeting a resolution to dissolve the Company.

参考译文：

股东会有权通过决议解散和清算公司。持有公司三分之一以上表决权的股东可以在股东会上提出解散公司的建议，以供股东会审议。

范例三：

The Company may be dissolved when the circumstances for dissolution as stipulated by laws and regulations occur.

参考译文：

在法律法规规定的诸种解散事由出现时，可以解散。

范例四：

The Company shall establish a liquidation committee and commence liquidation within 15 calendar days of the date of occurrence of the grounds for dissolution. The liquidation committee shall be composed of the shareholders of the Company and shall exercise the following functions and powers during liquidation:

(1) to thoroughly examine the property of the Company and prepare a balance sheet and a schedule of property, respectively;

(2) to notify creditors by notice or announcement;

(3) to dispose of and liquidate relevant unfinished business of the Company;

(4) to pay all outstanding taxes in full as well as taxes arising in the course of liquidation;

(5) to clear the claims and debts;

(6) to dispose of the property remained after full payment of the Company's debts; and

(7) to participate in civil litigation activities on behalf of the Company.

参考译文：

公司应于解散事由出现之日起十五日内成立清算组，开始清算。公司的清算组由股东组成，在清算期间行使下列职权：

(1) 清理公司财产，分别编制资产负债表和财产清单；

(2) 通知、公告债权人；

(3) 处理与清算有关的公司未了结的业务；

(4) 清缴所欠税款以及清算过程中产生的税款；

(5) 清理债权、债务；

(6) 处理公司清偿债务后的剩余财产；

(7) 代表公司参与民事诉讼活动。

范例五：

Once the liquidation panel is set up, the Company shall stop all business activities irrelevant to liquidation.

参考译文：

清算组成立后，公司应停止从事与清算无关的经营活动。

范例六：

The sequence by which assets are paid to settle debts is: 1. Liquidation cost; 2. Employee salary, labor insurance cost and severance fee; 3. Taxes owed; 4. Company debts.

The remaining assets, after costs and debts are paid according to the preceding paragraph, shall be distributed to shareholders in proportion to their respective capital contributions in the case of a limited liability company and in accordance with the ratio of share in the case of a company limited by shares.

参考译文：

财产清偿顺序如下：1. 支付清算费用；2. 支付职工工资、劳动保险费用、经济补偿金；3. 缴纳所欠税款；4. 清偿公司债务。

公司财产按前款规定清偿后的剩余财产，有限责任公司按照股东的出资比例分配，股份有限公司按照股东持有的股份比例分配。

范例七：

Once the liquidation is finished, the liquidation panel shall prepare a liquidation report, submit the report to the shareholders' meeting and relevant competent authorities for approval, apply for deregistration with the registration authority, and publicize the Company's termination.

参考译文：

公司清算结束后，清算组应制作清算报告，报股东会及登记主管机关确认，向公司登记机关申请注销登记，并公告公司终止。

◆ 知识点汇总

有关公司解散、清算的术语表达方式如下：

Dissolve, dissolution	解散
Liquidation	清算
Liquidation committee/panel/group	清算组
Liquidation cost/expenses	清算费用
liquidation report	清算报告
Apply for deregistration	申请注销登记
Distribute the remaining assets to shareholders in proportion to their respective capital contributions	按照股东出资比例分配剩余财产

七、附则（Supplementary Provisions）

附则部分一般写明章程签署的时间、备案情况、修订情况等。

范例一：

This Articles of Association shall be made in six originals, with each shareholder keep one counterpart, and one original shall be submitted to the company registration authority.

参考译文：

本章程一式六份，每位股东各持一份，并报公司登记机关一份。

范例二：

This Articles of Association is hereby executed in ________ City, China by all the shareholders.

参考译文：

本章程由全体股东于________市签署。

范例三：

This Articles of Association/Incorporation is hereby agreed to and signed on ________ (date) by all the promoters of the Corporation, and the first Amendment was approved by the shareholders' meeting on ________ (date), the second Amendment on ________ (date).

参考译文：

本章程经本公司全体发起人一致同意，于________（日期）签署，于________（日期）通过股东会第一次修订，________（日期）第二次修订。

范例四：

Any resolution for additional provision to the Articles of Associations as approved by the shareholders' meeting shall be deemed an integral part hereof, and shall be filed with company registration authority.

参考译文：

公司股东会通过的有关公司的章程的补充决议，均为本章程的组成部分，应当报公司登记机关备案。

范例五：

These articles of association shall be construed by the Company's shareholders' meeting, and shall become valid upon registration of the Company.

参考译文：

本章程的解释权归公司股东会，本章程于公司核准登记注册后生效。

第三节　董事会决议（Resolutions of the Board of Directors）

董事会决议是公司董事就公司重大事项召开董事会进行表决而形成代表董事会意见的文件，英文写为英文为 Resolutions of the Board of Directors 或者 Board Resolutions。董事会是公司的执行机构，尤其对于股份有限公司，所有权和经营权分离程度较高，使得董事会的权力很大，董事会决议的写作十分严肃，且需具备一定的规范格式，有点类似于要式文件。本节将主要展示五份中英文对照的董事会决议、董事会会议记录、董事会决议公告等，以供参考学习。

________________ Co. , Ltd.
Resolutions of the Board of Directors
Action by Unanimous Written Consent
________________有限责任公司
以书面一致同意形式通过的
董事会决议

The undersigned Directors of ________________ Co. , Ltd. (the "Company") hereby adopt by this written consent, in accordance with the Company Law of PRC and the Articles of Association of the Company, the following resolutions with the same force and effect as if they had been adopted at a duly convened meeting of the Board of Directors of the Company and direct that this written consent be filed with the Minutes of Proceedings of the Board of Directors:

根据《中华人民共和国公司法》和《公司章程》的有关规定，________________有限责任公司（以下简称“公司”）的董事签署通过下列决议，该决议与按照法定程序所召集的公司董事会通过的决议具有同等效力，且已按指示与公司董事会会议记录一并存档。

WHEREAS, ________________/鉴于，________________;

WHEREAS, ________________; /鉴于，________________;

NOW THEREFORE IT IS RESOLVED that ________________________;

因此，公司董事会决议________________________。

FUTHER RESOLVED that ________________________.

进一步决议________________________。

IN WITNESS WHEREOF, the undersigned, being all of the Directors of the Company, have executed this Action by Unanimous Written Consent effective as of ________________.

以昭信守，公司所有董事通过书面一致同意签署履行本决议。本决议自____年____月____日起生效。

Signatures of all Directors of the Board of Directors

全体董事签字：

范例二：

Resolutions of the Meeting of the Board of Directors

The Board of Directors of the AAA Co. , Ltd. (“The Company” hereinafter) delivered the meeting circulars by means of written and fax notices on December 7, 2019. The meeting of the Board of Directors was held in the meeting room of the Company in the morning of December 17, 2019. / AAA 有限公司（以下简称“公司”），于 2019 年 12 月 7 日通过书面或传真方式向全体董事发出了《AAA 有限公司关于召开董事会会议的通知》。2019 年 12 月 17 日上午，公司在会议室召开了董事会。

Five directors shall attend the meeting and five directors were present. Some officers of the Company attended the meeting without voting right. The meeting was convened and held in compliance with laws, regulations, rules and the Articles of Association of the company. Directors attending the meeting, after careful deliberation and voting, had approved and adopted the following resolutions with four (4) votes for it, zero (0) vote against it and one (1) vote waived: / 本次会议应到董事 5 位，实到董事 5 位，公司部分高级管理人员列席了本次会议。会议召集和召开符合法律、法规、规章及公司章程规定。与会董事经认真审议并表决，以 4 票同意、0 票反对、1 票弃权审议通过如下决议：

1. xxx.

2. xxx.

IN WITNESS WHEREOF, these board resolutions have been executed, and deemed to be passed, by the board members of the Company in person or by proxy effective on the date of execution hereof. / 以昭信守，本董事会决议由公司董事会成员亲自或在本决议签署之日有权的代理人签字并通过。

Directors (signature) /到会董事签名

AAA Co. , Ltd. / AAA 有限公司

December 17, 2019/2019 年 12 月 17 日

范例三：

Resolutions of the Board of Directors of ____________

______________公司董事会决议

It is hereby certified that the following Resolutions of the Board of ________________ (company name) were duly passed at a Meeting of the Board held on ________ (date), and that they are in accordance with the Memorandum and Articles of Association of the said Company and have been duly recorded in the Minutes Book of said Company.

兹证明下述________________（公司名称）董事会之决议在________（日期）召开的董事会会议适时通过，并与该公司章程及备忘录相符且已在该公司的备忘录中予以适时记录：

Resolved/决议如下：

That ________ is/are hereby authorized on behalf of the Company/在此授权________（一人或多人）代表公司：

a. to withdraw or deal with any of the Company's property or securities/提取或处置公司的任何财产或有价证券，

b. to sign any indemnities or counter-indemnities to the Bank/向银行签署任何赔偿书或反赔偿书，

c. to arrange for the granting of credits or the issue of guarantees by the Bank at home or abroad/安排国内或海外银行批准贷款或出具担保，

That these Resolutions shall be communicated to the Bank and remain in force until an amending Resolution shall be passed by the Board of Directors, and a copy thereof, certified by any one of the Directors or the Secretary, shall have been received by the Bank/凡此类决议须告知银行并在董事会通过修订决议之前保持效力。因此，须将一份经一位董事或秘书认定的决议副本交予银行。

Director's Name 董事姓名 ________________ Signature 签字________________

Director's Name 董事姓名 ________________ Signature 签字________________

Director's Name 董事姓名 ________________ Signature 签字________________

Chairman/主席 ________________ Secretary/秘书________________

范例四：

MINUTES OF MEETING OF BOARD OF DIRECTORS
OF ________________ (Company Name)
________________（公司）董事会会议记录

TIME（时间）：
VENUE（地点）：
AGENDA OF THE MEETING（会议议程）：TRANSFER OF GENERAL MANAGER OF ________________（Company name）/ ________________（公司）总经理调动
MEMBERS PRESENT（与会人员）：

Mr.	Chairman of Board
Mr.	Deputy Chairman of Board
Mr.	Director
Mr.	Director
Mr.	Director

董事长：
副董事长：
董事：
董事：

The following resolutions are approved and adopted among the directors regarding the transfer of key personnel：/董事会关于关键人事调动的决议如下：

1. Mr. ＊＊（Resident ID No：＊＊＊＊＊＊＊＊＊＊），the present General Manger of the ________________（Company name），will be transferred to another position of China ________________（Company name）./ 原________________（公司）总经理＊＊同志（居民身份证号：＊＊＊＊＊＊＊＊＊＊）调任________________（公司）其他岗位；

2. Mr. ＊＊＊（Resident ID No：＊＊＊＊＊＊＊＊＊＊）is appointed the new General Manager of the ________________（Company name）and has full discretion in handling the affairs of the company./ 任命＊＊同志（居民身份证号：＊＊＊＊＊＊＊＊＊＊）为________________（公司）总经理，全权处理________________（公司）事宜。

In addition，other matters are discussed in the meeting. The meeting ended at 11：00 satisfactorily. The meeting minute is stamped with the official seal and signatures of all directors below：/ 会议还讨论了其他相关事宜，于上午 11：00 圆满结束。此会议记录需加盖公章并由董事会成员签字。

________________（CompanyName）（seal）
________________（公司）（公章）

Chairman of the board：________（Signature）/董事长：________（签字）
Deputy Chairman of Board：________（Signature）/副董事长：________（签字）
Director：________（Signature）/董事：________（签字）
Director：________（Signature）/董事：________（签字）
Director：________（Signature）/董事：________（签字）

范例五：

Share's code：　　Share's Name：　　No. ：
股票代码：　　股票名称：　　公告编号：

Public Announcement on Resolutions of the Board of Directors
董事会决议公告

Note：________ Joint Stock Corporation, Ltd. and its Board members undertake that the information disclosed herein is truthful, accurate and complete and does not contain false statements, misrepresentations or major omissions of any kind.
注：________股份有限公司及董事会全体成员承诺所披露的信息是真实的、准确的、完整的，没有任何虚假记载、误导性陈述或重大遗漏。

I. Informing of the Meeting/会议通知情况

The Board of Directors of ________ Joint Stock Corporation, Ltd. (hereinafter referred to as "Company") sent out the 2019 Annual Report of JMC and relevant proposals to all the directors on March 20, 2019. /________股份有限公司董事会于2019年3月20日向全体董事发出了公司《2018年年度报告》及相关决议案。

II. Time, Place & Form of Holding the Meeting/会议召开时间、地点、方式

The Board meeting was held in form of paper meeting from March 20 to March 31, 2019. The procedure of convening and holding the meeting complied with the stipulation of the relevant laws, regulations and the Articles of Association of ________. /本次董事会会议于2019年3月8日至3月16日以书面表决形式召开。会议的召集、召开符合有关法律、法规和公司章程的规定。

III. Status of the Directors Attending the Meeting/董事会出席会议情况

Eleven directors shall attend this Board meeting and eleven directors were present. /应出席会议董事11人，实到11人。

续表

IV. Resolutions/决议 The directors present at the meeting approved and adopted the following resolutions in form of paper meeting: /与会董事以书面表决形式通过以下决议: 1. The Board of Directors approved to submit to the 2019 Annual Shareholders' Meeting the following proposal on year 2018 profit distribution: /批准向公司 2019 年度股东大会提交 2018 年度利润分配及分红派息预案如下: (1) to appropriate for the dividend distribution from the profit available for distribution, which shall be equal to RMB ________ per share and shall apply to the Company's total share capital; and/自可供分配利润中，按总股本及每股________元计提分红基金; (2) to carry forward the un-appropriated portion to the following fiscal year. / 剩余未分配利润结转下一年度。 Profit distribution proposal: /分红派息预案: A cash dividend of RMB ________ (including tax) per 10 shares will be distributed to shareholders. Based on the total share capital of ________ shares as of December 31, 2018, total cash dividend distribution amounts shall be RMB ______. /每 10 股派送______元（含税）现金股息，按 2018 年 12 月 31 日总股本______计算，共计提分红基金______元。 The Board decided not to convert the capital reserve to the share capital this time. /本次不进行公积金转增股本。 There were 11 votes in favor of this proposal, 0 vote against it, and 0 abstention. /同意: 11 票; 反对: 0 票; 弃权: 0 票。 2. The Board of Directors approved the 2018 Annual Report of the Company and the Extracts from such Annual Report. /批准公司《2018 年年度报告》和《2018 年年度报告摘要》。 There were 11 votes in favor of this proposal, 0 vote against, and 0 abstention. /同意: 11 票; 反对: 0 票; 弃权: 0 票。 The announcement is hereby published. /特此公告。 Board of Directors ________ Joint Stock Corporation, Ltd. March 31, 2019 ________股份有限公司 董事会 2019 年 3 月 31 日

第四节　委托持股协议

委托持股协议，又称股权代持协议，是指委托人和受托人之间签订的一份股权代持协议书，英文可写为 Share Entrustment Agreement 或 Shareholding Entrustment Agreement。实际出资人因为各种原因选择委托他人代持股份，因而与受托人签订委托持股协议。实际出资人被称为隐名股东（实际股东），代持人被称为显名股东（名义股东）。英文委托持股协议中，一般用 actual shareholder, actual owner, actual investor, sleeping shareholder, shadow shareholder, the entrusting party 等词指委托人、隐名股东、实际股东；用 dummy shareholder, registered shareholder, nominee shareholder 和 the entrusted party 等词指名义股东、显名股东、受托人。

本节将主要围绕委托持股协议常见的典型条款。

一、委托持股及股权归属（Shareholding Entrustment and Equity Ownership）

范例一：

The Entrusting Party hereby agrees to comply with the terms and conditions stipulated in this Agreement and entrusts the Entrusted Party to hold the one hundred percent (100%) stock equity in ________ Company (hereinafter referred to as "Designated Equity"); the entrusted party hereby agrees to accept the entrusting party's entrustment in compliance with the terms and conditions stipulated in this Agreement and holds the Designated Equity in its own name.

参考译文：

委托方同意根据本协议规定的条款和条件，委托受托方以受托方名义持有委托方所有的________公司 100% 的股权（以下简称“指定股权”）；受托方同意根据本协议规定的条款和条件接受委托方委托，以自己的名义持有指定股权。

范例二：

Party A hereby entrust Party B to nominally hold its investment in the Company, which represent fifty percent (50%) shares of the Company. Party B hereby agrees to accept the shareholding entrustment and exercise shareholder's rights for Party A.

参考译文：

甲方委托乙方在名义上代持甲方在公司的出资，占公司股份的50%。乙方同意接受甲方的持股委托，并代甲方行使股东权利。

在股权代持协议中，名义股东仅仅代表实际股东持有股份，隐名股东享有股东权利，并享有股权收益和承担亏损，如以下例子所述：

范例三：

Since ________ (date), the Entrusting Party shall enjoy all the shareholder's rights and interests and assume all the obligations and responsibilities arising from the ownership of the Designated Equity; the Designated Equity shall not belong to the proprietary property of the Commissioned Party. The Commissioned Party will only serve as the nominal shareholder of the Company and will neither be entitled to the corresponding shareholder's interests nor bear losses and liabilities arising from the ownership of the Designated Equity.

参考译文：

自________（日期）起，因持有指定股权而产生的在公司的股东权利、利益、义务和责任均由委托方享有并承担；指定股权不属于受托方自有财产，受托方仅作为公司名义上的股东，不享有因持有指定股权而产生的相应股东权益，亦不承担相应的亏损和责任。

范例四：

Party B confirms that the shares are actually owned and invested by Party A, and Party B shall hold it in the name of Party B on behalf of Party A. Party B, in its own name, acts as an agent for Party A to hold shares, and exercises the rights of shareholders on the basis of Party A's wishes, and Party A actually enjoys equity income.

参考译文：

乙方确认股份实际上是甲方实际拥有和投资，乙方以甲方的名义代表甲方持有。乙方以甲方的名义代理甲方持有该股份，并根据甲方的意愿行使股东权利，甲方实际上享有股权收益。

范例五：

The entrusting party is the actual owner of the stock equity. As for the stock equity, unless otherwise provided in this Agreement, the entrusting party is entitled to all the rights provided in the Articles of Association, laws and regulations as well as to the corresponding obligations. Trustee does not actually get the status of the Company's shareholders and does not enjoy any rights of the shareholders.

参考译文：

委托方为代持股权的实际拥有人，就代持股权而言，除本协议另有规定外，委托方享有公司章程以及法律、法规所规定的全部股东权利并承担相应的所有义务。受托方并不实际取得公司股东地位，不享有任何股东权利。

◆ 知识点梳理

Entrusting party	委托方
Entrusted party/ Commissioned party/trustee	受委托方
Entrust sb. to hold shares in the Company	委托某人持有在公司的股份
Hold shares in the name of……	以……的名义持股
Nominal shareholder	名义股东
Exercise shareholder's rights on behalf of Party A	代甲方行使股东权利
Equity income	股权收入
Neither be entitled to the corresponding shareholder's interests nor bear losses and liabilities arising from the ownership of the Designated Equity	不享有因持有指定股权而产生的相应股东权益，亦不承担相应的亏损和责任

二、委托权限（Scope of Entrustment）

范例一：

According to this agreement, Party A entrusts Party B in Party B's name to exercise shareholders' rights including: named in the register of shareholders; participate in the meeting of shareholders and exercise the voting rights in accordance with Party A's will; exercise shareholder's rights provided in the Company Law and the Articles of Association of the company; take or pay related profit and investment; sign legal documents in the name of Party B.

参考译文：

根据该协议，甲方以乙方的名义委托乙方行使股东权利，包括：在股东名册中具名；参加股东大会并按照甲方的意愿行使表决权；行使公司法和公司章程赋予的股东权利；接收或支付相关的利润和投资；以乙方名义签署法律文件。

受托方不能直接收取股权收益的条款如下：

范例二：

The entrusting party entrusts the commissioned party to exercise other shareholders' rights on the entrusted shares except the right to earnings in the name of the commissioned party, including, but not limited to the shareholder's right to information, the right to convene the shareholders' meeting, proposals and voting. However, the commissioned party shall have the prior consent of the entrusting party, or based on the indication of the entrusting party, so as to exercise the rights of shareholders. The commissioned party shall exercise these rights accurately, effectively, without delay and shall promptly inform the entrusting party of the results of exercising the shareholders' right subject to the entrusting party's consent and instructions.

参考译文：

委托方委托受托方以受托方名义就代持股权行使除股东收益权以外的其他股东权利，包括但不限于股东的知情权、股东会召集权、提案权和表决权。但受托方应当在事先已经得到委托方的同意，或者系根据委托方指示的情况下，方得行使上述股东权利。受托方并应准确、有效、不迟延地行使上述权利。受托方应当将其根据委托方的同意和指示就代持股权行使上述股东权利的结果，及时告知委托方。

受托方可以直接接受股权收益的条款如下（但代为接受完需返还委托

方）：

范例三：

Trustee is not entitled to the corresponding right to earnings of the share, and any and all dividends, gains and all other bonuses paid by the company on the entrusted share shall be owned by the entrusting party, while the trustee shall take necessary and possible measures to return all of these dividends, gains and other bonuses produced by the entrusted share to the entrusting party promptly.

参考译文：

受托方不享有代持股权所对应的收益权，公司就代持股权支付的任何和全部股息、红利以及代持股权产生的其他收益均应归委托方所有，受托方应采取必要和可能的措施保证上述股息、红利以及代持股权产生的其他收益被及时支付给委托方。

◆ 知识点梳理

与委托权限相关的表达方式如下：

Register of Shareholders/ Share Register/Register of Members	股东名册
Named in the Register of Members of the Company	在公司股东名册具名
Exercise the voting rights in accordance with the entrusting Party's will	按照委托方的意愿行使表决权
Take or pay related profit and investment	接收或支付相关的利润和投资
The right to earnings	股东收益权
The right to information	知情权
The right to convening the shareholders' meeting	股东会召集权
The right to proposals	提案权
The right to voting	表决权
Be entitled to ……	有权……
Return dividends, gains and all other bonuses produced by the entrusted share to the entrusting party	将代持股权产生的股息、红利以及其他收益返还委托方

三、委托方的权利与义务（Rights and Obligations of the Entrusting Party）

（一）委托方的权利

1. 享有实际收益权

范例一：

As the actual investor of the entrusted shares, Party A enjoys the actual shareholder right in the ________ Company and the right to earnings produced by the entrusted shares; Party B owns the equity in its own name on behalf of Party A, but does not enjoy any right of earnings or disposition (including but not limited to disposition such as equity transfer, pledge, transfer etc.)

参考译文：

甲方作为代持股权的实际出资者，对________有限公司享有实际的股东权利并有权获得相应的投资收益；乙方仅以自身名义代甲方持有该代持股权所形成的股东权益，而对该等出资所形成的股东权益不享有任何收益权或处置权（包括但不限于股东权益的转让、质押、划转等处置行为）。

范例二：

As the actual owner, Party A enjoys the actual shareholder rights of the company based on the investment amount and has the right to obtain all corresponding investment earnings; for the shareholder's equity formed, Party B does not have any right to earnings or disposition (including but not limited to transfer, gift and waiver of equity, or any form of guarantee such as pledge etc.)

参考译文：

甲方作为代表股份的实际出资者，依据出资额对公司享有实际的股东权利并有权获得相应的全部投资收益；乙方仅可以自身名义代甲方向公司出资及代甲方持有该等投资所形成的股东权益，乙方对该等出资所形成的股东权益不享有任何收益权或处置权（包括但不限于股东权益的转让、赠与、放弃或设置质押等任何形式的担保等处置行为）。

2. 知情权

范例：

Party A has the right to know the company's operating status, such as the company's actual business status, financial status, decisions made, and profit distribution plan.

Party B represents Party A to participate in the company's shareholders' meeting as a nominal shareholder. In the event that it involves matters that require Party B to vote at the company's shareholders' meeting, Party B shall exercise voting rights in accordance with Party A's instructions. At the request of Party A, Party B shall notify Party A in writing of the voting result of the shareholders' meeting or provide Party A with a copy of the resolutions of the shareholders' meeting.

参考译文：

甲方享有对公司经营状况的知情权，有权了解公司的实际经营状况、财务状况、决策以及利润分配方案等情况。

乙方以名义股东身份代表甲方参加公司股东会，如涉及需要乙方在公司股东会上表决的事项，乙方应根据甲方的指示行使表决权。乙方应当应甲方要求将股东会表决的情况书面告知甲方或向甲方提供股东会决议的复印件。

3. 股份转让权

范例：

During the period of entrusted shareholding, Party A has the right to request Party B to transfer the shares held by it and the shareholders' rights involved to its own name or to any third party nominated by it as it deems appropriate. For the formalities, relevant legal documents involved therein, without prejudice to Party B's substantive interests, Party B must unconditionally agree and accept. In case Party B refuses to cooperate with the transfer of shares in violation of this agreement, Party A has the right to request Party B to continue the performance and requires Party B to pay a penalty of RMB 10,000.

参考译文：

在委托持股期间，甲方有权随时要求乙方将其代持的股权及相关股东权益转移到自己或自己指定的任何合适的第三人名下，乙方应无条件予以同意并及时予以配合协助和办理相关法律手续，届时涉及的相关法律文件，在不损害乙方实质利益的条件下，乙方须无条件同意并无条件承受。乙方违反本条约定拒绝配合办理过户的，甲方有权要求乙方继续履行，并要求乙方支付10万元的违约金。

4. 监督权

范例：

As the actual owner of the shares, Party A has the right to supervise and rectify the inappropriate fiduciary behavior of Party B according to this agreement and has the right to claim compensation from Party B for the actual losses caused by the inappropriate fiduciary behavior of Party B according to this agreement.

甲方作为代持股权的实际所有人，有权依据本协议对乙方不适当的受托行为进行监督与纠正，并有权基于本协议约定要求乙方赔偿因受托不善而给自己造成的实际损失。

5. 撤销委托权

范例一：

The entrusting party has the right to revoke at any time the entrustment to the trustee and to demand that the trustee transfer related equity to the entrusting party or any third party nominated by it.

参考译文：

委托方有权随时撤销对受托方的委托，并有权要求乙方依法将相关股权转至委托方或委托方指定的任何其他第三方。

范例二：

Where Party A believes that Party B cannot perform the fiduciary duty faithfully or diligently, it has the right to terminate the entrustment to Party B (but must notify Party B and the company 10 days in advance), and requests Party B to transfer the corresponding "entrusted shares" to Party A or the new trustee designated by Party A.

参考译文：

甲方认为乙方不能忠实或勤勉履行受托义务时，有权解除对乙方的委托（但须提前10日通知乙方及公司），并要求乙方依法转让相应的“代持股份”给甲方或甲方指定的新受托人。

（二）委托方的义务

1. 缴纳出资的义务

范例：

As the entrusting party, Party A has the obligation to make timely capital contributions in accordance with the company's Articles of Association, this contract and the *Company Law*. Should the company's shareholders' meeting make decisions to increase the registered capital in the future, Party A is obliged to increase the capital contribution in accordance with the value-added amount (if any) determined by the resolution of the shareholders' meeting.

Party A shall bear all the consequences (including the actual losses caused to Party B) caused by Party A's failure to perform its capital contribution obligations in time.

参考译文：

作为委托人，甲方负有按照公司章程、本合同及《公司法》的规定进行及时出资的义务。如将来公司股东会作出增加注册资本的决定后，甲方有义务及时按照股东会决议确定的甲方增资额（如有）来增加出资。

因甲方未能及时履行出资义务而导致的一切后果（包括给乙方造成的实际损失）均应由甲方承担。

2. 承担税费的义务

范例：

During Party B's shareholding period, all relevant fees and taxes (including but not limited to attorney's fees, audit fees, assets evaluation fees, etc.) related to the holding of shares shall be borne by Party A; when the shareholding person is changed to Party A or any third party designated by Party A, the fees incurred in change of registration shall also be at the expense of Party A.

参考译文：

在乙方代为持股期间，因代持股份产生的所有相关费用及税费（包括但不限于与代持股份相关的律师费、审计费、资产评估费等）均由甲方承担；在乙方将代持股份转为以甲方或甲方指定的任何第三方持有时，所产生的变更登记费用也应由甲方承担。

3. 风险承担义务

范例：

Party A shall bear all the investment risks to the company to the limit of its capital contributions entrusted. Party B is not deemed to bear the obligation of maintaining and increasing the value of the capital entrusted by Party A. Therefore, Party A shall not claim compensation or indemnification from Party B in respect of the loss from the assets contributed.

参考译文：

甲方应以其委托出资的数额为限，承担对公司出资的一切投资风险，乙方不对甲方委托的出资承担保值增值义务，甲方不得就出资财产的盈亏要求乙方承担补偿或赔偿责任。

◆ 知识点梳理

有关委托方的权利和义务的条款如下：

Entrusted shares/entrustment shares	代持股份
Fiduciary behavior	受托行为
Perform the fiduciary duty faithfully or diligently	忠实或勤勉地履行受托义务
Be obliged to……	有义务……
Without prejudice to	不损害……的情况下
Claim compensation or indemnification from sb.	要求某人补偿或者赔偿
Revoke/terminate the entrustment	撤销/解除委托
Transfer the equity to its own name or to any third party nominated by the entrusting party	将股权转让给委托方自己或者委托方指定的第三方

四、受托方的权利与义务（Rights and Obligations of the Entrusted Party）

（一）受托方的权利

参与股东会并表决的权利

范例：

The entrusting party entrusts the entrusted party to exercise shareholders' rights on the entrusted shares in the name of the entrusted party, including, but not limited to the shareholder's right to information, the right to convene the shareholders' meeting, proposals and voting. However, the entrusted party shall have the prior consent of the entrusting party, or based on the indication of the entrusting party, so as to exercise the rights of shareholders. Entrusted party shall exercise these rights accurately, effectively, without delay.

参考译文：

委托方委托受托方以受托方名义就代持股权行使股东权利，包括但不限于股东的知情权、股东会召集权、提案权和表决权。但受托方应当在事先已经得到委托方的同意，或者系根据委托方指示的情况下，方得行使上述股东权利。受托方并应准确、有效、不迟延地行使上述权利。

（二）受托方的义务

1. 不得对代持股权转让、处分或者设置担保的义务

范例：

Within the period, without prior consent or notification of the entrusting party, the trustee shall not transfer the shares, or set any mortgage, pledge, other security, priority, property preservation measures, seizure, custody, leasing rights, options or other forms of encumbrance (hereinafter collectively referred to as "encumbrance"), or conduct any other forms of disposition. Any debt of the trustee shall not affect the entrusted shares adversely.

参考译文：

在代持期限内，未经委托方的事先同意或通知，受托方不得转让代持股

权，不得对代持股权设置任何抵押、质押、其他担保、优先权、财产保全措施、查封、托管、租赁权、期权或其他形式的权利负担（以下合称“权利负担”），或者进行任何其他形式的处分。受托方的自身任何债务不应对代持股权产生不利影响。

2. 不得转委托的义务

范例：

Without Party A's prior written consent, Party B shall not sub-entrust the above shares and the equity to any third party.

参考译文：

未经甲方事先书面同意，乙方不得转委托第三方持有上述代持股权及其股东权益。

3. 办理相关手续的配合义务

范例一：

If the entrusting party requests the trustee to set pledge or other forms of burden on the entrusted shares, the trustee shall provide necessary cooperation in transacting related formalities subject to the requirements of the entrusting party.

参考译文：

如果委托方要求受托方对代持股权设置质押或者其他形式的负担，受托方应当按照委托方的要求，在办理相关手续方面提供必要配合。

范例二：

During the term of entrustment, Party A has the right to transfer the relative shareholder's rights to its own name or to any third party nominated by it as it deems appropriate, and Party B shall agree and cooperate to sign any relevant legal documents unconditionally.

参考译文：

在委托持股期限内，甲方有权将相关股东权益转移到自己或自己指定的任何第三人名下，届时涉及的相关法律文件，乙方须无条件同意，并无条件承受。

4. 会议通知义务

范例：

After receiving any notification of meetings (including but not limited to the shareholder, board of directors and the board of supervisors) from the Company, Party B shall inform Party A three working days in advance, and give Party A detailed information about the nature, content, time, place and attendees of the meeting, so that Party A could send people or authorize Party B send people to attend the meeting. Any person from Party B shall not vote on matters and/or resolutions without party A's written authorization.

参考译文：

乙方在收到任何有关公司召开会议（包括但不限于股东大会、董事会及监事会）的通知后，应于三个工作日内转告甲方，并详细说明该会议的性质、内容、拟召开的时间、地点及拟出席的人员等资料，以便甲方派人员或授权乙方选派人员出席该会议。任何乙方选派参加该等会议的人员在未取得甲方书面授权前，不得对该等会议的事项和/或决议进行表决。

5. 股权收益返还义务

范例：

Party B undertakes to transfer all future investment earnings (including cash dividends, bonuses or any other earnings) arising from the shareholdings it receives in the future to Party A and guarantees to forward the investment earnings to the bank account designated by Party A within three days after receiving the same.

参考译文：

乙方承诺将其未来所收到的因代持股权所产生的任何全部投资收益（包括现金股息、红利或任何其他收益分配）均全部转交给甲方，并承诺将在获得该等投资收益后 3 日内将该等投资收益划入甲方指定的银行账户。

6. 保护股权不受损害义务

范例：

Should the Designated Equity be frozen, sealed up, auctioned, sold off or any other losses incurred due to any dispute or litigation arising from the Entrusted Party's own debt problems, the Entrusted Party shall notify the Entrusting Party of the foregoing incident or losses and inform relevant creditors and the court of the nature of the Designated Equity to ensure that the Designated Equity do not suffer the aforesaid losses.

参考译文：

受托方因自身债务而导致纠纷、诉讼可能导致指定股权被冻结、查封、拍卖、变卖或受到其他损失时，应书面通知委托方，并向相关债权人、诉讼法院说明指定股权的性质，确保指定股权不被冻结、查封、拍卖、变卖或遭受损失。

◆ 知识点梳理

有关委托方的权利和义务的条款如下：

Set any mortgage, pledge, other security, priority, property preservation measures, seizure, custody, leasing rights, options or other forms of encumbrance	设置任何抵押、质押、其他担保、优先权、财产保全措施、查封、托管、租赁权、期权或其他形式的权利负担
Disposition	处分
Sub-entrust	转委托
Provide necessary cooperation in transacting related formalities	在办理相关手续方面提供必要配合
Equity be frozen, sealed up, auctioned, sold off	股权被冻结、查封、拍卖、变卖

五、代持费用（Entrusting Fee）

股权代持费用可以由双方自由约定，没有强制性的标准。当然也可以免费代持，如下例：

范例一：

The entrusted party has the entrusting right of shares in line with the agreement free of charge.

参考译文：

受托方根据本协议的约定代持股权，不收取任何报酬。

范例二：

The following cost and fee occurred to the entrusted party in the course of implementing the agreement shall be charged to the account of the entrusting party upon the confirmation and consent of the entrusting party:

(1) Service charges, stamp tax, capital gains tax (if applicable), other taxes and dues occurred;

(2) Other reasonable costs and fees resulted from the implementation of this agreement.

参考译文：

在受托方履行本协议的过程中，发生的以下成本和费用，经委托方确认和同意后，应计入委托方的成本，由委托方承担：

(1) 发生的交易手续费、印花税、资本利得税（如适用）以及其他税费；

(2) 因履行本协议发生的其他合理成本和费用。

六、委托期限（Term of Entrustment）

范例一：

The term of this Agreement (the "Entrusting Term") is five years, starting from the effective date of this Agreement. Unless otherwise directed by the entrusting party, the agreement will automatically renew for another five years upon the expiration of the period, and so forth.

参考译文：

本协议的有效期（简称"代持期限"）为五年，自本协议生效日起算。除非委托方另有指示，否则本协议在代持期限届满时自动续展五年，依此类推。

范例二：

The term of this agreement starts from the effective date of this agreement and terminates when Party A instructs Party B to transfer the entrusted shares to Party A or any third party nominated by Party A.

参考译文：

甲方委托乙方代持股权的期间自本协议生效开始，至乙方根据甲方指示将代持股权转让给甲方或甲方指定的第三人时终止。

范例三：

The term of entrustment commences from the day of validation of this Agreement and terminates on the day when any of the following circumstances occurs：

（1）The formalities for the transfer of equity ownership have been completed for all the Entrusted Equity which has been registered in the name of the Entrusting Party or any other Party nominated by the Entrusting Party；

（2）In compliance with the instructions of the Entrusting Party，the Entrusted Party has sold out the Entrusted Equity and transferred the equity transfer payment to the account designated by the Entrusting Party；

（3）This Agreement is revoked by the Entrusting Party.

参考译文：

委托期限自本协议生效之日开始至下述情形之一发生之日终止：

（1）代持股权已全部完成股权交割过户手续，已登记至委托方或委托方指定的他方名下；

（2）受托方按照委托方指令，将代持股权全部出售，并将股权转让款全部划至委托方指定账户；

（3）本协议被委托方解除。

◆ 知识点梳理

委托期限条款写作句式

· The term of entrustment commences from the day of validation of this Agreement and terminates on the day when any of the following circumstances occurs.

· The term of this Agreement（the "Entrusting Term"）is five years，starting from the effective date of this Agreement.

· Unless otherwise directed by the entrusting party，the agreement will automatically renew for another five years upon the expiration of the period，and so forth.

· The term of this agreement starts from the effective date of this agreement and terminates when Party A instructs Party B to transfer the entrusted shares to Party A or any third party nominated by Party A.

第五节 股权证书（Share Certificate）

股权证书，也成股权凭证，是一个公司在出售股份时向认购人颁发的一种所有权凭证，英文表达一般为：share certificate，stock certificate，equity credential 等。

我们直接通过几个中英文版本对照的例子学习一下股权证书的写作规范：

范例一（适用于股份有限公司）：

Share Certificate

Certificate No. ________　　　　20000 Shares

________ Joint Stock Co.，Ltd.

Incorporated in ________

Outstanding share capital RMB ________

Divided into ________ ordinary shares of RMB ________ each

This is to certify that (name，ID number) from (country) is the registered holder of Twenty Thousand (number of shares) ordinary shares of RMB (price) per share，in the above named Company，numbered 1 – 20000，subject to the Articles of Association of the Company，given under this Official Seal of the above company，this (date).

President (signature) ________

Company Seal ________

Secretary (signature) ________

No transfer of any the above-mentioned shares can be registered until the certificate has been deposited at the registered office of the Company.

参考译文：

股份凭证

证书编号________　　　　　　　　　　　　　　　　　　　　　　　　　　　　　　　　2 0000 股

________股份有限公司

注册成立于________

已发行股本________元

划分为________份普通股，每股________元

兹证明，（持有人姓名及身份证号码），国籍（国家），是前述公司所发行的贰万（持股数量）股普通股的登记在册的所有权人。股份编号为第1号至第20000号，每股（价格）元。该股份适用公司章程的规定。本股份凭证加盖前述公司公章，于____年____月____日签发。

董事长（签字）________________

公司盖章________________

秘书（签字）________________

上述股份的任何转让，须在向公司注册营业地交存本凭证后方可获得转让登记。

范例二（适用于有限责任公司）：

Share Certificate

Company Name: ______________Co. , Ltd.　　Domicile: ______________

Registration date: ______________　　Registered capital: RMB ________

Name of shareholder: __________　　Type of Share: original share

Shareholding ratio: RMB ______ , accounting for ________of the registered capital

It is to certify that (name and ID number of the holder) holds the above shares and is the original shareholder of ________Co. , Ltd.

________ Co. , Ltd. (Official Seal)

Chairman of the Board: (signature)

Shareholder: (signature)

Date of Issue: ________________

Note:

1. The share certificate is a certificate of shareholding of the shareholder. The shareholder shall enjoy the rights stipulated in the company's Articles of Association and company regulations and assume corresponding obligations. This share certificate shall not be altered, forged, privately mortgaged, transferred, or sold; otherwise, it will be invalid.

2. When shareholders transfer equity in accordance with the company's Articles of Association and the company's related regulations, the original shareholder must go to the company in person with the share certificate and go through the relevant procedures with the company. This share certificate allows for no handwriting save the signatures on it.

3. This certificate is valid only if it is signed by the shareholder and the chairman and stamped with the company's official seal, with a cross-page seal consistent with the counterpart held by the board of directors. This share certificate is in duplicate, with the shareholder and the board of directors holding one copy respectively.

参考译文：

股权证书

公司名册：_______________有限公司　　　　住址：_________________________
注册日期：_______________　　　　　　　　注册资金：人民币_______________
股权人姓名：_______________　　　　　　所属股权类型：原始股
股权占比：人民币_______，占注册资金比例为_______%

兹证明，____（姓名和身份证号码）____是_______________有限公司的原始股东，持上述股份。

_______有限公司（公章）

董事长：____（签名）____
股权人：____（签名）____
签发日期：_____________

备注：
1. 股权证书为股东持股凭证，股东凭此证享受公司章程和制度规定的权利，并承担相应的义务。本股权证书不得涂改、伪造、私自抵押、转让、买卖无效。
2. 股东依据企业章程和公司有关制度转让股权时，须持股权证书和原始股本人到公司办理有关手续，本股权证制作除签名处外其他地方不得手写。
3. 本证书经股权人、董事长签字及加盖企业公章并与董事会留底股权证书一致加盖骑缝章方为有效，一式二份，股权人和董事会各执一份。

范例三（适用于有限责任公司）：

Share Certificate

Company name: ________________ Co. Ltd.
Registration date: ________________
Registered capital: ________________
Place of business: ________________

Name of shareholder: ________________
Identity Number: ________________
Capital contribution: ________________
Means of contribution: ____cash____
Shareholding ratio: ________%________
Contribution date: ________________

Legal Representative: ________ (signature)
________ Co. Ltd. (official seal)
Date of Issue ________________
Place of Issue ________________

参考译文：

股权凭证

公司名称：________________有限公司
注册日期：________________
注册资金：________________
营业地：________________

股东姓名：________________
身份证号码：______________
股东出资额：______________
股东出资方式：____现金____
股东所占比例：_____%_____
股东出资日期：____________

法定代表人：________（签字）
________有限公司（盖章）
签发日期：________________
签发地点：________________

◆ 要点小结

从上面三份股权凭证中，我们可以看出股权凭证的格式和内容大同小异，主要分为以下信息内容：公司基本情况；股东基本情况；认购股份情况或者出资情况；落款（签发时间、地点、公司授权代表签字等）。

◆ 知识点梳理

Share certificate, stock certificate, equity credential	股权证书、股权凭证、股份证书
Means of contribution	出资方式
Shareholding ratio	持股比例
Be altered, forged, privately mortgaged, transferred, or sold	涂改、伪造、私自抵押、转让、买卖
Cross-page seal	骑缝章

第六节　银行资信证明（Bank Credit Certification）

银行资信证明指银行接受客户申请，在银行记录资料的范围内，通过对客户的资金运动记录及相关信息的收集整理，以对外出具资信证明函件的形式，证明客户信誉状况的一种证明文件，是投标时需要出具的资质。

也有定义为：资信证明是指由银行或其他金融机构出具的足以证明他人资产、信用状况的各种文件、凭证等。此类证明文件不论以何种名义、形式出具，核心是证明他人拥有某项资产、债权或具有何种程度经济实力等等。

本节将通过几个例子探讨如何进行银行资信证明的规范英文写作。

范例一：

Bank Credit Certification

It is to certify that ____________ Co. Ltd. established the basic deposit account with our bank on ________ (date), account number: ____________. Since the company opened the account, the capital transactions have been normal, and the company has good record in the aspect of capital settlement. In addition, the company holds no loan or unpaid interest in our bank as of today.

________ Bank (Official Seal)
Authorized signature: ________
Issue date: ________

Remarks: The bank shall only be responsible for the accuracy of the Company's record with the Bank in terms of loan and interest repayment, and capital settlement during the period as indicated hereinabove. The Bank shall not be responsible for any changes arising after the period as indicated in the certification.

参考译文：

银行资信证明

兹有____________有限公司基本存款账户，账号：____________，开户日期为________（日期）。该公司自开户以来，资金往来正常，结算信誉良好，且目前在我行无贷款或者未结利息。

________银行（公章）
授权人签名：________
日期：____________

备注：我行只对本证明所指期间内，被证明人在我行偿还贷款及利息、资金结算情况的真实性负责，我行对本证明所指期间之后上述情况发生的任何变化不承担责任。

范例二：

Credit Certificate

This is to certify that ________________ Joint Stock Co. , Ltd. is a legal entity registered in the People's Republic of China, with legal address at: ________. The enterprise has maintained an active and satisfactory account with our Bank (Agricultural Bank of China Zhuhai Branch) since ________ (date), the account number: ________, and performs RMB and USD settlement business.

The credit status of the company is in good standing without bad credit record, and it has performed well in the compliance with the regulations regarding settlement.

Agricultural Bank of China Zhuhai Branch (Official Seal)

Authorized signature: ________

date: ________

Note: this certification shall not be construed as a commitment, guarantee or warranty, nor shall it legally bind our bank in any way.

参考译文：

资信证明

____________股份有限公司，中华人民共和国注册的合法企业，法定地址：____________。该企业在自________（日期）在本行（中国农业银行珠海分行）开立账户，账号为：____________，账户往来正常，进行人民币和美元结算业务。

该企业信贷状况良好，无违反结算纪律的行为，无不良信用记录。

特此证明。

中国农业银行珠海分行（公章）

授权人签名：________

日期：________

注：本证明不得被解释为某种承诺、担保或者保证，也不得认为对我行具有任何法律约束力。

范例三：

Credit Rating Certificate

To: ________________

After careful evaluation and assessment, our Bank hereby awards your company with AAA credit rating. This certificate is intended to be used in the pre-qualification of project bidding of your company and it is valid until ________ (date).

Important statements:

1. This certificate can become effective after being stamped with the official seal of our Bank;

2. This credit rating is based on our Bank's evaluation of your business transactions maintained with our Bank before this certificate is issued;

3. During the validity of this certificate, the Bank reserves the right to reassess the credit rating of your company subject to the internal regulations of the Bank in the event that the credit worthiness of your company changes;

4. The relevant third party shall act based on its own independent judgment. Their behavior and the consequences resulted shall not be connected with this rating.

________ Bank (official seal)

Authorized signature: ________

Issue date: ________

参考译文：

信用评级证明

致：________

经慎重评估，我行将贵单位的信用等级评定为 AAA 级。本证明供贵单位在工程投标资格预审时使用。本证明有效期至________（日期）为止。

重要声明：

1. 本证明需加盖我行公章后方可使用；

2. 本信用等级系我行依据贵单位在本证明出具前与我行业务往来情况所作评价；

3. 本行保留在本证明有效期内当贵单位资信发生变化时，按照本行内部规定重新评定信用等级的权利；

4. 相关第三人应依据其独立判断行事，其任何行为后果均与本证明和木评价无关，本行概不负责。

________银行（公章）

授权人签名：________

签发日期：________

◆ 知识点梳理

与银行资信证明有关的表达方式归纳如下：

Establish/maintain/open an account with ________ Bank	在__________银行开立账户
The credit status of the company is in good standing.	公司信贷状况良好
The company has good record in the aspect of capital settlement.	公司结算信誉良好
Maintain an active and satisfactory account	账户往来正常
Perform well in the compliance with the regulations regarding settlement	无违反结算纪律的行为
Hold no loan or unpaid interest in our bank	在我行没有贷款或者未结利息
This certification shall not be construed as a commitment, guarantee or warranty, nor shall it legally bind our bank in any way.	本证明不得被解释为某种承诺、担保或者保证，也不得认为对我行具有任何法律约束力。
Credit rating certificate	信用评级证明
Credit worthiness	信誉，信用可靠性

第七章　接受客户委托类涉外法律文书

接受客户委托中所必不可少的两种基本文书是授权委托书（power of attorney）和委托代理协议（agency agreement）。

第一节　授权委托书（power of attorney）

授权委托书（power of attorney）是当事人把自己的民事权利授予委托代理人的证明文书，即指一个人授权他人作为代理人为授权人利益从事某类行为或某一特定行为的一种书面文件。

中外授权委托书的基本格式类似，主要分为三部分。第一部分：首部，主要包含“授权委托书”标题，民事委托人和代理人基本情况。第二部分：正文，写明代理事项的内容、权限和范围、委托权限、有无转委托和委托期限等，一定要列明代理权限范围，并写上“特别授权”或者“一般授权”。第三：尾部，委托人签字盖章，写明具书时间。

范例一：

Power of Attorney

This Power of Attorney (“POA”) is made on [11 May 2019] by Party A, a ______________ organized and existing under the laws of Singapore with its [registered address] at ____________________________ (hereinafter referred to as the “Principal”) to grant certain authority as prescribed in this POA to: ______________, a citizen of the People's Republic of China with ID Number ____________________________ (hereinafter referred to as the “Attorney”).

1. Powers and Appointment

1.1 The Principal hereby entrusts the Attorney to be its true and lawful Attorney with full power and authority to act on behalf of the Principal to handle the following matters in ____________, Guangdong, China:

(a) Signing and executing a Shareholders Agreement with Party A as well as related documents/agreements as contemplated therein;

(b) Undertaking all procedures relating to [ADMINISTRATIVE PROCEDURE], including without limitation the review, preparation, signing and submission of documents required by applicable laws, rules and regulations and relevant authorities;

1.2 The Principal hereby undertakes to ratify and confirm all that the Attorney may do or cause to be done in conformity with this POA.

2. Term

This POA shall take effect on the date stated above and shall remain effective until ____________, unless earlier terminated by the Principal on written notice to the Attorney.

3. Indemnity

The Principal shall indemnify the Attorney against all liabilities, costs, expenses, damages and losses of any kind whatsoever (collectively, "Losses") incurred in connection with any action taken in good faith pursuant to this POA. This indemnity shall not cover Losses arising from the gross negligence or wilful misconduct of the Attorney.

4. General Provisions

4.1 This POA shall be governed by and construed in accordance with the laws of Singapore.

4.2 This POA is executed in both the Chinese language and the English language. Both language versions shall be equally valid. In case of any discrepancy, the English version shall prevail.

IN WITNESS WHEREOF this POA has been executed on the date first written above.

参考译文：

授权委托书

本授权委托书（“授权委托书”）于【2019年5月11日】由甲方，一家根据新加坡法律成立并存续的________，【注册地址】__________________（以下简称“委托人”）签订，以向下列各方授予本授权委托书规定的某些权力：

一位身份证号码为______________的中华人民共和国公民（以下简称“代理人”）。

1. 权力与任命

1.1 委托人特此委托代理人为其真实合法的代理人，全权代表委托人在中国广东省内处理下列事项：

（a）与乙方签署合资公司章程以及该等文件中拟议的相关文件/协议；

（b）【填入行政程序或行政事项】，包括但不限于审查、准备、签署和提交适用法律、法规和规章以及有关部门所要求的文件；

1.2 委托人在此承诺批准并确认代理人可以按照本授权委托书的规定完成所有事宜。

2. 期限

本授权委托书自上述日期起生效，且直至______________持续有效，除非委托人向代理人发出书面通知提前终止本授权委托书。

3. 赔偿

委托人应赔偿代理人就根据本授权委托书善意实施的任何行为而招致的所有责任、成本、费用、损害赔偿和损失（合称“损失”）。本赔偿范围不包括因代理人的重大过失或故意不当行为造成的损失。

4. 一般规定

4.1 本授权委托书及其解释应适用新加坡法律。

4.2 本授权委托书以中文和英文签署。两种文本具有同等效力。当发生不一致时，以英文版本为准。

本授权委托书已于首页所载日期签署，以昭信守。

签字：________________

姓名：________________

职位：________________

范例二：

Power of Attorney

Principal：XXX，female，residence：XXXXXX，Tel：134XXXXXXXX.

Agent：XX attorney-at-law of Guangdong LangQian Law Firm，Tel：138XXXXXXXX，address：15th Floor，CITIC South Airlines International Plaza，42 Haibin South Road，Jida，Xiangzhou District，Zhuhai City，Guangdong Province.

The above-mentioned trustee is entrusted to act as our agent ad litem in the commercial housing sales dispute with Zhuhai XXX Co.，Ltd.

The proxy authority of the authorized agent ad litem are as follows：

1. Special authorization.

2. Conduct all litigation activities.

3. Deliver and sign relevant litigation documents.

4. Participate in reconciliation and mediation.

Principal：

Date：

参考译文：

授权委托书

委托人：XXX，女，住所地：XXXXXX，电话：134XXXXXXXX。

受托人：XX，广东朗乾律师事务所律师，电话：138XXXXXXXX，地址：珠海市吉大海滨南路42号中信南航国际广场15楼。

现委托上列受托人在我方与珠海XXXX有限公司商品房销售合同纠纷一案中，作为我方委托代理人。

委托代理人的代理权限为下列第1－4项：

1. 特别授权。

2. 进行全部诉讼活动。

3. 送达、签收有关诉讼文书。

4. 参与和解、调解。

委托人：

年 月 日

范例三：

Power of Attorney

Principal: XXXX Company, Document No. :

Address: XXXXX.

Legal representative:

Trustee: XXX, attorney-at-law of Guangdong XX Law Firm, License No. :

Address: XXXXX.

XX Animation Co. , Ltd. is the producer and copyright owner of "XXX" cartoon. The " XXX " cartoon is adapted from the comic book of "XXX", whose copyright is owned by YYY Production Co. , Ltd.

In order to safeguard the various civil rights of the Principal and deal with various disputes between the Principal and the third party, the Trustee aforementioned is authorized to act for the Principal in all matters related with the Principal, including but not limited to legal disputes such as litigation, arbitration and negations within the territory of the People's Republic of China (except for Hong Kong, Macao and Taiwan).

The legal disputes herein refer to infringement to various types of intellectual property rights, including but not limited to copyright (including but not limited to the comic books, cartoons, films and television dramas, publications and their character images of "XXX"), trademark (including but not limited to XXX and XXX portrait), the right of trade name, various types of contract disputes and other types of legal disputes.

The rights exercised by the Trustee in its sole discretion include, but are not limited to, the following rights (any trustee may exercise the following rights separately):

1. Apply to the notary office for the notarization of the evidence preservation related to all kinds of matters, submit relevant materials, sign relevant documents, and handle other matters;

2. Complain to the e-commerce platform, apply for the authentic information of relevant third parties and handle all matters related to the complaint;

3. Report and complain to relevant administrative departments. Check and retrieve the relevant files related to the complaint case, and handle all matters related to the complaint.

4. Submit, deliver, and sign relevant legal instruments;

5. File lawsuits, apply for property preservation, pay litigation costs, and participate in all litigation activities in the first instance;

6. Lodge appeals and petitions, pay litigation costs, participation in all litigation activities of the second instance and retrial;

7. Acknowledge, abandon, change the claim, reconcile or file a counterclaim in the first instance, second instance litigation, enforcement and appeal, and apply for additional defendants;

8. Apply for enforcement, receive court refund and receive implementation fund and properties;

9. Sign and receive all kinds of legal instruments such as the complaint, the property preservation application, the statement of appeal, the answer to complaint, the enforcement application, and the petition etc. in the course of the first instance, second instance, enforcement, petition etc procedures.

10. Inquire the correspondent registration file in relevant authorities;

11. Inquire relevant case files;

12. Handle various types of certification, investigation and evidence collection;

13. Issue a statement, issue lawyer's letter, and a legal opinion;

14. Participate in non-litigation mediation, negotiation, and sign settlement agreement with a third party;

15. Conduct other matters that are beneficial to the Principal.

This power of attorney is valid for three years as from the date of signing. The trustee has the right to sub-entrust a third party.

Principal:

Date:

参考译文:

授权委托书

委托人: XXXX 公司, 证件号:

住址: XXXXX。

法定代表人:

受托人: XXX, 广东 XX 律师事务所律师, 证件号:

住址: XXXXX。

本公司日本 XX 株式会社 (XXX Animation Co., Ltd.) 是《XXX》动画片的制作公司和版权所有者。《XXX》动画片是改编自 XXX Production Co., Ltd. 拥有著作权的《XXX》漫画书。

为了维护委托人的各类民事权利, 处理委托人与第三方之间的各类纠纷, 特授权上列受托人全权代表委托人在中华人民共和国 (港、澳、台除外) 境内代理一切与委托人相关的诉讼、仲裁、谈判等全部法律纠纷。

本委托书所指的法律纠纷包括但不限于著作权 (包括但不限于《XXX》漫画书、动画片、影视剧等各类出版物及其人物形象等)、商标权 (包括但不限于 XXX 及 XXX 肖像图等)、企业名称权等各类知识产权侵权纠纷、各类合同纠纷及其他类型的法律纠纷等。

受托人全权行使的权利包括但不限于以下权利 (任一受托人均可单独行使以下权利):

1. 向公证机构申请办理各类事项的保全证据公证, 提交相关材料, 签署相关文件, 处理一切事宜;

2. 向电子商务平台投诉, 申请调取相关第三方的真实信息及与投诉有关的一切事宜;

3. 向相关行政部门举报、投诉。查阅和调取投诉案件的有关案卷资料, 处理有关投诉案件的一切事宜。

4. 提交、送达、签收有关法律文书;

5. 代为起诉、申请财产保全，缴纳诉讼费用、参加一审的全部诉讼活动；

6. 提出上诉和申诉，缴纳诉讼费用，参加二审、再审的全部诉讼活动；

7. 在一审、二审诉讼、强制执行及申诉过程中，代为承认、放弃、变更诉讼请求、进行和解或者提出反诉，代为申请追加被告；

8. 代为申请强制执行，代为接收法院退费、执行款物；

9. 在一审、二审、强制执行、申诉等诉讼阶段中，代为签署起诉状、财产保全申请书、上诉状、答辩状、强制执行申请书、申诉书等相关法律文件；

10. 代为到相应机关查询相应登记档案；

11. 代为查阅相关案件档案资料；

12. 代为办理各类认证、调查取证；

13. 代为发表声明、出具律师函、法律意见书；

14. 代为参加与第三人的非诉讼调解、谈判、签署和解协议；

15. 代为办理其他有利于委托人的事项。

本授权自签署之日起三年内有效。受托人有转委托权。

委托人：XXXXX
XXXX 年 X 月 X 日

范例四：

Power of Attorney

We, CC Garments Company, a corporation duly organized and existing pursuant to the Company Law of the People's Republic of China with its office in Xiangzhou District, Zhuhai, hereby appoints and empowers DDD from ABC Law Firm to be our agent ad litem in the first and second instances and/or retrial respectively, with respect to the case of Kaka Trade Company v. CC Garments Company.

We further appoint and empower the abovementioned attorney:

1. to prepare the answer and appear before a competent court;

2. to counter-claim, to investigate, collect, and deliver to the relevant court any related evidence;

3. to arrange reconciliation;

4. to accept any mediation presided over by the court;

5. to admit, waive or modify claims;

6. to prepare the statement of appeal and file an appeal;

7. to apply for retrial;

8. to apply for measures of evidence preservation and measures of property preservation during or before the proceedings;

9. to apply for enforcement of valid court orders;

10. to accept service of court documents;

11. to sign and receive verdicts, judgments, summons, decisions and any other court documents;

12. to handle all other issues in connection with the said matters.

In particular, we appoint and empower Mr. DDD to nominate and authorize any other lawyer of the law firm to engage in, fulfill and implement any of the matters and issues as contemplated herein. We further grant our recognition to the acts made and the documents signed by the attorney mentioned above within the limits of the powers granted herein.

We hereby confirm that this Power of Attorney shall remain in full force from the date of signature and/or seal through the completion of the matters as set forth in this Power of Attorney.

In witness whereof we cause this Power of Attorney to be duly signed and/or sealed.

Principal: CC Garments Company

Date:

参考译文:

民事授权委托书

本民事授权委托书委托方 CC 服装公司是依据《中华人民共和国公司法》成立的有限责任公司，办事处设在珠海市香洲区。该公司授权委托 ABC 律师事务所的 DD 先生就卡卡贸易公司诉 HCC 服装公司一案作为该方一审、二审或再审的诉讼代理人。

委托事项为:

1. 代为答辩，出庭；
2. 提出反诉，调查取证，并向有关法庭递送有关证据；
3. 进行和解；
4. 接受法庭调解；
5. 接受或放弃或变更诉讼请求；
6. 准备上诉状和提出上诉；
7. 申请再审；
8. 申请在审理中或审理前的证据保全及财产保全措施；
9. 申请强制执行法庭有效文件；
10. 接收送达法庭文件；
11. 签收裁决、判决、传票及任何其他的法庭文件；
12. 处理与所有与上述事务有关的相应问题。

DDD 先生有权提议和委托律师事务所的其他律师参与，履行并解决与此案相关的各事项。我们认可上述指定的委托人在授权范围内所做的行为及签署的文件。

我公司特此确认该授权委托书自签署之日起及执行期间有效。

我公司于证人面前在这份授权委托书上签字盖章。

委托人：CC 服装公司

日期：

◆ 授权委托书的写作要点：

第一，注意在授权委托书中使用正式程度较高的词语，如 appoint（委派），act on behalf of（代理），bring a file against（提起诉讼），pursuant to（依据），in regard to（就），in the event of（如果）等。

第二，注意法律专业术语的正确表达，如诉讼代理人（agent ad litem），答辩（answer），出庭（appear before the competent court），反诉（counter-claim），调查取证（investigate and collect evidence），递送（deliver），和解（make compromise），法院调解（mediation presided over by the court），放弃或变更诉讼请求（waive or modify the claims），上诉（appeal），再审（retrial），证据保全（evidence preservation），财产保全（property preservation），法院文书送达（service of court documents），一审法院（court of first instance），二审

法院（court of second instance）。

第三，注意套句的使用，如：

1. I，…，hereby appoint … to act on behalf of … in regard to … 我 XX 特此委托 XXX 就 XXX 一事代表 XXX。

2. We…hereby appoint and empower…to be our agent ad litem with respect to … 我们 XX 特此授权委托 XX 就 XXX 一事作为我们的代理人。

3. Now this deed witnesseth that I appoint…to be my corporation's true and lawful attorney and in the name of my corporation to do and execute all or any of the following acts, deeds and things… 现在所见证的委托书是我授权 XX 作为我公司的正式和合法的代理人，代理人得以我公司的名义行使和执行下列行为、文书和事务：…

4. We hereby confirm that this Power of Attorney shall remain in full force from the date of signature and/or seal through the completion of the matters as set forth in this Power of Attorney. 我公司特此确认该授权委托书自签署之日起及执行期间有效。

5. In witness whereof we cause this Power of Attorney to be duly signed and/or sealed. 我们于证人面前在这份授权委托书上签字盖章。

第二节　委托代理协议（agency agreement）

委托代理是指代理人依据被代理人的委托，以被代理人的名义实施的民事法律行为，其效力直接归属于被代理人。在涉外民事活动中，委托方为需要聘请律师的一方，受托方为律师事务所，律师事务所再指派某个律师担任案件的诉讼代理人。

一份完整的委托代理协议一般包含以下条款：当事人信息、委托事项、代理权限和代理期限、代理费用、双方的权利与义务、违约责任、争议解决等。

一、委托事项条款（Commitment）

委托事项常见表达方式如下：

Party A entrusts Party B to act as the attorney-at-law in its contractual dispute with YYY.

Party A hereby authorizes Party B to be the attorney-at-law in the case of…

Party A hereby with respect to ____ entrusts Party B as the agent of the above case.

二、代理权限条款（Scope of Power）

代理权限分为一般授权（general authorization）和特别授权（special authorization）。

一般授权代理，是指委托人只授予代理律师代理当事人进行一般性的诉讼活动，而不能代理当事人进行实体性权利处分的授权代理。例如，在一般代理过程中，律师可以代理起诉、应诉、提供有关证据、法庭质证、发表综合性代理词、参与法庭辩论等，但是对于代为承认、放弃、变更诉讼请求和进行和解等涉及当事人实体权利处分的事项就不属于一般代理的授权范围。

特别授权代理，是指委托人以特别授权的方式赋予律师除了一般代理权限以外，还具有代理当事人对案件实体问题的处理直接做出决定并明确表态的诉讼代理。我国《民事诉讼法》第59条规定，诉讼代理人代为承认、放弃、变更诉讼请求，进行和解，提起反诉或者上诉，必须有委托人的特别授权。因此，律师在诉讼过程中进行涉及处分实体权利的诉讼行为和其他一些重要的诉讼行为时，必须有委托人的特别授权。

范例一：

The agency authority of Party B is: to admit, waive or modify claims, to participate in reconciliation or mediation, to file a counterclaim or an appeal, to apply for execution, to sign or issue legal instruments on party A's behalf.

代理权限：代为承认、放弃、变更诉讼请求，进行和解、调解，提起反诉或者上诉，申请执行，代为签收、签发法律文书。

范例二：

The agency authority of Party B is item 2, 3, 4, 5:

1. General authorization;

2. File a lawsuit, apply for preservation of property, apply for authentication, apply for advanced execution, recognize, waiver or modify the claims, participate in reconciliation or mediation, file an appeal on Party's A behalf, sign and receive legal documents on Party A's behalf;

3. Apply for execution on behalf of Party A;

4. Acknowledge, give up or change the execution request, collect the execution payment and executed subject matter on behalf of Party A.

参考译文：

乙方的代理权限为第 2、3、4、5 项：

1. 一般代理；

2. 代为起诉、申请财产保全、申请鉴定、先予执行、承认、放弃或变更诉讼请求，参与和解、调解，提起上诉，代为签收法律文书；

3. 代为申请执行；

4. 代为承认、放弃或者变更执行请求，代为领取执行款以及执行标的物。

三、代理费用条款（Agency Fee）

律师收费方式有固定收费（fixed fee）、风险代理收费（no-win-no-fee arrangement）、固定收费 + 风险收费（fixed fee + contingency fee）等方式。

固定收费（fixed fee）举例如下：

In reference to the "Lawyers' Service Charge Standard of Guangdong Province", after negotiation between the two parties, Party A agrees to pay RMB 20, 000 Yuan within three days of signing this contract.

参考译文：

参照《广东省律师服务收费标准》，经双方协商，甲方同意于本合同签订后三日内支付人民币 2000 元。

固定收费 + 风险收费（fixed fee + contingency fee）举例如下：

范例一：

Party B's fees for all services under this Agreement shall be paid in two separate installments:

a. Fixed fee：RMB 100,000（before tax）to be paid in one installment within three days of the signing of this Agreement by bank transfer as designated by Party B, and Party B shall issue invoice to Party A; the fixed fee is the work cost of attorney for fulfilling the commitment.

b. Contingency fee：Party B shall be paid 20% of all Net Proceeds collected from enforcement of judgments resulting from cases under this Agreement. Net Proceeds is defined as follows：totally collected amount less case filing fee, including court fee of first and second instance, and court execution fee.

参考译文：

乙方根据本协议完成全部代理工作的代理费用由如下两部分组成：

（1）固定费用：人民币10万元整（含税），作为乙方律师工作成本费用。在本协议签订后3日内一次性通过银行转账至乙方指定账户；乙方出具发票。

（2）另行风险提成费用：乙方将根据本协议从本案最终执行回来的全部净收益中提取20%。净收益的含义如下：来自本案的全部金额，减去已经支付的案件费用。甲方扣除费用指的是从法院执行回款中扣除本案一审和二审的诉讼费以及法院执行费。

范例二：

According to negotiation between the two parties, Party A shall pay Party B the fixed lawyer's service fee of RMB 5,000 on the day of signing the agreement (in capital form：five thousand Yuan only), and contingency fee shall be paid to Party B within 3 days after receiving the proceeds collected from enforcement of judgement.

The payment standard of the contingency fee is：

a. if the commercial housing sales contract is cancelled, 1% of the returned house payment;

b. if the commercial housing sales contract continues to be performed, 15% of proceeds collected from enforcement of judgement.

参考译文：

根据双方协商，甲方于签约当日向乙方支付前期律师服务费人民币5000元整（大写：伍仟元整），后期风险代理律师服务费用于每次收到执行回款或权益后 3 天内支付给乙方。

风险代理律师服务费支付标准为：解除合同的按回款物中退房款的 1%；继续履行合同的按执行回款的 15% 向乙方支付。

附委托代理合同范本：

Agency Agreement for Civil Disputes

Principal：XXX（hereinafter referred to as Party A）

Trustee：Guangdong LangQian Law Firm（hereinafter referred to as Party B）

Party A entrusts Party B to act as the attorney-at-law in its contractual dispute with YYY. The two parties, through consultation, hereby agree upon, and shall be bound by, the following terms：

1. Party B accepts the entrustment of Party A and appoints Li Ping as the agent of Party A.

2. Term of agency：From the date of signing this contract, until the termination of execution of the above-mentioned case.

3. The agency authority of Party B is：to admit, waive or modify claims, to participate in reconciliation or mediation, to file a counterclaim or an appeal, to apply for execution, to sign or issue legal instruments on party A's behalf.

4. The rights and obligations of Party A are as follows：

4. 1 Party A has the right to know the progress of the entrusted case, the agency plan and relevant legal provisions from the lawyer appointed by Party B.

4. 2 Party A shall cooperate with Party B positively and provide necessary materials. Party A shall be responsible for the authenticity, legality, accuracy and completeness of the documentation provided.

4. 3 Party A must truthfully present the case to Party B and provide true and valid evidence.

4. 4 Party A shall pay the lawyer's fees as agreed in Article 6 of this contract.

5. The rights and obligations of Party B are as follows：

5. 1 Party B has the right to charge lawyer's fees according to the provisions of Article 6 of this contract.

5. 2 Party B shall perform its duties with due diligence to safeguard Party A's lawful rights and interests, and perform agency obligations such as evidence investigation and collection, and appear in the court on time.

5. 3 Party B shall promptly notify Party A of the progress of the case, explain the agency plan and relevant legal provisions to Party A at the request of Party A, and deliver the adjudicative documents to Party A in a timely manner.

6. Agency fees and payment methods

6. 1 In reference to the " Lawyers' Service Charge Standard of Guangdong Province ", after negotiation between the two parties, Party A agrees to pay RMB ____ Yuan within three days of the signing of this contract.

6. 2 Party A shall bear the transportation expenses, accommodation, catering and other necessary expenses incurred by Party B outside Zhuhai City, the investigation fees incurred in investigation to the relevant government authorities, and the translation fees, etc.

7. Liability for breach of contract

7. 1 Party A shall not terminate the contract halfway for no reason, otherwise the lawyer's fees already charged by Party B shall not be refunded; Party B shall have the right to recover from Party A the lawyer's fees that have not yet been paid.

7. 2 If Party A pays the lawyer's fees late, it shall pay the liquidated damages on the basis of five thousandths per day. If the payment is overdue for more than seven days, Party B has the right to terminate the contract, and has the right of not fulfilling the agency obligations such as appearing in court. All consequences arising therefrom shall be borne by Party A.

7. 3 If Party A provides false evidence or makes false statement on the case, Party B has the right to terminate the contract, and the lawyer's fee already paid shall not be refunded; in addition, Party B has the right to recover from Party A the lawyer's fees that have not yet been paid.

7. 4 Party B shall not terminate the contract halfway for no reason, otherwise the lawyer fees already collected shall be returned to Party A.

7. 5 Where Party B has serious faults that harm Party A's interests, including

the loss of the main evidence, the miss of time limits for submission of claims, the failure to appear in the arbitration tribunal or court, the failure to serve the judgment during the appeal period, and the failure to file an appeal in time etc. , Party A has the right to terminate the contract and ask Party B to return the lawyer's fees already charged.

8. Confidentiality

Party A and Party B shall not disclose the information and materials of the two parties to any third party in any way without the consent of the other party, unless otherwise required by national laws and regulations, otherwise both parties have the right to pursue the other party's legal liability.

9. Dispute Settlement

If the two parties have disputes arising from this contract, they shall resolve the dispute through negotiation as far as possible. If the negotiation fails, the two parties may file an arbitration to the Zhuhai Municipal Arbitration Commission. The arbitration fees and attorney fees arising from the arbitration shall be borne by the losing party.

10. Miscellaneous

10. 1 Concerning special entrust commitment, Party A shall issue a power of attorney to Party B in addition. The power of attorney is incorporated into this contract and has the same legal effect.

10. 2 This contract will enter into effect on the signature of both parties and the affixing of their official seals. The contract term is until the end of execution.

10. 3 This contract is in duplicate, and Party A and Party B each will hold one counterpart with the same legal effect. Those that are not included in this contract can be confirmed by both parties through further negotiation.

10. 4 This contract is executed in Chinese and English. The two versions have the same legal effect. In case of discrepancy between the two versions, the Chinese version will prevail.

Party A:	Party B:
Time:	Time:
Place:	Place:

参考译文：

民事纠纷委托代理合同

甲方：XXX

乙方：广东朗乾律师事务所

甲方因与 YYY 合同纠纷一案委托乙方代理。经双方协商一致，特订立下列各条款，双方应共同遵守：

1. 乙方接受甲方委托，指派李萍律师作为甲方的代理人。

2. 代理期限：自本合同签订之日起，至上述案件执行终结为止。

3. 代理权限：代为承认、放弃、变更诉讼请求，进行和解、调解，提起反诉或者上诉，申请执行，代为签收、签发法律文书。

4. 甲方的权利和义务：

4.1 甲方有权向乙方律师了解委托案件的进展、代理方案及相关的法律规定。

4.2 甲方必须积极配合乙方律师相关工作，提供必要的文件资料，并对所提供文件资料的真实性、合法性、准确性及完整性负责。

4.3 甲方必须如实向乙方律师陈述案情，提供有关本案真实有效的证据。

4.4 甲方应按本合同第 6 条的约定交纳律师费用。

5. 乙方的权利和义务

5.1 乙方有权按本合同第 6 条的约定收取律师费用。

5.2 乙方应尽职尽责维护甲方的合法权益，履行调查取证、按时出庭等代理义务。

5.3 乙方应将案件的进展及时通知甲方，应甲方的要求将代理方案及相关法律规定向甲方解释，并将裁判文书及时送达甲方。

6. 代理费用及付款方式

6.1 参照《广东省律师服务收费标准》，经双方协商，甲方同意于本合同签订三日内支付人民币____元。

6.2 乙方因到珠海市外所发生的交通费、食宿费等必要费用和到相关政府部门产生的调查费以及因本协议产生的翻译费由甲方承担。

7. 违约责任

7.1 甲方不得无故中途解除合同，否则乙方已收取的律师费用不予退回；乙方有权向甲方追讨应当支付而尚未支付的律师费用。

7.2 甲方如逾期缴纳律师费用，应按每日千分之五计付违约金。逾期超过七日，乙方有权解除合同，无需履行出庭等代理义务，由此产生的一切后果由甲方自行承担。

7.3 甲方提供虚假证据或对案情作虚假陈述的，乙方有权解除合同，已收取的律师费用不予退回；乙方有权向甲方追讨应当支付而尚未支付的律师费用。

7.4 乙方不得无故中途解除合同，否则应将已收取的律师费用全部退回甲方。

7.5 乙方有因重大过错损害甲方利益的情形，包括丢失主要证据原件、超过诉讼时效未及时起诉、未出庭参加仲裁或诉讼、超过上诉期间未送达裁判文书、未及时提起上诉等，甲方有权解除合同，要求乙方退回已收取的律师费用。

8. 保密

甲乙双方在未经过对方同意的情况下，不得以任何方式泄露双方的情报和资料给任何第三方，但国家法律法规有要求的除外，否则双方都有权追究对方的法律责任。

9. 争议解决

双方如果因本合同产生争议，应当尽量协商解决，如果无法协商解决，双方可向珠海市仲裁委员会提起仲裁，因提起仲裁产生的仲裁费、律师费等由败诉方承担。

10. 其他

10.1 涉及具体事项委托时，甲方以书面的方式另行对乙方进行授权。该授权文件构成本合同的一部分。

10.2 本合同经甲乙双方签字盖章后生效，合同期限到执行终结为止。

10.3 本合同一式两份，甲、乙双方各执一份，具有同等法律效力。本合同之未尽事宜，由甲、乙双方另行协商确定。

10.4 本合同以中文和英文两种文字拟定，具同等法律效力，两种文本的解释不一致时，以中文版本为准。

甲方：	乙方：
时间：	时间：
签订地：	签订地：

第八章　其他非诉讼类涉外法律文书

本部分将重点关注常见的非诉讼类涉外法律文书，如公证文书、法律备忘录、尽职调查报告、法律意见书、律师函等。

第一节　常见公证文书

公证书是指公证机构对当事人申请的公证事项经过审查核实、按照法定程序制作的具有特殊法律效力的司法证明文书。

公证书主要用于以下目的：（1）用于办理出入境手续，证明出入境所要求的相关事项，如去国外留学需办理申请人的毕业证公证书（notarization of diploma）、学位证公证书（notarization of degreecertificate）和成绩单公证（notarization of academic transcript）。（2）用于跨国间的民事交往，如去日本、德国等国家探亲，需办理亲属关系公证书（notarization of family relation）。（3）用于涉外经济活动，如与外商洽谈贸易、签订涉外经济活动，一般需要办理授权委托书（power of attorney）、注册资本验证（certification of registered capital）等的公证；在国外设立办事机构，一般需要办理公司章程（articles of association）、营业执照（business license）等的公证。（4）用于办理与财产、人身有关的民事法律事务，如亲属关系证明书（notarization of family relations）、出生公证书（notarization of birth）、死亡证明书（notarization of death）、委托律师的委托公证书（notarization of power of attorney）、结婚公证书（notarization of marriage）、收养公证书（notarization of adoption）、遗嘱公证书（testamentary notarization）等。（5）用于涉外诉讼，如在境外、港澳台地区形成的证据需要在境内作为诉讼证据使用，则需要履行相关的公证或者认证手续。

在实务中，有以下常见的公证文书：

出生公证书（Notarization of Birth）

毕业证公证书（Notarization of Diploma）

学位证公证书（Notarization of Degree Certificate）

成绩单公证书（Notarization of Academic Transcript）

亲属关系公证书（Notarization of Kinship）

婚姻状况公证书（Notarization of Marital Status）

无刑事犯罪记录公证书（Notarization of No Record of Criminal Offense）

（涉外）收养公证书（Notarization of Adoption）等。

无论何种类别的公证书，结构都是由首部（标题）、正文和尾部三个部分组成。

标题（Heading）一般为“公证书”，英文为“Notarization”或“Notarial Certificate”“Notary Public Certificate”。如果是具体的比如“毕业公证书”“收养公证书”等内容时，则为“Notarization of Diploma”和“Notarization of Adoption”，也可以直接写成“Notarization”或“Notarial Certificate”。

正文（Body Part）一般会出现“兹证明……”这样的表达，对应的英文表达为：This is to certify that…或者 It is to certify that…。

尾部（Close）一般包含以下信息：公证员（Notary）姓名和签名（Signature）或盖章（Stamp）；公证处名称及盖章；“中华人民共和国”（The People's Republic of China）字样；日期。日期的格式一般为月/日/年。

附各公证书范例如下：

一、出生公证书

Notarial Certificate

This is to certify that Xiao Wang (female) was born on August 20, 1996 in Zhuhai City, Guangdong Province, China. His father of Nan Wang and his mother is Xining Hao.

Notary Public: … (signature)
Zhuhai Notary Public Office
The People's Republic of China
(sealed)
September 10, 2019

参考译文：

公证书

兹证明王晓（女），于1996年8月20日出生于中国广东省珠海市，其父王楠，其母郝希宁。

中国人民共和国
珠海市公证处
公证员：
（盖章）
2019年9月10日

二、婚姻状况公证书

Notarization of Marital Status

This is to certify that Nan Wang (male, born on May 1, 1964) and Xining Hao (female, born on October 19, 1965) have been married since on October 1, 1992 at the registration office of Civil Affairs Department, Zhuhai City, Guangdong Province.

Notary Public: … (signature)
Zhuhai Notary Public Office
The People's Republic of China
(sealed)
June 9, 2019

参考译文：

公证书

兹证明王楠（男，1964年5月1日出生）和郝希宁（女，1965年10月19日出生）于1992年10月1日在广东省珠海市民政局注册结婚。

特此证明。

中华人民共和国
珠海市公证处
公证员：
（盖章）
2019年6月9日

三、毕业证公证书

Notarial Certificate

This is to certify that the photocopy attached hereto conforms to the original of the Graduation Certificate allocated the certificate No. 100071200505003499 and issued to Zhang Fang by Beijing Institute of Technology Zhuhai Campus on July 1st, 2005, and both the official seals of Beijing Institute of Technology Zhuhai Campus and the signature of President on the original are found to be genuine and authentic.

Notary Public: … (signature)
Zhuhai Notary Public Office
The People's Republic of China
(sealed)
June 8, 2019

参考译文：

公证书

兹证明该复印件与北京理工大学珠海学院于二零零五年七月一日发给张芳的编号为100071200505003499的毕业证书的原件相符。原件上北京理工大学珠海学院的钢印、印章和校长的签章均属实。

中华人民共和国
珠海市公证处
公证员：
（盖章）
2019年6月8日

四、学习经历证明

Notarial Certificate

(2002) Yu Zheng Zi No. 6

This is to certify that Zhang Yuan (female, born in 1975) was enrolled in the Foreign Languages Department of Henan University (four-year course) in September 1993 and graduated in July 1997.

Notary Public: Zhu Jun (signature)
Kaifeng Notary Public Office
Henan Province
The People's Republic of China
June 26, 2002

参考译文：

公证书

（2002）豫证字第 6 号

兹证明张媛（女，一九七五年出生）于一九九三年九月入河南大学外语系，学习四年，一九九七年七月毕业。

中华人民共和国河南省
开封市公证处
公证员：朱军
二零零二年六月二十六日

五、成绩单公证书

Notarization

This is to certify that the photocopy attached hereto is in conformity with the original of Official Transcripts issued to Liang Yu by Beijing Institute of Technology Zhuhai Campus on July 1, 2019, and that the official seal of Beijing Institute of Technology Zhuhai Campus and "Special Seal for Students' Status of Beijing Institute of Technology Zhuhai Campus" affixed to the original are found to be genuine and authentic.

Notary Public: … (signature)
Zhuhai Notary Public Office
The People's Republic of China
August 9, 2019

参考译文:

公证书

兹证明前面的复印件与北京理工大学珠海学院学校于2019年7月1日发给梁宇的成绩单原件相符。原件上“北京理工大学珠海学院学校”的印章及“北京理工大学珠海学院学校学籍管理专用章”均属实。

中华人民共和国
珠海市公证处
公证员：…
2019年8月9日

六、委托公证书

Notarization

This is to certify that Wang Yuan and Yang Shun came to my office on April 6, 2003, and affixed their signatures (or their seals) in my presence, on the power of attorney attached hereto.

Notary Public: Zhang Yang (signature)
Xi'an Notary Public Office
Shaanxi Province
People's Republic of China
April 15, 2003

参考译文:

公证书

此证明王源、杨顺于二零零三年四月六日来到我处，在我的面前，在附着的授权委托书上签字（或盖章）。

中华人民共和国陕西省
西安市公证处
公证员：张阳
二零零三年四月六日

七、继承权公证书

Notarization of Inheritance

(88) Guang Zheng Zi No. 9

This is to certify as follows:

Heirs: Chen Xiang, female, was born in 1952, now residing at 89 Jinwan Rd., Guangzhou City; Lin Yu, male, was born in 1976, now residing at Jinwan Rd., Guangzhou City.

Decreased: Lin Qi, male, born in 1950, was a staff member of Hong Kong Toy Company.

It is found that Mr. Lin Qi died intestate on March 23, 1998 in Hong Kong. His estate is in Hong Kong. According to the law of the People's Republic of China, Mr. Lin's estate is to be inherited jointly by his wife Ms. Chen Xiang and his son Lin Yu.

Notary Public: Zhang Ming (signature)
Guangzhou Notary Public Office
The People's Republic of China
May 5, 1998

参考译文:

继承权证明书

(88) 粤证字第8号

继承人:陈香,女,一九五二年出生,现住广州市金湾路89号;林宇,男,一九七六年出生,现住广州市金湾路89号。

被继承人:林琦,男,一九五零年出生,生前为香港玩具公司职员,于一九八八年三月二十三日在香港死亡。

查林琦于一九九八年三月二十三日在香港死亡,死亡后在香港留有遗产。死者生前无遗嘱,根据中华人民共和国法律规定,死者林琦的遗产,应由林琦的妻子陈香和儿子林宇二人共同继承。

特此证明。

中华人民共和国
广州市公证处
公证员:张明
一九九八年五月五日

八、亲属关系公证书

Notarial Certificate

(2015) Zhu Zheng Wai Zi No. 86

Applicant: Liu Junyu, male, was born on November 3, 1998. ID card No.: 37078319981103 * * * *.

Related Persons: Liu Mingxiang, male, was born on February 19, 1973. ID card No.: 37072319730219 * * * *.

Related Persons: Yang Jie, female, was born on September 11, 1974. ID card No.: 37072319740911 * * * *.

Notarial matters: kinship.

This is to certify that Liu Yunyu is the son of Liu Mingxiang and Yang Jie.

NotaryPublic: Li Yanlin (signature)
Notary Public Office of Zhuhai City
The People's Republic of China
February 13, 2015

参考译文：

公证书

（2015）珠证外字 86 号

申请人：刘俊宇，男，一九九八年十一月三日出生，公民身份号码：3707831998-1103 * * * *。

关系人：刘明翔，男，一九七三年二月十九日出生，公民身份号码：3707231973-0219 * * * *。

关系人：杨杰，女，一九七四年九月十一日出生，公民身份号码：3707231974-0911 * * * *。

公证事项：亲属关系。

兹证明刘俊宇是刘明翔和杨杰的儿子。

中华人民共和国
珠海市公证处
公证员：李燕临
二〇一五年二月十三日

九、签名公证书

Notarial Certificate

(2019) Zhu Zheng Wai Zi No. 338

Applicant: Zhuhai Jiaxing Woods Industry Co. , Ltd.

Legal representative: Wang Jiaxing, male, was born on January 20, 1972. ID card No. : 47984519720120 * * * * .

Notarial Matters: signature, seal

This is to certify that Wang Jiaxing, the legal representative of Zhuhai Jiaxing Woods Industry Co. , Ltd. , came to our notary public office on April 8, 2019, and signed and sealed on the preceding Sales Contract in the presence of the notary public.

Remark: the content of the Sales Contract is not notarized in this certificate.

Notary Public: Li Yanlin
Notary Public Office of Zhuhai City
The People's Republic of China
April 8, 2019

参考译文：

公证书

（2019）珠证外字338号

申请人：珠海市家兴木业有限公司

法定代表人：王家兴，男，一九七二年一月二十日出生，公民身份号码：47984519720120 * * * * 。

公证事项：签名、印鉴

兹证明珠海市家兴木业有限公司的法定代表人王家兴于二〇一九年四月八日来我处，在本公证员的面前，在前面的《销售合同》上签名、盖章。

注：本公证书未对《销售合同》的内容进行公证。

中华人民共和国
珠海市公证处
公证员：李燕临
二〇一九年四月八日

十、境外公证认证文书

根据《中华人民共和国民事诉讼法》的规定，境外形成的证据材料，应该经过公证或者认证手续后，方可在国内法院作为证据使用。下面列举几种公证认证书以供学习和参考。

范例一：

> **认证书**
>
> （2019）摩领认字第0000111号
>
> 兹证明前面文书上摩洛哥王国外交与国际合作部的印章和 Mr. AAA 的签字均属实。
>
> 该文书内容由出文机构负责。
>
> 中华人民共和国
> 驻摩洛哥大使馆
> 二等秘书　XXX（签名）
> 2019年2月20日

参考译文：

> **China Authentication**
>
> (2019) Mo Ling Ren Zi No. 0000111
>
> It is to certify that the seal of the Ministry of Foreign Affairs and International Cooperation of the Kingdom of Morocco and the signature of Mr. AAA on the documents are authentic.
>
> The issuing organization is responsible for the contents of this document.
>
> People's Republic of China
> Embassy in Morocco
> Second Secretary XXX (signature)
> February 20, 2019

范例二：

认证书

（2019）新领认字第0005444号

兹证明前面文书上新加坡共和国外交部的印章和Mr. AAA的签字均属实。

该文书内容由出文机构负责。

中华人民共和国
驻新加坡大使馆
一等秘书　XXX（签名）
2019年05月09日

参考译文：

China Authentication

（2019）Xin Ling Ren Zi No. 0005444

I hereby certify that the seal of the Ministry of Foreign Affairs of Singapore and the signature of Mr. AAA on the documents are authentic.

The issuing organization is responsible for the contents of this document.

People's Republic of China
Embassy in Singapore
First Secretary XXX（signature）
May 9，2019

范例三：

港澳地区出具的发往内地使用的文书，如商业登记证明，分别需要中国法律服务（香港）有限公司和中国法律服务（澳门）公司公证后方可在内地使用，特列举商业登记公证书一份供参考。

公证书

（2018）中法澳证字第 1000 号

根据澳门特别行政区商业及动产登记局 2018 年 4 月 13 日出具的《商业登记证明》，兹证明登记号码为 4567 SO 号的商业登记资料如下：

公司名称：AAAA（澳门）有限公司

注册地址：澳门 XXX 路 50 号

所营事业：房地产买卖及出入口多种类货品

开业日期：2000 年 5 月 12 日

注册资本：澳门币壹佰万元整（MOP ＄1, 000, 000. 00 元）

股东及股份：1. AAA——MOP ＄800, 000 元；

2. BBB——MOP ＄200, 000 元.

行政管理：一名行政管理机关成员。目前成员为股东 AAA。

签名方式：公司行为可由该名成员单独作出，公司将对该名成员以公司名义作出的行为负责。

中国法律服务（澳门）公司

中国公证员________（签名）

2018 年 4 月 18 日

说明：

1. 本公证书有效期至 2018 年 7 月 12 日，期间如有商业登记资料变更的除外。

2. 后附澳门特别行政区商业及动产登记局出具的《商业登记证明》正本（6 页）。

参考译文：

Notarization

(2018) Zhong Fa Ao Zheng Zi No. 1000

According to the "Business Registration Certificate" issued by the Commercial and Movable Property Registration Bureau of the Macao Special Administrative Region on April 13, 2018, it is certified that the business registration information of registration number 4567 SO is as follows:

Company name: AAAA (Macau) Co., Ltd.

Registered address: 50 XXX Road, Macau

Scope of Business: Real estate trading, import and export of various types of goods

Registration date: May 12, 2000

Registered capital: MOP 1 million (MOP $ 1,000,000.00)

Shareholders and shares: 1. AAA——MOP $ 800,000;

2. BBB——MOP $ 200,000.

Administration: The administrative organ has one member. The current member is shareholder AAA.

Signature method: The corporate behavior can be made by the member alone, and the company will be responsible for the behavior of the member taken in the name of the company.

China Legal Services (Macau) Company

Chinese Notary Public ________ (signature)

April 18, 2018

Note:

1. This notarization is valid until July 12, 2018, except for any changes in business registration information during the period.

2. Attached is the original "Certificate of Business Registration" issued by the Commercial and Movable Property Registration Bureau of the Macao Special Administrative Region (6 pages).

附各种证书范本：

毕业证书范例一：

Certificate of Graduation

It is to certify that Mr. Zhao Ming, male, a native of Hubei Province, born on January, 1984, having specialized in English Language and Literature in the Foreign Language Department of Yangtze University from September, 2002 to July, 2006 and having completed the four-year undergraduate program with qualified standing, is hereby awarded this Certificate of Graduation.

(signature)
President of Yangtze University
June 30, 2006

参考译文：

本科毕业证书

学生赵明，性别男，一九八四年元月出生于湖北，于二〇〇二年九月至二〇〇六年七月在本校外语系英语语言文学专业四年制本科修业期满，考试合适，准予毕业。

长江大学
校长
二〇〇六年六月三十日

毕业证书范例二：

Certificate
of Graduation of Postgraduate Student

This is to certify that Wang Xue, female, born on February 12, 1972, majoring in International Law from September 1995 to July 1998, with length of schooling of three years, having fulfilled all the prescribed courses required in the cultivation program of postgraduate student with qualified standing, and having passed the dissertation defense, is hereby conferred this Certificate of Graduation.

President: Zhang Yonglin
Cultivation Institution: Chinese University of Political Science and Law
July 1st, 1998

参考译文：

硕士研究生毕业证
公证书

研究生王雪，性别女，1972 年 2 月 12 日生，于 1995 年 9 月至 1998 年 7 月在国际法专业学习，学制三年，修完硕士研究生培养计划规定的全部课程，成绩合格，毕业论文答辩通过，准予毕业。

校长：张永林
培养单位：中国政法大学
1998 年 7 月 1 日

学位证书范例：

Certificate of Bachelor's Degree

This is to certify that Miss Li Hong, female, a native of Hubei Province, born in January, 1984, having majored in Oil Logging in the Oil Exploration Department of Southwest Petroleum Institute for four years, has qualified for graduation. Upon the examination in accordance with the Regulations Regarding Academic Degrees of the People's Republic of China, she is hereby conferred the Bachelor's Degree of Science.

(signature)
President of Southwest Petroleum Institute
June 30, 2007

参考译文：

学士学位证书

李红，性别女，生于一九八四年元月，系湖北人，在本院石油开发系测井专业（四年制本科）修业期满，成绩合格，根据中华人民共和国学位管理条例，决定授予该生理学学士学位。

西南石油学院
校长
二〇〇七年六月三十日

职务证明范例一：

Certificate of Identity

This is to certify that Wang Xue, female, born on February 12, 1977, is an associate professor of the School of Law and Administration of our university. Her administrative post is associate dean.

Beijing Institute of Technology, Zhuhai
May 20, 2013

参考译文：

身份证明

兹证明：王雪，女，出生日期1977年2月12日，为我校法律与行政学院法学专业教师，副教授，行政职务为副院长。

特此证明。

北京理工大学珠海分校
2013年5月20日

职务证明范例二：

Certificate of Legal Representative

This is to certify that Mr. Chen Dong is the legal representative of our company.
His title in the company is: executive director.

Zhuhai Sunshine Electronics Co., Ltd.
May 20, 2013

参考译文：

法定代表人身份证明
陈东是我单位法定代表人。 职务：执行董事。 特此证明。
珠海阳光电子有限公司 2013 年 5 月 20 日

第二节 法律备忘录（Law Office Memo）

什么是法律研究备忘录呢？在一个项目的过程中或在起草一份合同时，合伙人或资深律师可能会遇到一个或几个法律问题，需要助手去研究，加以法律分析，找出答案，并写在备忘录中以供参考；或者客户要求就一个或几个事项或交易涉及的法律问题要求我们出具备忘录，对客户而言是提出解决方案，指导案件进程，是风险防范的保障。

法律备忘录是一种常见的法律文书，其实际上是一种书面的法律分析。作为书面文件，法律备忘录是根据当时有效实施的法律规定和司法实践所进行的法律分析的历史记录，通常具有如下功能或作用：（1）对法律问题进行书面分析；（2）借助常识、经验的积累，协助提出解决方案；（3）指导工作进程，包括程序、步骤等。

撰写法律备忘录的时候，一般遵循以下步骤：（1）整理事实/背景情况；（2）找出法律问题；（3）研究法律、分析问题、提出解决方案。

范例：

April 6, 2019

Memorandum to: Jeff Wood, Esq.

Debeviose & Plimpton (Hong Kong)
Chinese Court's Jurisdiction Over AT&T

Background

You have asked us to advise whether a Chinese court would have Jurisdiction over AT&T in the following transaction: * AT&T plans to invest in a Sino-foreign joint venture company (the "Joint Venture Company") through Pudong LLC, an offshore special purpose vehicle to be established and wholly owned by it. * Once established, Pudong LLC will enter into a joint venture agreement (the "Joint Venture Agreement") with two Chinese parties to form the Joint Venture Company. At the request of the Chinese parties, AT&T intends to provide a guarantee in the form of a comfort letter (the "Letter") to ensure the performance by Pudong LLC of its obligations under the Joint Venture Agreement. The Letter (a copy of which having been provided to us) expressly provides that it is governed by New York law and subject to the jurisdiction of New York or Federal courts in the United States. The letter is proposed to be signed by AT&T and countersigned by the Chinese parties to the Joint Venture Agreement.

Question

The question is whether AT&T will be subject to the jurisdiction of a Chinese court by executing the Letter in the manner as described above.

Short Answer

If a dispute arises from the interpretation or performance of the Joint Venture Agreement and, in the absence of a valid and enforceable arbitration agreement among the parties, a claim is made against Pudong LLC before a Chinese court having jurisdiction over the claim, it is likely that AT&T will be named as an indispensable party and the Chinese court may decide that, since the Letter is part and parcel of the Joint Venture Agreement, the court should have jurisdiction over AT&T.

Analysis

Under Chinese law, contracts or agreements such as the Joint Venture Agreement which will be filed with the relevant Chinese governmental authorities for the establishment of companies such as the Joint Venture Company must be governed by Chinese law. As a parallel, China's civil Procedural Law provides that, in the absence of a valid and enforceable arbitration agreement among the parties, the Chinese court will have jurisdiction over any dispute that may

续表

arise from the interpretation and performance of a contract such as the Joint Venture Agreement. Article 246 of the Civil Procedural Law states: "Actions concerning disputes arising from the performance of contracts for Sino-foreign equity joint ventures, or Sino-foreign cooperative exploration and development of the natural resources in the PRC shall be under the jurisdiction of PRC courts".

Since AT&T, by virtue of the Letter, provides a guarantee for the performance by Pudong LLC of its obligations under the Joint Venture Agreement, it is likely that AT&T will be named as an indispensable party to the dispute. If so, the question is whether the Chinese court will decide that it has jurisdiction over AT&T even though AT&T does not have any presence in China other than providing the guarantee.

Under article 243 of the Civil Procedural Law, a foreign person may be subject to the jurisdiction of the Chinese court if, among other things, (i) it has representative office in China, or (ii) it is a party to a contract which is the subject matter of the litigation, or (iii) it has assets located in China that can be attached. For example, parties to the Joint Venture Agreement will have to choose Chinse law as the governing law and, in the absence of an arbitration agreement, the Chinese court will have jurisdiction over a dispute arising from the Joint Venture Agreement by virtue of Article 246 of the Civil Procedural Law and over the parties if any of the conditions set forth under Article 243 of the Civil Procedure Law is met. On the other hand, Chinese law also permits parties to a contract to choose the governing law and the forum of dispute resolution (including foreign courts) if such a choice is not inconsistent with the mandatory rules under Chinese law that provides otherwise.

Conclusion

Based on the above analysis, we are of the view that the Letter, as so drafted, in and by itself does not constitute a contract that is mandatorily governed by Chinese law or over which the Chinese court will have jurisdiction in respect of any dispute arising therefrom. Chinese courts should honor the parties' choice of law and jurisdiction in respect of the Letter. On the other hand, however, if the Chinese court determines that a dispute arising from the Letter constitutes a dispute of the Joint Venture Agreement, it may decide that it has jurisdiction over AT&T.

Suggestions

In view of the above analysis, we would suggest the following: First, parties to the Joint Venture Agreement agree that any dispute arising therefrom should be submitted to arbitration before a well-established international arbitration institution, such as the London Court of International Arbitration or the International Chamber of Commerce Court of Arbitration. By law, Chinese courts should honor the parties' choice of arbitration and reject filing of a lawsuit by any of such parties in respect of a dispute aris ing from the Joint Venture Agreement.

一份完整的尽职调查报告主要包含以下方面的清单内容：

范例：

1. 企业基本情况、发展历史及结构：The basic information, evolvement and organizational structure of the company

法定注册登记情况 Registration

股权结构 Ownership structure

下属公司 Subsidiaries and branches

重大的收购及出售资产事件 Key events of purchasing and selling assets

经营范围 Business scope

2. 企业人力资源 Human resources

管理架构（部门及人员）Management structure (Departments and staffing)

董事及高级管理人员的简历 Resume of Directors of the Board and members of the upper management team

薪酬及奖励安排 Policies on compensations, rewards and penalties

员工的工资及整体薪酬结构 Salary structure

员工招聘及培训情况 Recruitments and training arrangements

退休金安排 Benefits Policy, e. g. Pensions

3. 市场营销及客户资源 Marketing, Sales and Customer resources

产品及服务 Products and services

重要商业合同 Important business contracts

市场结构 Market structure

销售渠道 Distribution channels

销售条款 Sales policies and terms

销售流程 Sales management procedure

定价政策 Pricing policy

信用额度管理 Credit & Risk exposure management

市场推广及销售策略 Marketing and sales strategy

促销活动 Promotion activities

售后服务 Post-sales services

客户构成及忠诚度 Customer base composition and customer loyalty

4. 企业资源及生产流程管理 Enterprise resources and production management

加工厂 Factory and plant

生产设备及使用效率 Equipments and production capacity

研究及开发 Research and development

采购策略 Purchasing policy

采购渠道 Purchasing channels

供应商 Suppliers

重大商业合同 Important business contracts

5. 经营业绩 Business performance

会计政策 Accounting policy

历年审计意见 Auditing results of the last years if available

三年的经营业绩、营业额及毛利详尽分析 Analysis on business performance, sales revenue and gross profit of the last three years if available

三年的经营及管理费用分析 Analysis on operation and administration expenses of the last three years if available

三年的非经常项目及异常项目分析 Analysis on Non-frequent and abnormal activities of the last three years if available

各分支机构对整体业绩的贡献水平分析 Analysis on the contribution of each subsidiary to the overall business performance

6. 公司主营业务的行业分析 Industry analysis

行业现状及发展前景 Current situation and anticipation of industry development trend

中国特殊的经营环境和经营风险分析 Analysis on the business environment and operational risks in China

公司在该行业中的地位及影响 The subject company's position and influence in the industry

7. 公司财务情况 Financial status

三年的资产负债表分析 Balance Sheet of the last three years if available

资产投保情况分析 Analysis on assets insurance status

外币资产及负债 Assets and liabilities in foreign currency

历年财务报表的审计师及审计意见 Auditors' opinion on the financial reports of the past years

最近三年的财务预算及执行情况 Financial budgets and performing status of the last three years if available

固定资产 Fixed assets

或有项目（资产、负债、收入、损失）Contingent items on assets, liabilities, income, losses

无形资产（专利、商标、其他知识产权）Intangible assets, e. g. patent, trademark and other intellectual property rights

8. 利润预测 Profitability forecast

未来两年的利润预测 Profit forecast of the next two years

预测的假设前提 Assumptions of the forecast

预测的数据基础 Foundation of the forecast

本年预算的执行情况 Current year's budget performing status

9. 现金流量预测 Cash flow forecast

资金信贷额度 Commercial and bank credit limits

贷款需要 Needs on loans

借款条款 Borrowing terms

10. 公司债权和债务 Creditor's rights and liability

（1）债权 Creditor's Rights

债权基本情况明细 Details of rights

债权有无担保及担保情况 Collateral/guarantee status on the rights

债权期限 Duration of the creditor's rights

债权是否提起诉讼 Legal actions pursued

（2）债务 Debts and Liabilities

债务基本情况明细 Details of the liability

债务有无担保及担保情况 Collateral/guarantee status on the Liabilities

债务抵押、质押情况 Mortgage and pledge

债务期限 Duration of the liabilities

债务是否提起诉讼 Legal actions pursued

11. 公司的不动产、重要动产及无形资产 Properties, valuable assets and intangible assets

土地权属 Land property

房产权属 House property

车辆清单 Automobiles list

专利权及专有技术 Patents and self-developed technologies

以上资产抵押担保情况 Mortgage and collateral status on the above listed assets

12. 公司涉诉事件 Lawsuits

作为原告诉讼事件 Lawsuit put out by the subject company, as Plaintiff

作为被告诉讼事件 Lawsuit against the subject company, as Defendant

13. 其他有关附注 Other issues and comments

公司股东、董事及主要管理者是否有违规情况 Violations by any of the shareholders, directors and executives if there's any

公司有无重大违法经营情况 Significant business operational violations by the company

上级部门对公司重大影响事宜 Impact and influence from government administrative departments on the subject company

14. 企业经营面临主要问题 Business obstacles and operational difficulties

困难或积极因素 Obstacles & difficulties and the negative impacts or positive if there's any

应对措施 Solutions

第四节　法律意见书（Legal Opinion）

法律意见书是律师提供法律服务的一种综合性的书面文件，其内容包括向咨询者提供法律依据、法律建议以及解决问题的方案。律师以出具法律意见书的方式解答法律询问，应当注意为咨询者提出的法律问题作出准确、肯定、有法律依据的回答，为咨询者的决策提供具体、明确、可靠的参考意见。

一份法律意见书包括首部、正文、结尾、附件几部分。

首部主要包括：1. 标题，即在文书顶端居中标明“法律意见书”字样；2. 致送单位（或人）的称谓，在标题的下一行顶格写明接受文书的单位名称或人的名称。如：“××有限责任公司”“尊敬的×××先生（女士）”“××总经理”等；3. 说明解答内容的缘起和依据，要求用简明扼要的文字概括交待解答的是什么内容，即就提出的什么问题予以答复。如下例：

范例一：

We have been asked to provide this legal opinion with regard to the laws of the People's Republic of China (the "PRC"), excluding those of the Hong Kong Special Administrative Region, Macau Special Administrative Region and Taiwan, in connection with:

(a) a facility agreement (the "Facility Agreement") dated [ ] entered into by and among [ ] (the "Borrower"), as borrower, [ ] (the "Guarantor"), as guarantor, and [ ], as lender amended by the First Amendment Agreement to the Facility Agreement dated [ ];

(b) an accounts agreement (the "Accounts Agreement") dated [ ] entered into by and between the Borrower and the Lender as amended by the First Amendment Agreement to the Accounts Agreement dated [ ]; and

(c) an accounts assignment agreement (the "Accounts Assignment Agreement") dated [ ] entered into by and between the Borrower and the Lender as amended by the First Amendment Agreement to the Accounts Assignment Agreement dated [ ].

范例二：

This legal opinion is confined to and given on the basis of the published and publicly available PRC laws and administrative regulations (excluding the laws and regulations of Hong Kong, Macau Special Administrative Regions and Taiwan) effective as at the date hereof. We do not guarantee that any change in such laws or in their interpretation after the date hereof will not affect any of the opinions expressed below. We have not investigated, and we do not express or imply any opinion on the laws of any other jurisdiction, and we have assumed that no such other laws would affect the opinions expressed below.

正文部分是法律意见书的主体部分。正文通过法律、法规来详细解答询问人所提出的问题。一般而言，这一部分需要进行严密的论证，科学的分析，从而给询问人一个圆满的答案。正文的内容既可单列一项，就问做答，也可以分为若干个问题，用分题标号形式一一作答，具体如何写，要根据询问人所提问题的多少来决定。

依据法律法规的规定或具体交易的内容或客户的要求，每一份法律意见书正文的内容都不同。法律意见书需要包括什么内容需依具体交易而确定。

结尾部分主要是对所述问题进行总结，加以概括，起到归纳全文的作用。还要在文末右下角写出律师的工作单位、职务及姓名，并注明制作日期。

一般性交易的法律意见书仅为了特定的交易目的，是不公开的，不可作扩大解释，也不可被引用并在任何其他公开文件中提及，且只适用于法律意见书中明确提及的交易方及交易事项，因此在法律意见书的最后会对意见书的使用作出限定，常用的表达方式有以下：

This legal opinion is addressed to you for your own benefit only and solely for the purpose of the Transaction Documents. It is strictly limited to the matters stated herein and is not to be read as extending by implication to any other matter in connection with any of the Transaction Documents, any other documents mentioned in any of the Transaction Documents, and any other documents executed and/or delivered in connection therewith. Further, it is not to be transmitted to any other person nor is it to be relied upon by any other person or quoted or referred to in any public document or filed with any governmental or other regulatory authority or agency or any other person other than you and your legal counsels without written consent.

附件一般指审阅文件清单，实际上是对已审阅文件的简单列举。法律意见书如有附件，应在正文之后列出附件名称，并编好顺序。

范例三：

Date: June 16, 2019

Legal Opinion for the Labor Dispute

Zhuhai XXX Co. , Ltd. ,

We have reviewed and studied the materials related to the labor dispute case Mr. XX delivered us three days ago. Based on the actual situation of the case and related laws and regulations, we hereby offer you our legal opinion and suggestions about the case for your reference.

------------------------ (Body)

It is only our preliminary legal advice. If your need more assistance, please do not hesitate to contact us.

Guangdong LangQian Law Firm

Lawyer XXX

Tel: 86 – XXXXXXX

范例四：

Legal Opinions
on XXX's Intention to Recruit Workers
with Non-Competition Restrictions

In respect of XXX (Guangzhou) Co. , Ltd. 's (hereinafter referred to as "XXX Company") plan to recruit a worker with Non-competition restrictions, XXX Company entrusts attorney XXX from Beijing Jingsh (Zhuhai) Law Firm to issue legal opinions on this matter.

According to China's *Labor Contract Law*, *Anti-Unfair Competition Law*, *General Rules of the Civil Law*, *Tort Liability Law* and other laws and regulations (please refer to related laws and regulations in Appendix One), combined with the information provided by XXX's management personnel, I hereby issue the following legal opinions for your reference:

Part One Analysis of Legal Risks

With regard to the currently valid legal rules, combined with the currently known information, XXX's recruitment of this worker involves at least three types of legal risks, namely, purely Non-competition restrictions risk, risk of infringement of trade secrets and liability for unfair competition, and risk of violations of the principle of good faith and corporate values.

续表

Ⅰ. Purely Non-competition Restrictions Risk

According to the *Labor Contract Law* and other legal provisions, the employer may reach a Non-competition agreement (or clause) with a worker with confidentiality obligations. During the period of Non-competition, workers with Non-competition restrictions cannot work for other employers in the same or similar trade that compete with the current employer. In case a worker violates the Non-competition agreement, he/she shall pay liquidated damages according to the Non-competition agreement. In case losses are incurred to employer, he/she shall also be liable for economic compensation. At the same time, the employer has the right to request the worker to terminate his/her labor relationship with other enterprises.

The dispute on Non-competition restrictions belongs to the scope of labor disputes. The worker that XXX Company plans to recruit has signed "Confidentiality and Non-Competition Restrictions Agreement" with his previous employer YYY, and he is currently within the period of Non-competition restrictions, and bears obligations of Non-competition. If the previous employer YYY initiates labor arbitration on disputes over Non-competition due to the breach of duty of the worker and investigates into his legal liability for breach of the Non-competition obligation, it will be supported by the labor arbitration tribunal, that is, the laborer will return the compensation for Non-competition obligation, pay liquidated damages, continue to fulfill the Non-competition restrictions, and the labor contract relationship with XXX Company will also be discharged.

For XXX, the purely Non-competition restrictions dispute does not involve the liability for damages of XXX, but XXX ultimately cannot achieve the purpose of recruiting the worker.

Ⅱ. Risk of Infringement of Trade Secrets and Liability for Unfair Competition

In practice, disputes on Non-competition restrictions are often not pure labor disputes. The issue of Non-competition restrictions is often complicated by its involvement of trade secrets, technical secrets etc. confidential information, as well as its involvement of intellectual property rights and unfair competition. Therefore, the laws and regulations involved are not limited to labor law.

The Non-competition restrictions agreement often stipulates the confidentiality of trade secrets. The confidentiality of trade secrets can be protected not only through the relevant laws of the labor field, but also through the *Anti-Unfair Competition Law*, such as Articles 9, 17 and 32. That is to say, in case an employer is aware that the worker knows the trade secrets of other companies and has the duty of confidentiality after he leaves the precedent company, it continues to recruit the worker and use the trade secret that the worker knows, it will constitute an infringement of trade secret.

Therefore, if a company hires such a worker, it may constitute an infringement of trade secret and be charged by a company that the employee previously served. In such cases, the court usually will rule that the worker stop the infringement act and compensate the previous employer for economic losses. The employer that deliberately recruits such a worker shall also bear the liability for compensation.

续表

Ⅲ. Risk of Violations of the Principle of Good Faith and Corporate Values

China's *General Rules of the Civil Law* stipulates the principle of good faith. This principle requires that parties to a contract shall uphold creditworthiness, keep their promise and do not deceive others in market activities. At the same time, in pursuing one's own interests, one shall not harm the interest of others and the society. This principle requires civil subjects to maintain the interest of both parties and balance the interests of the parties concerned and the interests of society. In other words, when XXX Company recruits workers, it shall not damage the legitimate rights and interests of other companies. If a company is aware that a worker is within the Non-competition period and still recruits the worker, it is obviously contrary to the law.

At the same time, most companies advocate adherence to discipline and compliance with the law, honesty and trustworthiness in their core values and core cultural concepts. XXX Company is no exception. The values advocated by XXX Company include Trust and Integrity, and the code of conduct includes Legal Compliance, Business Ethics, Confidentiality, Compliance and Reporting of Misconduct etc. If the company violates these values and codes of conduct in recruiting staff, it will be extremely unfavorable for the management of employees and the establishment of corporate image.

In addition, in terms of business ethics, if a lawsuit is incurred due to recruitment of workers with Non-competition obligations, the adverse impact in the same trade cannot be ignored.

Part Two Probability Analysis of YYY in Safeguarding Its Legal Rights

Through retrieval via professional legal search software, the affiliated companies of YYY are involved in a total of 401 civil litigations, of which 56 were labor dispute cases (please refer to the statistics table in Appendix 3), and there are three verdict documents related to three precedents on Non-competition restrictions. It can be seen that the YYY company has a tradition of investigating into the liability of those who violate the Non-competition obligations. Moreover, in examining these three judgments, we found that YYY's investigation is often thorough, and the cases run through the first instance, the second instance and retrial; in addition, the company often alters the grounds of lawsuit in order to continue the investigation of the liabilities of those who violates the Non-competition obligations. The strength of its investigation is obviously large. The case name is as follows (please refer to the reference cases in Appendix Two):

……

From the above case analysis, we believe that YYY attaches great importance to protecting its legal rights in respect of labor disputes and civil and commercial disputes, including but not limited to Non-competition disputes. The probability of safeguarding its legal rights is very high.

续表

Part Three Conclusion

Through the above legal risk analysis and analysis of YYY in safeguarding its legal rights, XXX will face relatively large potential legal risks if it recruits workers with Non-competition restrictions, including but not limited to the termination of labor relations with the prospective worker and liability for damages etc.

Beijing Jingsh (Zhuhai) Law Firm
Attorney XXX
March 12, 2020

参考译文：

关于
XXX 公司拟招录负有竞业限制义务的劳动者之
法律意见书

XXX 有限公司（以下称“XXX 公司”）计划招录某个负有竞业限制义务的劳动者。XXX 公司委托北京京师（珠海）律师事务所 XXX 律师就此事出具法律意见书。

根据我国《劳动合同法》、《反不正当竞争法》、《民法通则》、《侵权责任法》等法律规定（见附录 1 相关法律规定），结合 XXX 公司管理人员提供的信息情况，提供如下法律意见供 XXX 公司参考：

第一部分　法律风险分析

就现行有效的法律规则，结合目前已知的信息，XXX 公司招录该劳动者涉及至少三类法律风险，即单纯的竞业限制风险、侵犯商业秘密与不正当竞争风险、违反诚实信用原则及企业价值观的风险等。

一、单纯的竞业限制风险

根据《劳动合同法》等法律规定，用人单位可与负有保密义务的劳动者约定竞业限制协议（或条款）。在竞业限制期内，负有竞业限制义务的劳动者不能在与本单位生产或者经营同类产品、从事同类业务的有竞争关系的其他用人单位从业，或者自己开业生产或者经营同类产品、从事同类业务。劳动者违反竞业限制协议的，应当按照约定向用人单位支付违约金，给用人单位造成损失的，还应当承担赔偿责任，用人单位并有权要求劳动者解除与其他单位的劳动关系。

单纯的竞业限制纠纷属于劳动争议范畴，XXX 公司计划招录的该名劳动者，与其原用人单位 YYY 公司签订有《保密及竞业限制协议》，且目前处在竞业限制期限内，负有竞业限制义务。若原用人单位 YYY 公司因劳动者违约而提起竞业限制纠纷的劳动仲裁，追究其违反竞业限制义务的法律责任，将会得到劳动仲裁委的支持，即劳动者

续表

返还竞业限制补偿金、支付违约金，并继续履行竞业限制义务，解除与 XXX 公司签订的劳动合同关系等。

对 XXX 公司而言，单纯的竞业限制纠纷虽涉及不到 XXX 公司的赔偿责任，但 XXX 公司最终无法达成招用该劳动者的目的。

二、侵犯商业秘密、不正当竞争赔偿责任风险

实践中竞业限制纠纷往往不是单纯的劳动争议，竞业限制问题往往因为涉及商业秘密、技术秘密等保密信息，涉及知识产权以及反不正当竞争等而复杂化，涉及的法律规范也不限于劳动法律。

竞业限制协议往往会约定商业秘密的保密问题，关于商业秘密的保密义务，不仅可以通过劳动领域相关法律保护，也可也通过《反不正当竞争法》寻求保护，在该法第九条、第十七条、第三十二条中就有相关规定（见附录 1 相关法律规定）。也就是说，如果用人单位明知劳动者知悉其他公司商业秘密、在其离职后还具有保密义务，仍录用该劳动者并使用他所知悉的商业秘密，则构成侵犯商业秘密。

因此，如果 XXX 公司录用这样的劳动者，则可能构成侵犯商业秘密进而被劳动者之前任职的公司追诉。此类案件，一般会判决劳动者停止侵权行为，并赔偿原用人单位经济损失，录用劳动者的用人单位也需要承担赔偿责任。

三、违反诚实信用原则及企业价值观的风险

我国《民法通则》规定了诚实信用原则，这一原则要求当事人在市场活动中应讲信用，恪守诺言，诚实不欺，在追求自己利益的同时不损害他人和社会利益，要求民事主体在民事活动中维持双方的利益以及当事人利益与社会利益的平衡。也就是说 XXX 公司在招录劳动者时，不能损害其他单位的合法权益，如果明知劳动者尚处在竞业限制期内仍进行录用，显然与法相悖。

同时，大多数企业在核心价值观、核心文化理念中都会倡导遵纪守法，诚实守信等观念，XXX 公司也不例外，XXX 公司倡导的价值观包括 Trust and integrity，行为准则包括 Legal Compliance、Business Ethics、Confidentiality、Compliance and Reporting of Misconduct 等，若公司在人事招录上违反这些价值观与行为准则，对于员工的管理与企业形象的树立都将是极其不利的。

另外，从商业道德上来说，如果因招录负有竞业限制义务的劳动者而涉讼，在同行业中的不良影响也不容忽视。

第二部分　YYY 公司维权概率分析

通过法律专业检索软件进行检索，YYY 旗下公司共涉及 393 件民事诉讼，其中，关于劳动争议案件有 66 件（见附录 3 统计表），有关竞业限制的案例有三份裁判文书。可见，该公司具有追究违反竞业限制人员责任的先例。而且，考查这三份判决书追究责任的力度，我们发现，YYY 公司追诉往往是一追到底，案件经历一审、二审与再审，并且，更换案由后继续追诉，可见其追究力度之大。案例名称如下（见附录 2 参考案例）：

……

……

续表

从以上案例分析，我们认为 YYY 公司在包括竞业限制纠纷在内的劳动争议和民商事诉讼等方面维权意识强、力度大，维权概率相当高。 **第三部分 结论** 通过以上法律风险及 YYY 公司维权情况分析，XXX 公司如招录负有竞业限制义务的劳动者则存在较大的法律风险，包括但不限于解除与拟招录劳动者的劳动关系以及民事赔偿责任等。 北京京师（珠海）律师事务所 XXX 律师 2020 年 3 月 12 日

第五节 律师函（Lawyer's Letter）

律师函（Lawyer's letter）是指律师接受客户的委托就有关事实或法律问题进行披露、评价，进而提出要求以达到一定效果而制作、发送的专业法律文书。用律师函对某一事实进行法律评价和风险估计，其目的在于以法律尺度和律师的判断，对送达对象晓之以法律事实，动之以利弊得失，让送达对象得出自己的“法律评价”，即“传法达意”。

律师函只代表声明作用，并不代表法院认可，如果委托人，以及律师利用权力伪造，造假律师函给受害者，属于违法犯罪行为。受害者收到恐吓、威胁、损失等，应当报警处理，追究委托人，律师的责任。

律师函可以笼统的分为首部、正文和尾部三大组成部分。

首部一般由三个部分组成：具体包括标题、函号和送达对象。

正文一般由四个部分组成：具体包括委托声明、事实简述、法律评论和律师意见。委托声明由委托来源及委托事项两部分组成。委托声明主要是向送达对象表明律师向其出具律师函的合法授权来源，以及委托人的委托事项，即委托人想让送达对象做什么或不做什么。

尾部一般是附件、落款和联系方式。律师函的落款具体包括律师事务所的名称、发函律师姓名和发函时间。律师函的联系方式包括发函律师的联系方式及委托人的联系方式。

范例一：

Date: June 16, 2019

Lawyer's Letter

No. :

To: Zhuhai Sunshun Co., Ltd.

As entrusted by XX Ltd. (hereinafter referred to as "XX Company"), I hereby issue to you this Lawyer's Letter regarding the payment for goods owed by you to XX Company.

On May 5, 2018, you gave a purchase order (order No. :) to XX Company, to purchase from XX Company 5,000 pieces of computer housing at the unit price of 120 yuan/piece (inclusive of VAT) and the total price of 600,000 (inclusive of VAT), with the payment terms of 60 days upon your receipt of the invoices. After the said purchase order was confirmed by XX Company, a contract for purchase and sale of goods between you and XX Company was concluded.

Subsequently, XX Company, pursuant to the purchase order, delivered to you all goods with good quality under the purchase order, and further more, on May 26, issued to you the special invoices for VAT at the total value of 600,000. However, after your receipt of the goods, you failed to make payment timely pursuant to the purchase order. Although XX Company urged you to make full payment for many times, you only paid part of the amounts, i. e., 200,000 yuan, and has been refusing to pay off the balance of 400,000 yuan so far.

It is my opinion that, your failure in payment has constituted a material breach under the purchase order. Now, as entrusted by XX Company, I hereby require you to, within 7 days upon your receipt of this Lawyer's Letter, pay off the said balance of 400,000 in a lump sum to XX Company.

If, within the said time period upon your receipt of this Lawyer's Letter, you fail to pay off the said balance or actively seek solutions through consultation with XX Company, I will, as directed by XX Company, bring a civil lawsuit against you, so as to recover from you the principal of the said amount and the interests and damages resulting from your failure of payment, and apply to the court for seizing or freezing your relevant properties.

For avoidance of burdensome litigation and in consideration of your goodwill, it is advisable for you to attach much importance to this case and promptly make response to us after your receipt of this Lawyer's Letter.

XXXX Law Firm

Attorney-at-law: XXX

范例二：

Lawyer' Letter
Regarding XXX's Illegal Termination of
the Labor Contract of YYY

March 20, 2020

Dear Sirs/Madams,

Regarding the labor dispute between XXX Co., Ltd. (hereinafter referred to as your company) and YYY, YYY has entrusted Beijing Jingsh (Zhuhai) Law Firm to represent her in labor arbitration, and Beijing Jingsh (Zhuhai) Law Firm appointed attorney XXX to handle the case. I am writing to inform your company about the case as follows:

I. Basic Facts

On June 1, 2018, your company signed a "Labor Contract" with YYY, with the duration from June 1, 2018 to June 1, 2021.

Since January 1, 2019, in view of the performance of your company and the achievements of YYY in 2018, your company increased the salary of YYY for 2019.

However, your company suddenly issued "Notice of Termination of Labor Contract" on June 15, 2019, and released the employment relationship with YYY on the same day, together with the issuance of "Dismissal Form". The reason of your company's termination of the labor contract is that YYY issued the "Salary Adjustment Scheme" arbitrarily.

II. Your company's unilateral termination of the labor contract is a violation of regulations, and the labor contract relationship shall be resumed according to law. The illegitimacy of your company's conduct is mainly reflected in the following four aspects:

1. Violation of regulations

The unilateral termination of the labor contract by your company is illegal. The reasons include at least: A. Lack of grounds. The "Employee Handbook" did not go through the publicity procedure; B. Lack of facts of YYY's serious violation of discipline. The grounds for the termination of labor contract are erroneous, and there exists no fact of the so-called ultra vires issuance of company policy. The "Salary Adjustment Scheme" was signed by the general manager of your company, who gave it to YYY to publicize it; C. Lack of legal procedure. The termination of labor contract did not go through the procedure of notifying the labor union.

The "XXX Compliance Requirements" on your "Employee Handbook" clearly states that "compliance is an important part of our company. It is the responsibility of everyone from newcomer to CEO in doing everything in their daily work."

As a transnational company in the world, XXX shall not go back on its word. Any Non-compliance shall be corrected. The consequences of violation of laws and regulations will definitely damage the reputation, credit and goodwill of XXX.

续表

2. Non-compliance with the procedure

On June 15, 2019, the director of Human Resources, during the absence of the general manager who was on business trip, arbitrarily ordered official seal keeper to stamp the official seal on the "Notice of Termination of Labor Contract", which is in serious violation of the "Regulations on the Use and Management of Official Seals" of your company.

It can be clearly seen that this unilateral termination is individual will kidnapping company will, and the act of stamping the official seal violates your company's rules and regulations and is unethical. Article 5. 5. 1 of the "Regulations on the Use and Management of Official Seals" stipulates that "anyone who violates these regulations shall be punished by the company in accordance with the internal management regulations of the company; those whose behavior causes serious losses to the company, or even constitutes a crime shall be sent to the judicial authorities."

3. Compounding mistakes

Your company didn't face up to the mistake in the above unilateral termination of labor contract. What's more, under the instigation of the director of Human Resources, your company immediately recruited a human resources manager to replace the post of YYY instead of repenting your mistake. It can be seen that your company intends to go further and further on the wrong road.

I would like to remind your company that the *Labor Contract Law of the People's Republic of China* and other laws and regulations stipulate that in case of illegally terminating labor contract relationship, the employee has the right to request the restoration of labor relationship, and this request will not be altered in spite of the re-employment of another person.

I hope that your company realize what is the correct road to take. The consequence of using one mistake to cover up another mistake is to lift a rock only to drop it on your own toes.

4. Procrastination in providing evidence

On March 30, 2020, the Zhuhai Labor Dispute Arbitration Commission held tribunal hearing. On this preparatory hearing, your company should have submitted full, complete and standardized evidence regarding the termination of labor contract. However, the agent-ad-litem of your company ignored the arbitration procedure and failed to submit evidence on the grounds of lack of enough time to translate a large amount of English materials. After the arbitral tribunal determined that the formal tribunal hearing would be opened on April 13, 2020, I requested your company to provide related evidence materials in advance once more. However, your agent-ad-litem hasn't provided any evidence so far.

In summary, we believe that your company's termination of labor contract is illegal, and no individual's private rights can override the company's management practices. I hope that your company will correct the mistake and alter the violation of regulations. We hereby propose two requirements:

续表

1. In order to effectively reduce the impact of illegal behavior, your company is requested to recall your decision as soon as possible and restore YYY's labor contract relationship, so that YYY can return to her post, and all the staff can be affected by the compliance management of your company.

2. According to the company's rules and regulations, your company is requested to investigate into the liability of relevant personnel, crack down on the private desires of individuals, and earnestly safeguard the good image of your company in management and standardization.

Pease consider the above suggestions carefully.

Attorney XXX
Beijing Jingsh (Zhuhai) Law Firm

参考译文：

关于 XXX 公司违法解除 YYY 劳动合同事宜的
律师函

敬启者：

XXX 有限公司（以下称贵司）与 YYY 劳动争议纠纷案件，YYY 委托北京京师（珠海）律师事务所代理其劳动仲裁案件，北京京师（珠海）律师事务所指派本所 ZZZ 律师代理该案。现就案件有关事宜致函贵司如下：

一、基本事实

2018 年 6 月 1 日贵司与 YYY 签订《劳动合同》，合同期限自 2018 年 6 月 1 日至 2021 年 6 月 1 日。

自 2019 年 1 月 1 日起，鉴于贵司业绩和 2018 年 YYY 的成绩，贵司对其 2019 年薪资予以增加。

但是，2019 年 6 月 15 日贵司突然作出《解除劳动合同通知书》，并于当日解除与 YYY 的劳动合同关系，《退工单》亦同日开出。贵司解除劳动合同的理由是 YYY“无故发布了《工资调整方案》”。

二、贵司本次单方解除劳动合同系违规解除，依法应恢复劳动合同关系。贵司违法违规行为主要包括如下四点：

1. 不合规

本次贵司单方解除劳动合同系违规解除，理由至少包括：A 无依据。员工手册未履行公示程序；B 无严重违纪事实。解除所依据的事实错误，不存在所谓越权发布政策的事实，《工资调整方案》系贵司总经理签字后交由 YYY 发布；C 无合法程序。解除劳动合同未履行通知工会程序。

XXX 作为世界有影响力的大公司，不应自食其言。不合规就应该知错必改，违法法规的后果必将损害 XXX 的声誉。

续表

2. 不合程序

2019 年 6 月 15 日，人力资源总监趁贵司总经理出差之际，违反贵司《公章使用和管理规范》，未经总经理许可，未提交《盖章申请》，擅自指令公章保管人在《解除劳动合同通知书》上加盖贵司公章。

但很显然，本次单方解除系个人意志绑架了贵司意志，加盖公章的行为违反了贵司规章制度，系不道德行为。贵司《公章使用和管理规范》5. 5. 1 条规定："违反本规定的，由公司按公司内部管理规定以违纪进行处理，造成公司严重损失或情节严重的，并且构成犯罪的，公司将移送司法机关处理。"

3. 错上加错

贵司无法正视本次解除劳动合同的错误，更有甚者，在人力资源总监的鼓动下，贵司不思改过，而是急速招聘人力资源经理以替代 YYY 的工作岗位。可见，贵司意欲在错误的道路上越走越远。

希望贵司明确，《中华人民共和国劳动合同法》等法律法规规定，违法解除劳动合同关系的，劳动者有权要求恢复劳动合同关系，而这一要求不因为违法解除合同的用人单位再行招聘有关人员顶岗而改变。

希望贵司不要知错不改，用一个错误掩盖另一个错误的后果就是搬起石头砸自己的脚。

4. 拖延举证

2020 年 3 月 10 日，珠海市劳动争议仲裁委员会依法开庭，在本次预备庭上，贵司理应充分、完整、规范的提交解除劳动合同的证据，然而贵司委托的代理人却无视仲裁程序，以大量英文资料未能及时翻译为由，当庭未能提交证据材料。仲裁庭确定 2020 年 4 月 13 日开庭后，本律师再次要求提前提供有关证据材料，时至今日，贵司代理人也未提供任何证据。

综上，我们认为，贵司本次解除合同系违法行为，任何个人私权都不能凌驾于公司管理规范之上。希望贵司有错就改，违规必究，在此我们提出两点要求：

1. 为有效降低违法行为的影响，恳请贵司尽快收回错误决定，恢复 YYY 的劳动合同关系，让 YYY 回归工作岗位，让贵司上上下下看到贵司合规管理。

2. 根据公司规章制度，追究有关人员的责任，打击个人私权私欲，切实维护贵司依法管理、规范管理的良好形象。

以上，请贵司慎重考虑。

北京京师（珠海）律师事务所

ZZZ 律师

2020 年 3 月 20 日

范例三：

YYY Medical Care Co. , Ltd.
Global Intellectual Property
BLVD 6, Homburg
Telephone:
Fax:
Email:
September 10, 2019

Guangdong XXX Co. , Ltd.
Management Board
6 Jinhai Road
Jinwan District, Zhuhai, P. R. China
YYY Medial Care Deutschland GmbH.
Re: Infringement of AAA Trademark
Responsible manager: Mr. CCC
Dear Sir/Madam,

We are writing to you on behalf of YYY Medical Care Co. Ltd. , which is one of the world's leading providers of products and services for people with chronic kidney failure, with approximately 3. 2 million patients undergoing dialysis on a regular basis worldwide. YYY offers products and services along the entire value chain of dialysis from a single source. It serves more than 320, 000 patients in a global network of more than 3, 700 dialysis clinics. At the same time, with 41 production sites on all continents, YYY is the world's leading provider of dialysis products such as dialysis machines, dialyzers and the associated disposable accessories, including a sodium bicarbonate container for dialysis machines, labeled with the trademark AAA.

YYY Medical Care Co. Ltd. owns the trademark for the sign AAA in many countries around the world, including Germany, the European Union and China. Please find attached as Annex 1 for your reference of an overview of the relevant trademark portfolio.

With regard to all its trademarks, YYY Medical Care Co. Ltd. takes great efforts to market and advertise its products and, therefore, forcefully defends them against third party infringements.

YYY Medical Care Co. Ltd. noticed that Guangdong XXX Co. , Ltd. Co. , Ltd. exhibited during the ERA-EDTA Congress in Budapest a container to be used for YYY Medical Care dialysis machines. The below photograph was taken at the XXX's booth No. 123 in Exhibition Hall C on August 10, 2019.

As can be seen from the photograph, in the top right corner of the label the sign AAA is used. The use of an (almost) identical trademark for identical products within the European Community infringes upon the EU trademark of YYY Medical Care Co. Ltd. Under the EU

续表

Trademark Regulation, YYY Medical Care Co. Ltd. is *inter alia* entitled to request from XXX to cease-and-desist from using this sign, to release and destroy infringing products, to request information on the extent of sales and to claim damages.

To defendits rights, YYY Medical Care Co. Ltd. initiated seizure proceedings with the National Tax and Customs Administration of Hungary (NTCA). Accordingly, NTCA officers came to XXX's booth on 14 August 2019. Because XXX agreed to destroy and remove from the exhibition the product, YYY Medical Care Co. Ltd. withdrew its application for seizure and the seizure has not been executed. YYY Medical Care Co. Ltd. acknowledges and appreciates this cooperation of XXX.

At the ERA-EDTA Congress the parties agreed to enter into settlement negotiations following the Congress. A protocol signed at XXX's booth by YYY Medical Care Co. Ltd.'s local legal representative, XXX's representative and the customs officers is attached as Annex 2. In this protocol the actions at the booth and the mutual commitment of the parties to reach an overall settlement are noted.

The purpose of this letter is to make suggestion with regard to possible terms of an amicable settlement. Please find attached as Annex 4 a draft agreement for your kind consideration. Please kindly note that as a gesture of goodwill YYY Medical Care Co. Ltd. would offer to waive most of its claims if XXX undertakes to no more use the AAA trademark in an amicable settlement. For legal reasons, this undertaking needs to be secured by a contractual penalty. In order to allow XXX a smooth transition, YYY Medical Care Co. Ltd. would also be prepared not to insist on an immediate cease-and-desist undertaking but offers XXX a transition period of two months to make the necessary changes to its product labels.

Please note that if there is no amicable settlement, YYY Medical Care Co. Ltd. will have to enforce its rights in court proceedings. The cost of such proceedings had to be borne by XXX. However, we trust that this will not be necessary.

If you consent with the draft undertaking, please kindly return the original countersigned document together with Annex 1, both in duplicate——in advance by fax, to the attention of Mr. CCC by October 25, 2019.

If you have any comments, please let us have your feedback by this date.

Kind regards,

YYY Medial Care Co. Ltd.

上述函件是国外一家医疗设备公司就国内公司涉嫌商标侵权而发出的函，因为国外公司认为国内公司在展台的一个包装物上有 AAA 标识，而 AAA 标识是国外公司已经注册的商标，且目前还在保护期之内。据国内公司相关海外市场管理人员陈述，国内公司并没有故意侵权的意图，因为 AAA 标识在医疗行业是通用名，并非专有名，而且 AAA 标志的大小写设计等与 AAA 并非一致，并不具有混淆性。展会期间双方在现场进行了沟通，国内公司也进行了解释，展会结束后，国外公司马上发函给国内公司。估计国外公司也能判断出来国内公司并没有侵权的故意，出现相似标识纯属偶然，且在展会处理该事件的过程中，国内公司表现出重视和积极的态度，因此，该函写作语气不温不火，国外公司先介绍自己公司的规模和在世界上的影响力，再介绍 AAA 标志被用在公司多款畅销产品等，之后介绍事件的经过，但是整个函件可谓柔中带刚，结尾的时候才说明本函的目的，即建议双方达成友好的和解协议，通过订立书面和解协议约束国内公司，以防再发生类似事件。国外对于知识产权的重视和保护力度可谓非常严格，在侵权行为还没有发生，或者根本就不可能发生侵权行为的情况下，他们就已经把可能的苗头扼杀在摇篮。

针对上述函件，本作者作为国内公司的海外市场法律顾问，作出了以下回复，仅供学习参考：

Guangdong XXX Co. , Ltd.
6 Jinhai Road
Jinwan District, Zhuhai, P. R. China
September 20, 2019

YYY Medical Care Co. , Ltd.
Global Intellectual Property
BLVD 6, Homburg
Telephone:
Fax:
Email:

Dear Mr. CCC,

In reply to your email dated June 26, our company attaches great importance to it, and gives the explanation and commitment as follows:

XXX is a listed company in China with independent research and development team and capacity, and it possesses a leading position in China in the area of medical apparatus and instruments. XXX has always emphasized the protection of intellectual property and respected the research and development fruit of others.

The product that uses "AAA" mark is called "aaa" in Chinese, which means "ccc". AAA is a generic name instead of special name for this type of product, so we didn't realize the use of a generic name would result in potential infringement on other's intellectual property,

续表

because a generic name is not qualified to be registered as a trademark according to the *Trademark Law of the People's Republic of China*. In addition, the "AAA" mark of XXX is distinguishable from your trademark in respect of layout, design etc. You trademark is spelled as "AAA", but we use "A-AA". We use a cross-bar, and this difference is distinguishable. Finally, we use the letter "A" because of the following two reasons: first, the name of XXX begins with "A"; second, the English word "biological" also begins with "bi", which gives some implications about the industry we are in. Therefore, by using the mark "A-AA", we do not intend to imitate the trademark of your company, and the misunderstanding between us in ERA-EDTA Congress in Budapest is only a coincidence. Based on the above three reasons, we don't think it necessary to sign the settlement agreement. However, in order to show our sincerity and commitment, and eliminate your worry, our company has decided to change "A-AA" to "ZZZ", which is far from being identical with or similar to "AAA". What's more, based on your request, we will make some adjustment by removing the "A-AA" mark from all of our products, and ensure that the word "A-AA" will not appear on our products any more. We ask for six months' transition period to finish the adjustment. We do appreciate your efforts in the protection of intellectual of property and we look forward to your reply. Yours sincerely,

第九章　仲裁类涉外法律文书

如果发生民事纠纷，当事人可以协商解决，也可以通过仲裁委员会进行仲裁，还可以向人民法院提起诉讼。仲裁与诉讼都是解决合同纠纷和其他财产权益纠纷的法律形式，但是有显著的区别：

一是管辖权的取得不同。诉讼过程中，一方当事人向有管辖权的法院起诉，法院依法受理后，另一方须应诉；而通过仲裁委员会申请仲裁，则必须要有一个有效的仲裁协议，即合同中订立仲裁条款，或纠纷发生后双方当事人达成一个请求仲裁的协议。

二是审理者的产生方式不同。诉讼案件的审判员根据案件的不同类型由法院指定，不能由当事人自行选择，但当事人有法定理由的可以申请回避；而仲裁案件，双方当事人除可以协商选定仲裁委员会、约定仲裁庭的组成人数外，还有权选定仲裁员。

三是开庭审理的原则不同。法院开庭审理一般公开进行，涉及国家机密、商业秘密或个人隐私的案件，可以不公开审理；仲裁庭审理案件一般不公开进行，以保护当事人之间的商业秘密和维护其商业信誉。

四是审理程序及当事人的能动作为不同。诉讼过程中当事人应当严格按照诉讼法的规定进行；仲裁过程中当事人则有较大的处分权，几乎每一步骤当事人都能主动作为，如约定由三名仲裁员还是一名仲裁员组成仲裁庭，是否开庭审理等都可由当事人自由选择，不得强迫。

五是监督程序不同。我国法院实行两审终审制，对于已经发生法律效力的判决，发现确有错误的，可适用审判监督程序。我国仲裁委员会则实行一裁终局制，并适用司法监督程序，即（1）当事人提出证据，证明符合撤销裁决条件的，可向仲裁委员会所在地中级人民法院申请撤销裁决；（2）被申请人提出证据，证明有不予执行条件的，经人民法院合议庭审查核实，裁定不予执行。

通过以上对比，可知仲裁具有以下优点：第一，灵活性（仲裁不像诉讼需遵循严格的程序要求）；第二，快捷性（仲裁一裁终局）；第三，保密性（仲裁可不公开审理，有助于保护当事人的商业秘密，仲裁裁决书也无需在网上公开）；第四，中立性（双方可分别选择仲裁员，可自由选择仲裁地）。

第一节　仲裁协议（Arbitration Clause）

基于仲裁以上的优点，在国际商务活动中，发生争议后常见的争议解决方法是国际商事仲裁。将争议提交仲裁解决的一个前提条件是：当事人之间签订有效的仲裁协议。

根据《联合国贸易法委员会国际商事仲裁示范法》（UNCITRAL Model Law on International Commercial Arbitration）的定义，仲裁协议是指合同双方将合同中或者其他法律关系中发生的所有争议或者部分争议提交仲裁解决的约定（Arbitration agreement is an agreement made by the parties to submit to arbitration all or certain disputes which have arisen or which may arise between them in respect of a defined legal relationship, whether contractual or not）。仲裁协议可以是合同中的一个条款，也可以是一个单独的协议。

在一个仲裁协议中，应包含以下内容：双方将争议提交仲裁解决的意图（the intent to arbitration）、仲裁范围（the matters to be arbitrated）、仲裁机构的选择（selection of arbitration institution）。如根据以下仲裁协议："disputes arising from the performance of a contract shall be submitted to arbitration"，管辖争议范围仅限于与合同履行相关的争议，排除了有关合同解释、合同效力等方面所发生的争议，即因合同解释、合同效力所发生的争议，不得通过仲裁解决。

很多仲裁机构都提供了可直接适用的仲裁协议，如国际商会（International Chamber of Commerce, ICC）提供的仲裁协议表述如下："All disputes arising in connection with the present contract shall be finally settled under the Rules of Conciliation and Arbitration of International Chamber of Commerce by one or more arbitrators appointed in accordance with the said Rules."

参考译文：因该合同所产生的一切争议均应依据国际商会调解和仲裁规则解决，并根据上述规则指派一名或者多名仲裁员组成仲裁庭。

联合国贸易法委员会的仲裁协议版本如下："Any dispute, controversy or claim arising out of or relating to this contract, or the breach, termination or invalidity thereof, shall be settled by arbitration in accordance with the UNCITRAL Arbitration Rules at present in force".

参考译文：因该合同所产生的任何争议、冲突或者索赔要求，或者有关该合同的违约、终止或者效力，应依据联合国贸易法委员会现行有效的仲裁规则通过仲裁解决。

有时候，在以上简明版本的基础上，会增加更具体的内容，如："The number of arbitrators shall be …（one or three）; the place of arbitration shall be …（city or country）and the language（s）to be used in the arbitral proceedings shall be …"。

目前比较知名的国际仲裁机构有：中国国际经济贸易仲裁委员会（China International Economic and Trade Arbitration Commission, CIETAC），香港国际仲裁中心（Hong Kong International Arbitration Center, HKIAC），深圳国际仲裁院（The Shenzhen Court of International Arbitration, SCIA），上海国际仲裁中心（Shanghai International Arbitration Center），澳洲国际贸易仲裁中心（Australia Centre For International Commercial Arbitration, ACICA），新加坡国际仲裁中心（Singapore International Arbitration Center, SIAC）等。

华南国际经济贸易仲裁委员会又名深圳国际仲裁院，简称 SCIA（英文全称分别为 South China International Economic and Trade Arbitration Commission, The Shenzhen Court of International Arbitration，曾名中国国际经济贸易仲裁委员会华南分会、中国国际经济贸易仲裁委员会深圳分会），是设立于中国深圳经济特区的仲裁机构。当事人在仲裁协议中约定争议由华南国际经济贸易仲裁委员会、深圳国际仲裁院、中国国际经济贸易仲裁委员会华南分会或中国国际经济贸易仲裁委员会深圳分会进行仲裁的，或约定的仲裁机构名称可推定为 SCIA 的，均应视为同意由 SCIA 进行仲裁。

附：深圳国际仲裁院（The Shenzhen Court of International Arbitration, SCIA）仲裁协议范本：

范例一：

Any dispute arising from or in connection with this contract shall be submitted to

Shenzhen Court of International Arbitration（SCIA）for arbitration.

参考译文：

因本合同所产生的任何争议，应提交深圳国际仲裁院仲裁解决。

范例二：

Any dispute arising from or in connection with this Contract shall be submitted to South China International Economic and Trade Arbitration Commission Mediation Center for mediation. If the mediation is successful, the parties agree to submit the settlement agreement to SCIA to request that an arbitral award be rendered in accordance with the Arbitration Rules and based on the terms of the settlement agreement. If any party is unwilling to mediate or the mediation fails, the dispute shall be referred to SCIA for arbitration.

参考译文：

因本合同所产生的任何争议应提交华南经济贸易仲裁委员会调解中心进行调解。如果调解成功，双方同意将和解协议提交华南经济贸易仲裁委员会并要求根据仲裁规则、依据和解协议的内容出具仲裁裁决。如果任何一方不愿意调解或者调解失败，应将争议提交华南经济贸易仲裁委员进行仲裁。

范例三：

Both parties agree that any party may submit the settlement agreement to the South China International Economic and Trade Arbitration Commission and request for rendering an arbitral award in accordance with the terms of the settlement agreement pursuant to the Arbitration Rules. The arbitral award is final and binding upon both parties.

参考译文：

双方同意将和解协议提交华南经济贸易仲裁委员会，并要求依据和解协议的内容，按照仲裁规则出具仲裁裁决。仲裁裁决是终局的，并对双方具有约束力。

将争议提交仲裁解决所需要的文书有：授权委托书（Power of Attorney）、法定代表人证明书（Statement of Legal Representative）、仲裁申请书（Request for Arbitration）、仲裁答辩状（Statement of Defense）、仲裁反请求书（Request for

Counterclaim）、财产保全申请书（Application for Preservation of Property）、仲裁员选定书［Appointment of Arbitrator（s）］、和解协议（Settlement Agreement）。

第二节　仲裁中常见文书范本

一、授权委托书（Power of Attorney）

Power of Attorney

Principal：

Legal Representative：

Attorneys：

（1）Name：

Position：

Company：　　　　Tel：

Zip code：

The scope of the authorization：

（2）Name：

Position：

Company：　　　　Tel：

Zip Code：

Position：

Address：

The scope of the authorization：

The principal hereby appoints and gives power of attorney to each of the above Attorneys to act on behalf of the Principal in its dispute with ________________.

Principal：（Stamp）

Legal representative：（signature）

Date：

Attach：scope of the authorization：

1. to submit the request for arbitration, to amend or waive the arbitration claims;

2. to submit the Statement of Defense, to submit the request of counterclaim, to amend or waive the counterclaims;

3. to appoint the arbitrator;

4. to attend hearings, give presentations, make statements, to investigate the facts of the case and to collect evidence;

5. to conduct mediation and conciliation with the opposing party and reach a settlement;

6. to receive the notification and other file relating to arbitration case;

7. to submit the application for property preservation and protection of evidence;

8. to apply for the enforcement of an arbitral award;

9. to handle other legal matters relating to the dispute.

二、法定代表人证明书（Statement of Legal Representative）

Statement of Legal Representative

This is to certify that （name） is presently （position） and the legal representative of this company.

Attach:

Legal representative' Address:

Telephone number:

N. B. Should there be no legal representative of this company, Chief Executive Officer will be available.

三、仲裁申请书（Request for Arbitration）

Request for Arbitration

Claimant: ________

Address: ________　　E-mail: ________　　Tel: ________

Fax: ________

Legal Representative: _______ Position: _______ Agent: _______、_______

Agent's Contact Information:

(hint: If there are more than one Claimant, please list as Claimant A、Claimant B)

Respondent: ________

Address: ________　　E-mail: ________　　Tel: ________

Fax: ________

Legal Representative: _______ Position: _______ Agent: _______、_______

Agent's Contact Information:

(hint: If there are more than one Respondent, please list as Respondent A、Respondent B)

Arbitration Agreement:

Claims:

1.

2.

……

The facts and grounds:

……

To

Shanghai International Economic and Trade Arbitration Commission/ Shanghai International Arbitration Center

Claimant: ××× (seal)

Legal Representative: ________ (signature)

Date:

四、仲裁答辩状 (Statement of Defense)

Statement of Defense

Respondent: __________________________

Address: ________ E-mail: ________ Tel: ________

Fax: ________

Legal Representative: ______ Position: ______ Agent: ______、______

Agent's Contact Information:

Claimant: ________________________

Address: ________ E-mail: ________ Tel: ________

Fax: ________

Legal Representative: ______ Position: ______ Agent: ______、______

Agent's Contact Information:

Statement of Defense:

To

Shanghai International Economic and Trade Arbitration Commission/ Shanghai International Arbitration Center

Respondent: ××× (seal)

Legal Representative: ________ (signature)

Date:

五、仲裁反请求书（Request for Counterclaim）

Request for Counterclaim

Claimant: ________________________

Address: ________ E-mail: ________ Tel: ________

Fax: ________

Legal Representative: ________ Position: ________

Agent: ________

Agent's Contact Information: ________

Respondent: ________

Address: ________ E-mail: ________ Tel: ________

Fax: ________

Legal Representative: ________ Position: ________

Agent: ________

Agent's Contact Information: ________

Counterclaims:

1.

2.

……

The facts and grounds:

……

To

Shanghai International Economic and Trade Arbitration Commission/ Shanghai International Arbitration Center

Claimant: ××× (seal)

Legal Representative: ________ (signature)

Date:

六、财产保全申请书（Application for Preservation of Property）

Application for Preservation of Property

Claimant: ________

Address: ________ E-mail: ________ Tel: ________

Fax: ________

Legal Representative: ________ Position: ________

Agent: ________

Agent's contact information: ________

Respondent: ________

Address: ________ E-mail: ________ Tel: ________

Fax: ________

Legal Representative: ________ Position: ________

Agent: ________

Agent's contact information: ________

Requests:

1.

2.

……

The facts and grounds:

……

To

Shanghai International Economic and Trade Arbitration Commission/ Shanghai International Arbitration Center

Claimant: ××× (seal)

Legal Representative: ________ (signature)

Date:

Property clue:

The court that proceeds with the application:

七、仲裁员选定书 [Appointment of Arbitrator (s)]

Appointment of Arbitrator (s)

With regard to the arbitration case (No. ________), we have appointed Mr. / Ms. as arbitrator, and recommended Mr. /Ms. as the presiding/sole arbitrator.

To

Shanghai International Economic and Trade Arbitration Commission/ Shanghai International Arbitration Center

Claimant/Respondent: ××× (seal)

Legal Representative: ________ (signature)

Date:

八、和解协议 (Settlement Agreement)

Settlement Agreement

Party A: ×××

Party B: ×××

With regard to the arbitration case (No. ________), the parties have reached a settlement agreement, and request the arbitral tribunal to render the arbitral award in accordance with the terms of the settlement agreement:

1. ……

2. ……

3. ……

This Agreement shall come into force upon the undersigning by both Parties. This Agreement shall be executed in triplicate. Party A and Party B shall take one original and the third original shall be kept by Shanghai International Economic and Trade Arbitration Commission/Shanghai International Arbitration Center.

Party A: ××× Attorney (signature)

Party B: ××× Attorney (signature)

Date: ________

◆ 知识点梳理

Request for Arbitration	仲裁申请书
Statement of Defense	仲裁答辩状
Request for Counterclaim	仲裁反请求书
Application for Preservation of Property	财产保全申请书
Appointment of Arbitrator (s)	仲裁员选定书
Settlement Agreement	和解协议
Presiding/sole arbitrator	首席仲裁员
Sole arbitrator	独任仲裁员
Claimant	仲裁申请人
Respondent	仲裁答辩人
Arbitral tribunal	仲裁庭
Facts and grounds	事实与理由
Render the arbitral award	出具仲裁裁决书

参考文献

一、中文著作类

［1］李克兴，张新红著：《法律文本与法律翻译》，中国对外翻译出版公司 2005 年版。

［2］李克兴著：《高级合同写作与翻译》，北京大学出版社 2016 年版。

［3］刘洪泉著：《英语应用文写作》，上海外语教育出版社 2009 年版。

［4］乔焕然著：《英文合同阅读指南》，中国法制出版社 2015 年版。

［5］全国国际商务单证专业培训考试办公室著：《国际商务单证理论与实务》，中国商务出版社 2014 年版。

［6］宋红波，朱明炬著：《实用文体翻译教程》，清华大学出版社 2016 年版。

［7］王相国著：《鏖战英文合同》，中国法制出版社》2018 年版。

［8］熊云英，任小军著：《涉外法律文书写作》，中国政法大学出版社 2013 年版。

［9］余世明著：《国际商务单证实务》，暨南大学出版社 2005 年版。

［10］张法连著：《法律英语术语双解》，中国法制出版社 2013 年版。

［11］中国政法大学法律英语教学与测试研究中心著：《法律英语写作教程》，中国法制出版社 2013 年版。

［12］张学森著：《国际商法》，复旦大学出版社 2016 年版。

二、中文论文类

［1］陈新仁：《语法隐喻的认知语用解读》，载《外国语》2014 年第 2 期。

［2］候芹英：《试论法律英语的模糊性》，上海海事大学 2004 年硕士毕业论文。

［3］胡壮麟：《语法隐喻》，载《外语教学与研究》1996 年第 4 期。

［4］李剑波：《论法律英语的词汇特征》，载《中国科技翻译》2003 年第 5 期。

［5］李萍：《法律英语的词汇特征研究》，载《中国科技翻译》2017 年第 4 期。

［6］李萍：《从法律英语的词汇特征评〈民法总则〉的英译》，载《中国科技翻译》2018 年第 2 期。

［7］李萍：《语法隐喻在法律汉语英译中的应用》，载《课程教育研究》2018 年第 13 期。

［8］王晋军：《名词化在语篇类型中的体现》，载《外语学刊》2003 年第 2 期。

［9］杨敏：《法律语篇权力意志剖析》，载《外语与外语教学》2004 年第 5 期。

［10］隋萍萍：《涉外公证文书汉英翻译报告》，西南科技大学 2017 年硕士毕业论文。

［11］种夏，李剑波：《法律英语教学模式比较研究》，载《西南政法大学学报》2007 年第 6 期。

［12］朱永生：《名词化、动词化与语法隐喻》，载《外语教学与研究》2006 年第 2 期。

三、外文著作类

［1］Alix Adams. Law for Business Students ［M］, Ninth Edition, Pearson Education Limited. , 2016.

［2］Catherin Mason. The Lawyer's English Language Coursebook ［M］, England: Global Legal English Ltd. , 2014.

［3］D. Crystal & D. Davy. Investigating English Style ［M］, London: Longman Group Ltd. , 1969.

［4］Mellinkoff. Language of the Law ［M］, Boston: Little, Brown and Company, 1963.

［5］O' Barr & William M, Linguistic Evidence: Language, Power and Strategy in the Classroom [M], New York: Academic Press, 1982.

[6] Quirk, R. et al. A Comprehensive Grammar of the English Language [M], London: Longman, 1985.

[7] HAN Yonghong. International Business Law (Second Edition) [M], Beijing: University of International Business and Economics Press, 2018.

图书在版编目（CIP）数据

涉外法律文书写作 / 李萍著 . —北京：中国法制出版社，2020. 5
ISBN 978 -7 -5216 -0800 -7

Ⅰ. ①涉… Ⅱ. ①李… Ⅲ. ①法律文书 - 写作 - 中国 Ⅳ. ①D926. 13

中国版本图书馆 CIP 数据核字（2020）第 019962 号

责任编辑：程思　　封面设计：周黎明

涉外法律文书写作

SHEWAI FALÜ WENSHU XIEZUO

著者/李萍

经销/新华书店

印刷/三河市国英印务有限公司

开本/710 毫米 ×1000 毫米　16 开　　印张/24. 5　字数/314 千

版次/2020 年 5 月第 1 版　　2020 年 5 月第 1 次印刷

中国法制出版社出版

书号 ISBN 978 -7 -5216 -0800 -7　　定价：86. 00 元

北京西单横二条 2 号

邮政编码 100031　　传真：010 -66031119

网址：http：//www. zgfzs. com　　编辑部电话：010 -66066620

市场营销部电话：010 -66033393　　邮购部电话：010 -66033288

（如有印装质量问题，请与本社印务部联系调换。电话：010 -66032926）

续表

Second, the language of the Letter should be adjusted so as to eliminate any suggestions or impression that AT&T is the actual party (in lieu of Pudong LLC) that makes the investment in the Joint Venture Company. Third, subject to the agreement among the Parties, the Letter should be as explicit as possible that the guarantee by AT&T is a general guarantee, and not a joint and several guarantee. Under Chinese law, in the absence of a joint and several guarantee, a party may not sue the guarantor until and unless it has exhausted its remedies against the primary obligator. This may add some additional protection for AT&T. If you have any questions, please feel free to call any of the undersigned. （该范例来源于金杜律所事务所的网上发布）

第三节　尽职调查报告（Due Diligence Report）

尽职调查报告是由中介机构在企业的配合下，从法律、会计、财务、商业、技术、税务和业务方面，对企业的历史数据和文档、管理人员的背景、市场风险、管理风险、技术风险和资金风险做全面深入的审核，多发生在企业公开发行股票上市和企业收购。通过尽职调查，可以达到了解商业伙伴和交易对方的目的，发现其业务上的优势和弱点，找出其现存和潜在的各种重大问题和影响交易的重要因素，以便作出是否与之进行拟议的合作或交易的决定，同时为讨价还价甚至交易完成后的整合计划提供依据和基础，所谓知己知彼，百战不殆。

尽职调查报告一般包括：引言（introductory remarks），概要（executive summary），分析（review and analysis）等部分。

引言（introductory remarks）部分主要是介绍交易的背景信息、交易目的、尽职调查范围、信息来源等内容。常见的表达方式为：This legal due diligence is conducted by [　] in view of the proposed investment from [　] in [　] Co., Ltd. (hereinafter "[　]") by equity investment and loan. [　] is a company validly incorporated and existing under the laws of the PRC.

We have been requested to conduct a legal due diligence on [　] in light of the above transaction, and this report summaries the results of the legal due diligence.